Man on the Run

Man on the Run
The Life and Death of Marco Pantani

Manuela Ronchi

and Gianfranco Josti

Translated by Daniel Friebe

ROBSON BOOKS

First published in Great Britain in 2005 by Robson Books, The Chrysalis Building, Bramley Road, London W10 6SP

An imprint of **Chrysalis** Books Group plc

Originally published in Italy in 2004 by RCS Libri S.p.A., Milan

Printed by Creative Print & Design (Wales), Ebbw Vale

Contents

Introduction: 'He's Gone Away'   1

1 *Enfant Prodige* Meets *Enfant Terrible*   5

2 The Makings of a Superstar   16

3 The Comeback and the Glory   28

4 My Meeting with Marco Pantani   45

5 Madonna di Campiglio, Drama and Intrigue   57

6 The Beginning of the Nightmare   78

7 The 'Substance'   104

8 Back with a Whimper   116

9 A New Team for the Pirate   134

10 The Slow Road Back   162

11 Presumed Guilty   176

12 The Lonely Pirate   200

13 The Long Goodbye   211

Introduction

'He's Gone Away'

For five years my life was intertwined with that of Marco Pantani. Our relationship began as a professional one, but later underwent a radical and profound change, to the point where it was difficult to sum up in just a few words; those five years were filled with friendship, trust and mutual support, sometimes passing in the blink of an eye, and sometimes seeming to have lasted a lifetime.

Marco Pantani ought to have been the author of this book. We had spoken about it at length, particularly in December 2003, as we strolled through the Trenno park near Milan, pushing my son Filippo's pram. Marco wanted to write about his life, focusing on that torrid battle to reclaim his identity, to bring some balance back into his life both on and off the bike. When we were ready, we were planning to entrust Gianfranco Josti with the task of committing Marco's thoughts to paper. Gianfranco, the cycling correspondent for the *Corriere della Sera*, was and is a true authority on the world of sport and also a heartfelt admirer of Marco's. We believed he would be the right man to order Marco's notes and thoughts and fashion them into a book with a message for young people in particular.

Marco didn't make it: he left on his tiptoes without making a sound. Nonetheless, his tragic death was accompanied by a deafening commotion and confusion which overcame everyone: his family above all, but also me and everyone else who loved him.

With the full blessing of Marco's mother, father and sister, I took it upon myself, together with Gianfranco, to write this book. Ever since I arrived in the sport, the Deacon, as Gianfranco is nicknamed in the press room, has been a point of reference for me. Not only that, but he was one of the few journalists that Marco respected; he never tried to steer his thinking, only to capture and convey it.

With Gianfranco, I will try on these pages to represent as faithfully as possible the defining thoughts, moods and experiences of Marco's life – the life of a sporting idol who happened also to be a very fragile and, as we have seen, mortal human being. This book is about paying tribute but also setting the record straight after so many lies were told and written about Marco in the last few years of his career. After Marco's autopsy, which disproved once and for all the malicious gossip linking his death with performance-enhancing drugs, it's also about restoring some pride, even if only to the memories Marco left behind. That said, nothing will fill the void Marco has left in the hearts of those people who really loved him.

The dramatic announcement

St Valentine's Day, 14 February 2004. For me it was a normal working Saturday, the only difference being the sense of unease which invariably used to stalk me whenever I had no news of Marco. Our last telephone conversation took place on Monday 9th: he had announced that he would drop by my house to pick up the car and that he was going to his villa in the spa town of Saturnia, in the far south-west of Tuscany. I had called a friend of mine who often used to spend the weekend in that part of Italy to ask her to check everything was under control. There was a science-fiction film being shown on TV and I was looking forward to a quiet evening at home with my husband Paolo and baby Filippo.

It was before eleven when my mobile rang. It was my brother, Massimo: 'Lela... Marco's dead!' Blood started pumping through my brain like an electric current. It couldn't be, there must have been a mistake.

But when Paolo switched over to another channel and I heard the newsreader say: 'Marco Pantani has been found dead in a hotel in Rimini' all my senses were numbed. Then the tears started – endless, inconsolable tears. I collapsed into Paolo's arms with Filippo clasped to my chest, drowning in a sense of emptiness. It was as though I just didn't want to accept that it was real.

Within a few minutes, every phone in the house was ringing off the hook. The boss of component manufacturer Shimano's Italian arm, Amadeo Colombo, called, also in tears. The motorcyclist Max Biaggi, my former client, called from Australia, not believing what he had just heard: 'Manu, is it true? Is Pantani really dead?'

I was in a trance, incapable of holding my tears in check, but knowing that I had to find Marco's parents immediately. Tonina's mobile was ringing but no-one was answering. I tried Marco's Dad's number. 'Paolo, have you heard?' At the other end there was an interminable silence before Paolo spoke with a hushed voice, as though scared of hearing what I was about to say. 'No, what's happened, Manu?' It dawned on me that they didn't know. I was the one who would have to tell them the dramatic news. I drew a breath... 'Paolo, Marco is dead!' I shrieked those words, and the only reply was an ear-splitting cry of anguish and the sound of the line going dead.

In that precise moment I realised the scale of the tragedy that had just struck Marco's family and the torment which was to follow. Paolo and Tonina had lived through five years of torture, but they could have survived another hundred if it meant helping Marco. We had been frightened that this moment would arrive for some time but we kept the thought at bay by hoping that a light in his head would suddenly switch itself on and bring him back to reality. I also tried to contact Manola, Marco's sister. She had already heard the news. She was at home, where she had laid on a birthday party for her son Denis and a dozen or so of his friends. Denis turned fourteen that very day. Manola had screamed so loudly, so despairingly that she had terrified them all. She was confused, lost, disorientated. She couldn't bring herself to speak to her parents and she was getting telephone calls from people she didn't even know.

While all of this was going on, I kept saying 'it's not true, it's not right, it can't be true. They've got it wrong.' In my mind, I was reliving the three days that Marco – il Panta – had spent at my house when, rocking my baby Filippo in his arms, he seemed to be revelling in his new role as 'Uncle Fester', as he had nicknamed himself. But of course the TV was oblivious to this and carried on making the announcement for the benefit of those who didn't already know, throwing in some speculation for good measure: 'It is not known whether it was a natural death or suicide.'

No, it couldn't be suicide. Even the last time Marco called me he had spoken about his plans for the future. There were often more than mere hints of desperation in his voice, but I was sure that he was going to get back on his feet. Not for the first time, what had happened could not be undone and I had to hurry to Rimini, where the investigating magistrate, Paolo Gengarelli, had found the last letter I had given to Marco.

I think that it was the longest and most difficult night of my entire life. I gathered up a few things for Filippo, threw them into a bag and, in the middle of the night, dropped him off at my mother's house before my husband, Paolo, and I headed straight for Rimini.

In the long hours that we spent in the car, while my husband was driving, I remembered the years I had spent by Marco's side. Happy days, dark days, days full of hope and days of blistering disappointment. I got to know his personality, his nature – a mixture of incredible generosity and crude selfishness. I relived the persecution that for five years he had suffered at the hands of too many people. I felt anger but also frustration at not having been able to lift him out of that black hole he had fallen into. I was also slightly envious, as I thought of the people, like Gianfranco Josti, who had seen him at the pinnacle of his career during his glorious 1998 season.

I remembered his stories, and imagined the days of childhood whiled away with his beloved grandfather Sotero, long before the trouble started.

1

Enfant Prodige Meets *Enfant Terrible*

Understanding Marco Pantani's complicated but fascinating personality isn't an easy task. We have to start a long way back, with the story as told by Marco's mother Tonina:

> Manola was only five years old when I became pregnant with Marco. On one hand I was happy, because I always loved children, but on the other hand I was worried because times were hard and I had to work. I decided to go to Bellaria, where my parents lived, so that my mother could look after the little one while I brought some money in as a hotel chamber maid. Although the work was tough, I had to keep things moving along at home, so, with my big belly, I used to go shopping on my bike with Manola in the basket. One day, all three of us went head over heels; I suppose Marco was destined to fall down even before he was born. My husband, Paolo, was brimming with pride when he was born – he even brought his friends to the hospital in Cesena: 'Look how big his feet are. Isn't he handsome? Black hair, dark skin, but blue eyes.'

It wouldn't be the simplest childhood for either Marco or his sister Manola. Both were mischief-prone. Marco's escapades, in particular, left him with some of his best memories but also came close to causing his parents several heart attacks. In later years, Marco would explain: 'To say that I was a little tyke would be a major under-statement; I was a real pain in the backside, a tearaway. I was difficult to control and I never stopped causing trouble. I was a ringleader, I liked to be number one.'

One day, on his way home, holding hands with his mum and dad, Marco saw his granddad Sotero and ran towards him. A car was coming from the other direction. Marco wound up underneath the wheels getting off lightly with just a bump to the shoulder. While Tonina was rearranging hotel rooms, he would run off onto the beach and jump into the sea, and it was the hotel guests who went to fetch him. One day Tonina caught him in the nick of time while he was climbing up the railing of a balcony intending to throw himself off, convinced that he was a parachutist. Another time, he threw himself off a car roof trying to impersonate Zorro in a costume made by Tonina for a fancy dress party. Only years later did he own up to other exploits: Bicio and Massimo, two friends who often came to call for him after school, had bought some live eels for the August bank holiday and Marco had beaten them to death. That time he got a good clip round the ear for his troubles.

Yes, he was a little scamp, but he was also one that was well liked by everyone: a ringleader from his days at nursery, when his little pals used to look to him to solve any problem. Among his closest friends was a disabled boy called Fabio. They remained good friends throughout Marco's career, when Marco would often visit him at his family home. And what about school? Tonina picks up the story:

He had been given the label of 'problem child' and, even later, this used to grate with him. Signora Neri, his teacher, wanted an assistant teacher just to keep him under control and Marco never got on well with her because of that. When he became famous, Signora Neri came to see him; she had moved to Forlì and she was pleased to see him again because, for all his mischief, she always thought that he'd be successful in life. At Marco's funeral her bunch of flowers lay next to the coffin.

Marco had to be pushed to go to school because he didn't like the idea of being sat down behind a desk for hours or having to do homework. His reports never made it home. It was his granddad, Sotero, who used to pick him up because Paolo and I had to work and it was Sotero who would put his signature on the reports.

After school, keeping him on a leash was a challenge. He would meet his friends then lead them on their usual capers. A favourite prank was catching lizards and pretending to shoot them at his mother like bullets. He played in the courtyard with Tonina keeping him under surveillance from the window. When he took off his T-shirt to tie it around his waist it was a sure sign that he had wet his pants – a desperate measure to get yet more attention! For years this was the pattern and he only stopped when the tellings off also stopped. He was a show-off, but smart with it: 'Marco do your homework, do your homework.' 'Yes, I'll do it in a bit.' He never looked at his books at home because he memorised everything he heard in the classroom. When he was eight years old, his report read as follows:

> Uncertain start, a very clear intelligence which is counteracted by an unruly, restless temperament. He is overly energetic, very aggressive, irremediably careless and disorganised. With class-mates, he always wants to be ahead of the rest and he never accepts defeat. He does almost no work at home, but at school he shows an interest in everything and is willing to contribute to discussions on any subject. Poor in language due to lack of care over writing and spelling; good and very individual ideas. In arithmetic he gets by. Is improving. Always willing in drama lessons.

It wasn't easy to make ends meet for the Pantani family. Indeed, under the strain of work and raising two children, Tonina became ill with depression and was hospitalised for a long period. The dastardly duo of son and bike added to her headaches:

> We lived on the canal. When he was very small, his granddad gave him a red bike and I never stopped worrying that he would end up in the water. I felt these things inside, just like in my nightmares I always imagined that Marco drowned in a washing tub and died. It was there, in our house on Via Garibaldi, that Marco was taught to ride by my brother-in-law and the president of the Fausto Coppi club, Signor Ciani. He was an old man and Marco became very fond of him.

When work called, Tonina would scoop up the children and put them on the bike, Marco in front, Manola behind. 'Promise me you'll keep your legs wide apart because if they get caught up in the wheels we'll fall,' she would say before every journey. One day, on the bridge on Viale Roma, Manola couldn't resist: she threaded a foot between the spoke and all three finished up in a bundle on the tarmac. Manola's foot was permanently damaged. Much to the disapproval of her doctors, however, it wouldn't stop her escaping to the beach with Marco whenever she could.

Paolo and Tonina certainly had anything but a quiet life. They did however have the satisfaction, after years of sacrifice, of being able to afford a large flat in a block on Viale dei Mille.

Marco, like all boys of his age, had learned to play football. His parents had bought him some studded boots ('they cost an arm and a leg') and he wanted to show that he could play, although his whippet-like physique made him an obvious candidate for the subs bench. Cycling was his way out, and the fact that the square underneath his apartment block was the local rider's meeting place added to the appeal. It was also where the Fausto Coppi's *directeur sportif*, Nicola Amaducci, lived, where the team bus loaded with bikes would set out for races, and where the training sessions would start: no more than twenty or thirty kilometres on the road with Amaducci keeping watch from behind the steering wheel of his car.

One day, Marco made what seemed like a rash decision: he took his mother's bike and decided to tag onto the bunch. He had to sweat blood, but somehow managed to follow the wheels and make it home in a semi-conscious state several hours later. After that feat of endurance, the calls for Marco to join the chain gang on a more permanent basis became unanimous.

Although he certainly didn't lack enthusiasm money was in short supply. Mindful of this, Marco found it hard to argue the case for his new interest, which had taken the place of football, swimming and running. One day, having spoken to Tonina first, he decided to tackle his father:

'Dad, I want to race bikes.'

'Yeah, it will be like the football – you'll get bored and give up. What's more, to race you need a bike, and that doesn't come cheap.'

'Don't worry, they'll give me everything at the Fausto Coppi, a bike too.'

The bike, Marco's first, turned out to be a Vicini painted in metallic grey and donated second-hand by the Italian Cycling Federation. Before finding an owner, it was on display in the Bar del Corso in Cesentaico. It was too big for Marco, whose feet only just reached the pedals. He writhed around on his saddle and was made the butt of endless jokes. It didn't matter; he had won his battle and now he could let his pedals do the talking. The arrival of the bike also bought about a change in Marco's father. Paolo began to spend what little spare time he had behind his son's bicycle. 'I have two jobs to do,' Pantani senior used to complain to his wife, 'to keep up with you and keep up with Marco.'

The beginning of a love affair

Marco Pantani had a unique relationship with Sotero, his paternal grandfather. Sotero had taught him how to fish in the sea and the river, sometimes took him along on hunting trips, and the two spent hours going on walks together. It seemed natural that he would give his grandson his full backing in his new passion. On his thirteenth birthday, Sotero presented Marco with a blood red Vicini Tour de France which was considerably more expensive than the one his parents had been considering. 'Don't worry, I'll pay the difference,' Sotero said, calming his son's protests.

Marco was in seventh heaven. No bike was cleaner than his: after training rides, he would bring the bike into the flat and, if it had got muddy, take it straight to the bath tub. Tonina, by now selling *piadine* – a flatbread sandwich which is a speciality of Romagna – in a bar in Cesenatico, reacted exactly as one would expect.

Neither is it hard to imagine how Marco spent his afternoons: on his bike, in search of new mountains. Drawing on the local knowledge that Paolo had picked up on hunting trips over the years, Marco would discuss routes with his dad and then go out to test them. He would return home at dusk, with 130 or 140 kilometres in the legs. There wasn't a hill or mountain in the whole of Romagna that he hadn't climbed. Plus, he had a great time going off with the boys from Fausto Coppi; him invariably tucked in at the back until the road started to rise. At that stage he would overtake them, look them in the eye one by one and finally ride away into the distance. Years later, after Marco had turned pro and had already collected some of his most famous victories at the Tour and Giro, the journalist Gianfrano Camerini asked him: 'Who are you when you drop everyone? Does the climb empty your mind of all thoughts?' Marco replied: 'I am my own man. In training I can't bear to be dropped. I want there to be nothing but fresh air behind me, whether it's in races or just on a gentle spin. Every day I want to get used to being alone: the rest have to worry about following me. Not until I've got rid of them all do I feel at ease. What's more, my body is made for climbing mountains.'

The date 22 April 1984 is etched in the memory of Paolo Pantani: in Case Castagnole, riding in the Under-14 category, Marco Pantani won his first race.

'I remember it well, because before the race I wrote a little note and slipped it into his jersey pocket. "Be brave, either you blow up or you make the others blow up." He found it when he was rummaging around in his pocket at the start line and read it out loud in front of Amaducci's wife. He listened to me: he got into a break and won.'

Successes like these were few and far between – races in the Under-14 category tended to be ridden on a flat course. But all Marco needed was a motorway bridge to drop everyone, which was precisely what happened in La Caserma, a village between Forlì and Cervia. If there was a real climb, like the one in Reggello, he took them all to the cleaners: three kilometres from the finish-line, one of his team-mates, Anthony Battistini, was out front, over a minute ahead of the nearest chasers. Among them was Marco, who, on the hardest part of the climb, suddenly accelerated, dropped the group like a piece of litter and, after catching his team-mate, breezed past him to cross the finish line alone.

After his initial doubts about Marco's choice of sport, his father found himself falling in love with cycling. This reinforced the bond between father and son, even though Paolo spent a lot of time away from home with work. Sometimes, Marco would follow his dad as he travelled the length of Italy to work on the construction of water works or industrial refuse plants. Paolo remembers:

> I was working down south, in Puglia, Lessina to be precise. Marco, who was fifteen by then and had moved into the next age group in races, had come with me. He was always out training, between Rodi Graganico and Peschici, or in the Foresta Umbrai; he was quite prepared to do more than 100 kilometres just to try some climb that one of the locals had told him about. A week later, we went home because Marco wanted to enter a race with a hilltop finish. He won by a huge margin.

The race started in Forlì and ended at the top of the Monte Corona, and Vittorio Savini remembers it fondly. Having spent three years as Marco's *directeur sportif*, Vittorio became the president of the 'Club Magico Pantani' when Pantani became the sport's most popular figure in the mid 1990s. Before that time, there wasn't too much silverware to buff the Pantani reputation. This was mainly due to Marco's bad habit of staying at the back of the bunch until the road started to climb: the decisive break had often already got away and, so, while making up prodigious ground, Marco had his work cut out to catch up with the leaders. There were spectacular crashes, too, adding to Tonina's anxiety when she knew that her son was out on his bike.

One such occasion was in 1986. On a descent not far from home, an oncoming car struck Marco head on and he was close to dying from a ruptured spleen. Another day, in a mock sprint with his training partners he collided with a van, cutting his face and leaving him with a scar that would never disappear. As if all this wasn't enough, Marco managed to find trouble even in winter, when he would rig his bike up with snow wheels, which he had invented to enable him to ride on icy roads. Although he was skinny, the ice on the canal or local pond didn't always hold his weight, making cold baths something of a ritual.

When he wasn't injured, Marco adored training with the pros who lived in the area, especially Alfio Vandi and Claudio Savini, Vittorio's brother. Both tried in vain to dissuade him from attempting to follow them, since their training was patently too intense for a junior. But Marco, stubborn as he was, latched on to their wheels and never allowed himself to come unstuck. They would try to trick him: Vandi attacking going uphill and Savini pretending that he was too tired to chase. 'If you want, I'll go after him,' Marco suggested. Off he went. It would then be Savini's turn to attack, with Vandi playing games, and the youngster chasing again. In the end, it would be Marco who upped the pace and be the first to quench his thirst at the water fountain at the summit. 'What does your Dad feed you?' Vandi and Savini once asked, stunned.

Although wrapped up in his son's possible future as a star cyclist, Paolo Pantani saw to it that Marco attended school until he obtained his diploma. After middle school, he enrolled in a technical institute in Cesena, where he specialised in radio technology after a failed attempt to earn a place on the agriculture course. It was a familiar story: not much studying, poor marks and a couple of exams to be retaken in October. Then came the umpteenth accident – a broken collarbone. No training but no studying either. 'Dad, I want to be a pro rider, I can't waste my mornings at school; at that time of the day I should be going to train.' His father replied curtly: 'Fine, try then, but remember that if you fail you'll be making *piadine* with your mother in the snack-bar or you'll be helping me as a plumbing technician.' It was the latest and so far biggest challenge, and Marco Pantani – the man from the sea who lived to climb mountains – would emerge as the clear winner.

On the brink of greatness

At nineteen years of age, having won the tug of war with his parents, Marco dedicated his life to cycling. He had marked his eighteenth birthday, literally, by having a likeness of the devil tattooed onto his right forearm and a butterfly on the opposite arm. 'Everyone of my age was having tattoos, so I joined in and went to Rimini to a bloke who they said was a specialist,' Pantani would explain later. He didn't need to explain to his Italian audience that the devil was also the symbol of his favourite football team, AC Milan.

After beating off the competition of the many other local teams who wanted to sign him, the Rinascita Ravenna amateur team welcomed Pantani into its ranks. The team's manager was Giuseppe Roncucci, another key figure in the development of Marco's career. Various other coaches who worked with Pantani claimed that he wasn't easy to manage, that he pretended to listen to them but ultimately did his own thing. Roncucci, on the other hand, seemed to be tuned in to the Pantani wavelength from the start.

'I can assure you,' says Roncucci 'that in the three seasons he spent with me he always followed my instructions. He knew how to get respect even from boys who were older than him. He lead the team with great confidence, which came from his strong personality, but when it was time to graft for the team he was at the front of the queue as well.'

He immediately made his mark on the amateur scene, winning twice in his début competition – a small stage race in a remote corner of Italy's deep South. But his thoughts were already dominated by the amateur version of the Giro d'Italia, which he would ride for the first time in 1990. It wasn't a happy experience. In the time trial, riding on disc wheels which he had never used before, he misjudged a curve and hit a wall, badly bruising his shoulder. That evening Roncucci called Paolo to ask whether he could come to fetch his son and take him home. Marco would recover from the injury in no time, but in his current state there was no sense in continuing the Giro.

'When I got there, I found Marco in tears,' Paolo recalls. "Dad, you tell him, I can carry on even with one hand. Please, let me stay." He insisted so much that he twisted both my arm and Roncucci's.'

They cooked up an ingenious solution: a special rubber armrest, fixed to the handlebars with sticky tape. He could brake with one hand but had to avoid putting pressure on his arm. He finished the Giro in third position behind eventual winner Wladimir Belli. It turned out to be a fruitful season, with a handful of victories and the Emilia regional championship title.

The following year, Marco made another step up, finishing the amateur Giro in second place behind Francesco Casagrande and pocketing a pair of stage victories at Agordo and Pieve di Cadore in the Dolomites. Only the time he lost to Casagrande on the flat denied him overall victory. The performance that really turned heads, however, came in another race, at Futa, in a mountain time trial open to both amateurs and professionals. Pantani recorded a time just a few seconds slower than Gianni Bugno who rode sporting the world champion's rainbow jersey he had earned the previous year in Stuttgart. Some conspiracy theorists even suggested that Bugno was allowed to slipstream behind motorbikes belonging to the race organisers, the theory going that they couldn't bear to see their bill-topping word champion upstaged by a 21-year-old amateur who was still unknown to the wider public.

Finally, in 1992, came the long-lusted after victory in the amateur Giro. Pantani's dislike for time trials was already common knowledge, and he came close to sabotaging his chances by losing four minutes against the clock. It was in the Dolomite mountain stages of Cavalese and Alleghe that he turned things around. Roncucci's account:

> Marco attacked on the first climb, dropping all of his closest rivals. The only rider who could follow him was a Colombian, who even did his share of the pace-making. To reward him for his help, Marco had promised to let him win the stage. But he double-checked with me and, realising that his advantage wasn't enough, I told him that he had to leave the Colombian behind and gain as many seconds as possible if he wanted to take the pink jersey and not just win the stage. He listened to me, rode away and crossed the line on his own. Sure enough, he won the Giro.

One mission was accomplished, but for around a year Pantani had already been sizing up an even more ambitious goal: turning pro. He had contacted Davide Boifava, manager of the Carrera team, and had Roncucci and his father at his side at their first meeting. Boifava says:

He wanted a contract straight away, but the rules made it impossible – with the Olympics coming up no amateur was allowed to move up into the pros. 'I'm not leaving here if you don't give me a contract to sign,' he moaned. Finally, I managed to convince him that, the following year, as soon as the regulations allowed it, I would call him. After his win in the amateur Giro d'Italia, he signed. I'll never forget what he said as he was leaving the room: 'You manage a big team, a team of champions and I have chosen this team. But remember: you're the one who has done the best business here by taking me on, not me by coming to you.'

On 5 August 1992, at the age of twenty-two years, seven months and four days, Marco Pantani made his official professional début at the Gran Premio di Camaiore in Tuscany.

2

The Makings of a Superstar

Marco Pantani completed his first season among the professional elite in 1993. Still timid in such exalted company, Davide Boifava felt that Marco needed some guidance, and asked Claudio Chiappucci to take him under his wing. Chiappucci was at this time recognised as one of the sport's best climbers and most colourful personalities, a reputation based largely on his kamikaze breakaways in the 1990 and 1992 Tours de France. Known as 'El Diablo', Chiappucci was Pantani's room-mate at his first Giro d'Italia with the pros. Chiappucci recalls:

I had met him a few months earlier, in a restaurant in Cesena. My first impressions were good because it was obvious that he knew what he wanted. Like me, he had chosen Carrera because it was the team which offered the most security. At first, he didn't say much, kept himself to himself; it was a struggle to get him to open up with me. I think he had a few problems fitting in with the older members of the team, especially Guido Bontempi, who were good pros but also had a tendency to get on your nerves. That's why I tried to protect him. What struck me most was his attention to detail in everything. He wanted his saddle height millimetre perfect, the cleats on his shoes millimetre perfect, and the length of every training session kilometre perfect. He was meticulous about everything, maybe too much. In that Giro he withdrew four stages from the end.

Tendonitis in his knees was slowing him up and Boifava insisted that he stop, waving away Marco's protests – there were big climbs still to come and he was looking forward to testing himself in the Sestriere mountain time trial. He had also broken two vertebrae in a fall. Thus, Pantani's first Giro d'Italia proved to be in keeping with his maiden season with the pros: few tangible rewards, some harsh lessons, several of which were invaluable, including the trip to Belgium and into the lair of the one-day race specialists in Liege-Bastogne-Liege.

The next year's Giro d'Italia was to mark the beginning of the end of Pantani's initiation period. His hairline receding every day, Pantani now had to prove that he was maturing quickly on the bike, too. A handful of good displays in the races leading up to the Giro – particularly his fourth-place finishes in the Giro del Trentino and Giro di Toscana – persuaded Boifava to give him some freedom within the team. Pantani didn't need a second invitation, finishing fifth at Campitello Matese, just four days into the race. That day's winner was a young, blonde-haired blue-eyed Russian, Euvgeny Berzin, who surged unexpectedly to the top of the overall race standings and was never overtaken. Berzin was a meteorite, a freak phenomenon who, in the years that followed, plunged to earth as quickly as he had risen.

The Giro was entering its second week. Miguel Indurain, the comfortable victor in the previous two years and the pre-race favourite, had looked in trouble against Berzin. The Russian, the same age as Pantani, had Indurain eating dust in the Giro's first time trial, where the Spaniard had previously reigned supreme, and on the medium-length climbs he had shown that he had another gear.

This particular year Italy's national tour was leaving the confines of the peninsula to make PR-friendly stopovers in Slovenia (Kranj) and in Austria (Lienz). In the second of these stages, a long-range solo victory by Michele Bartoli had overshadowed a sudden acceleration by Pantani on the Bannberg climb. No more than a leg-loosener, perhaps, but the attack had lifted Pantani by three places in the overall standings, into tenth.

Twenty-four hours later, this conqueror of mountains from the Italian plain was to finally make his grand entrance onto the world stage. Claudio Chiappucci, at the time Pantani's team captain, tells the story:

From Lienz, we were riding to Merano, climbing four mountain passes on the way. I was in a breakaway and behind us, the group containing all the main contenders had started to chase. They caught me three kilometres from the summit of the Giovo Pass and I saw that Pantani was with the leaders. I rode alongside him and said: 'I'm too tightly marked, you turn on the gas a kilometre from the top, and we'll see if the group breaks up. If we come back to you on the descent, I'll try an attack.' Marco still didn't have much of a reputation in the peloton so they let him go, but I knew that he was a good descender, almost as good as me. As he rode away to the finish, I acted as a stopper. Marco won the stage and I lost out to Bugno in a sprint for second place.

On the next day, a stunning action replay. The difference being that, this time, the mountains which provided the backdrop were pillars of cycling lore, and included the 2,758-metre Passo Stelvio, Italy's highest mountain pass. Chiappucci again:

As per usual, I was out front in a small breakaway, but at the end of the Stelvio descent only Wladimir Belli was still with me. As soon as the Mortirolo began, I heard on my earpiece that Pantani had taken off out of the chase group. It's the same scenario as the previous day: when he caught me, I told him to attack and he rode away. Berzin tried to stay on Marco's wheel while Indurain climbed at his own pace. Marco's changes of pace soon shook off Berzin, too, but on the descent Indurain and Belli came back to him. The three shared the work equally, because Indurain wanted to kill off Berzin on the overall standings.

On the final obstacle of the day, the Santa Cristina climb, Pantani spotted Indurain's increasingly leaden pedal-stroke, and launched yet another attack, finally braking free of the Spaniard to romp to his second straight stage win. The fanatical Italian fans – the *tifosi* – hailed their new idol at the finish in Aprica amid some of the most euphoric scenes ever witnessed at the Giro. Chiappucci, the now outgoing national hero, completed a perfect day for the home crowd by finishing second, having also put paid to Indurain on the Santa Cristina.

'That day, we showed that, by pooling our strengths, we could wreak havoc,' Chiappucci reflects. 'It wasn't to be because he was the rising star while I, having reached the top, was coming to the end of my career. The press, the *Gazzetta dello Sport* in particular, started to hype up a rivalry which, in reality, never existed. There was no animosity between us. They would stop at nothing to split us up and in the end they succeeded, even though Pantani and I never argued.'

On the morning of Monday 6 June, still giddy from Pantani's latest, inspirational cavalcade, Italians unfolded their favourite daily sports newspaper, the *Gazzetta dello Sport*, to be greeted by the front-page headline: 'Pantani, you're a legend'.

It was overlooked later that Chiappucci and the rest of the Carrera team hardly went out of their way to boost the youngster's chances of garnishing his double stage success with the overall victory in that Giro. His heroics at Aprica had fast-tracked Pantani up the general classification and within reach of the leader's pink jersey (although Berzin then consolidated his lead in the mountain time trial up the Bocco pass in Liguria). To turn the race to his advantage, Marco would need a special performance, of the kind he had often conjured up as an amateur.

There was a stage that looked ready-made, starting in Cuneo and taking the race to Les Deux Alpes, over the French border, and climbing the legendary trio of the Agnello, Izoard and Lautaret passes before the final rise to the ski resort. Pantani had taken his cue, attacking on the first climb and decimating the peloton. Sadly, he soon came up against a formidable coalition orchestrated by Moreno Argentin, Berzin's team captain and a shrewd tactician. Pantani's solo raid ended in Briançon, with a pair of mountains still to climb and a headwind sucking him up back towards a chasing group containing Berzin and Indurain. Also present were Pantani's Carrera team-mates, Chaippucci and Poulnikov, but both were clearly more interested in pursuing individual success than in helping the young climber.

So it was that Poulnikov succeeded in winning the stage while Pantani, sporting the white jersey awarded to the best-placed Under-25 rider, secured his place in the affections of both the public and the pundits. It hardly seemed to matter that it was Berzin who was parading in the pink jersey when the race ended in Milan, with Pantani having to settle for second ahead of the great Miguel Indurain. That day in Milan, the usually docile Spaniard vowed that, at the Tour de France, he would make Pantani – this little upstart – pay for subjecting him to such humiliation on the mountains of the Giro.

At the age of 24, Marco Pantani set out on his voyage of discovery in the sport's most famous and prestigious event, the Tour. He was a distant onlooker in the bunch sprints which characterise the first week of the race, and suffered during the team time trial. The race then crossed the Channel for a three-day stop in England, with Marco's compatriot, Flavio Vanzella, wearing the yellow jersey. Like everyone else, Marco was blown away in the first individual time trial by the whirlwind Indurain, clearly over his Giro disappointment and now the favourite for a fourth consecutive Tour victory. Finally the mountains came, first the Pyrenees, kicked off with the long climb to Hautacam, above Lourdes. As soon as the road began to rear up, Marco tried to get clear. For once his kick wasn't incisive and the metronomic Indurain caught and overtook him shortly before the line. As usual, 'Big Mig' wasn't interested in winning the stage and let the Frenchman Luc Leblanc, who was soon to be crowned world champion, take the stage. The Carrera team had lost on two fronts: Pantani was clearly dissatisfied with his third place, and Chiappucci, who had made no secret of his victory ambitions, had fallen ill with food poisoning and was forced to pull out the following day.

The second day in the Pyrenees saw another gruelling trek through the mountains. This time it was another climbing prodigy, the Frenchman Richard Virenque, who grabbed the headlines with a stage win.

Although he moved up several positions on the overall standings, Pantani gained just a handful of seconds on Indurain on the final climb of the day; stage wins were destined to elude him in that first Tour. He would have loved to open his account on the Mont Ventoux, where he launched yet another of his by now trademark attacks, only for the win to go to another Italian, Eros Poli, after an epic solo breakaway. On Alpe d'Huez, which would be a happy hunting-ground for Italians throughout the 1990s, fans watched Pantani soar but lose out again to a rider who had been allowed to escape much earlier in the day, Roberto Conti. Conti also hailed from the Romagna region, and later went on to be one of Pantani's most loyal team-mates and friends.

The pattern continued. At Val Thorens, Pantani, now already drawing comparisons with the 'Angel of the Mountains' Charly Gaul, was again inundated with praise and adulation. But no sooner had the stage began than Pantani fell heavily on his knee. The race doctor pointed him towards the following ambulance, but Pantani flatly refused. The pain only subsided after a few kilometres of unbearable discomfort. On the final climb, displaying the full expanse of his strength and courage, he shook off all of his main rivals but still didn't manage to taste victory on the day. Consolation came only in the knowledge that the podium was now within reach and, later, after beating Indurain in the mountain time trial to Avoriaz. Unfortunately, there too, someone had gone even faster: Piotr Ugrumov. The Latvian went on to finish second behind Indurain in Paris, with Pantani a brilliant third in his first Tour. A rapturous reception on the Champs-Elysées confirmed that Pantani had already won many French hearts.

The season of despair

After the performances of the previous season, it seemed natural that Marco Pantani's main objective in 1995 would be the Giro d'Italia, especially with Indurain announcing that he would be focusing on his quest for an historic fifth Tour win. Pantani also had a score to settle with Berzin, the Russian who owed a large portion of his success the previous year to team-mate Moreno Argentin's shrewdness. But Brezin could no longer lean on Argentin as the ex world champion had retired after the '94 Giro. Poulnikov's departure was the only major change in Marco's Carrera team: Chiappucci was still the captain, even though Pantani was earning more and more freedom. This was not least because Pantani had shown himself to be a good team player, while Chiappucci's difficult temperament was well known.

As always in the build-up to a major event, Pantani was training tirelessly. No more nightclubs, no more boat trips, hunting or fishing. A one-track mind. He had looked quickly at the race route: the climbs were well spread out to counterbalance the Maddaloni time trial, along with a forty-kilometre mountain time trial to Selvino. His legs were sending back promising signals, too: in the Giro dell'Appennino, a key warm-up race, Marco had set a new record split time on the famous Bocchetta climb, despite only crossing the finish line in fifth place.

The first of May was a bank holiday for everyone except the riders – the so-called convicts of the road – who had just twelve days to fine tune their form before the Giro. Marco had decided to do just that at the Tour of Romandy and in the afternoon was due to fly to Switzerland. He thought a brisk spin before a long car journey would be the perfect tonic, and what better place to do it than on his favourite, undulating route from Cesenatico towards Sant'Arcangelo and then on to the Republic of San Marino.

At the crossroads of Via Emilia, Marco glimpsed a Fiat Punto. There was a stop sign, so he didn't envisage any problems. The driver would have to brake. Maybe the driver was distracted – he was looking in the opposite direction to where Marco was coming from. Pantani locked his brakes and tried to steer but couldn't avoid the collision. He was sent sprawling over the tarmac and badly cut his cheekbone. The road immediately filled up with people who recognised the local hero and within minutes an ambulance had arrived. The guilty driver was inconsolable: he was a fan of Pantani and knew him well because he also lived in Cesentico.

When he got to the hospital in Rimini, Pantani was conscious and even had the presence of mind to phone his parents to tell them not to worry. The prognosis could have been much worse as the doctors reeled off a long list of bumps and bruises – including concussion, laceration wounds to the right temple, bruises to the right knee and lower spine, plus general grazing – but no breaks. In spite of his protests, Marco would stay in hospital for two days to undergo a series of tests including a computerized axialtomography (CAT scan of the brain), all of which were negative.

Marco spoke to Davide Boifava and Giuseppe Martinelli, his Carrera team managers several times a day. The question was always the same: 'Will I be better in time for the Giro?' No sooner had he returned home than he had retrieved his bike from the garage for a first fitness test. The results weren't encouraging: he was hurting all over, from his head to his knee. Naturally, he didn't give up and planned a long training session for the following day. But there was more disappointment when pains in his knee forced him to beat a premature retreat back to Cesenatico. A visit to a specialist in Brescia revealed the root of the problem: the impact with the car had badly bruised his cartilage and the fluid around it. In addition to the usual infrared and laser treatment, he was ordered to rest for at least ten days. He started to panic: how could he rest with the Giro on its way?

The race was due to get underway in Perugia on Saturday 13 May, and with three days to go Pantani had to take a decisive fitness test: Marco was on his bike with *directeur sportif* Boifava behind the wheel of his Carrera team car. A few turns of the pedals were all Boifava needed to confirm his and his rider's worst fears. Pantani had difficulty absorbing the blow but Boifava was sure that if he rode the Giro instead of treating his injuries as he should, Marco's career could be at risk. The best medicine, after all, was rest.

The Giro that Pantani had dreamed of winning started without him and was to be dominated from start to finish by Switzerland's Tony Rominger. Berzin was without doubt less impressive than in 1994 but recovered ground on the penultimate day to take second overall. Chiappucci again allowed the podium to slip through his grasp and Ugrumov came in third. At home, Pantani kept one eye on the TV but, with the Tour de France on the way, he was more worried about his injuries, which were taking longer than expected to heal. The Tour didn't inspire Marco like the Giro but he knew that it would bring more exposure than any other race and that he'd be expected to live up to the precedent he had set in 1994. He was also keen to win for the first time on French soil. To build his confidence before the Tour he entered the Tour of Switzerland, immediately reassuring his fans by winning the hardest stage of the race, a summit finish at Flumserberg after two tough mountain passes.

The 1995 Tour de France, the fifth and last instalment of the Indurain dynasty, was kind to the Italians. Fabio Baldato and Mario Cipollini each won stages, the Italian Gewiss–Bianchi outfit prevailed in the team time trial and the unfancied Ivan Gotti enjoyed two days in the yellow jersey. But it was Pantani who once again had the *tifosi* drooling, winning in record time on Alpe d'Huez and then at Guzet Neige in the Pyrenees. These events were overshadowed, however, with not just the Italians but the entire race rocked by the death of Fabio Casartelli. The 1992 Olympic champion, Casartelli crashed and died on the descent off the Col du Portet d'Aspet, blackening the mood and the entire race, in particular for his Motorola team-mates. One of these, Lance Armstrong, responded in the only way he knew, winning the stage to Limoges and dedicating his victory to Casartelli. The accident had the opposite effect on Pantani – arguably contributing more to his slide on the overall standings than a bout of gastroenteritis did.

The season served up one last, golden opportunity for Pantani in the shape of a world championship in Duitama, Colombia – a climber's paradise. Pantani knew that he would have few better chances of donning the rainbow jersey, so decided to prolong his season. He checked into the Italian team base a few days after his team-mates and within minutes was diving headlong into the hotel pool. In the evening, after dinner, Italian national coach Alfredo Martini invited him to take a stroll in the hotel grounds. 'You know, Marco, it's obvious that you're from the sea, because you swim like a fish,' Martini told him. 'You're used to it: a dip in the pool is relaxing, a bit of fun for you. But if you swim the others might want to as well and I can't stop them. Now think about some of the more fragile guys, like [Leonardo] Piepoli. They could catch cold and I might lose them for the race.' Pantani reassured him: 'Don't worry, Alfredo, I won't do it again, I promise.'

Twenty-four hours later, after a race won by the Spaniard Abraham Olano, coming in ahead of Indurain and Pantani, Martini found Pantani in his hotel room. The veteran Italian coach was in low spirits: Bugno had caved in immediately, Chiappucci seemed in good form but fell on the wet tarmac, while a slow-burning Pantani attack took out three Italians – Francesco Casagrande, Pelliccioli and Paolo Lanfranchi – who were supposed to protect him in the closing stages. 'Marco, you rode brilliantly, you're third place is more than deserved,' Martini said. 'You were right not to follow Olano: you could have wasted precious energy and maybe someone else would have attacked. It was the right choice to stay on Indurain's wheel.' Looking into the old man's eyes, Marco shrugged: 'Look, Alfredo, I only didn't go after Olano because, when he attacked, my rear-wheel slipped on the wet tarmac. Otherwise I would have gone with him and maybe the result would have been different. We could have been toasting another Italian rainbow jersey instead of a third place tonight.'

The near miss in Colombia would have been an oddly appropriate way to finish an unfortunate season. After the accident on 1 May, missing out on the Giro and the gastroenteritis at the Tour, 1996 should have been time for a fresh start and hopefully a more auspicious one. But fate had set one more cruel trap for Marco Pantani.

The fall in Milan–Turin

The season was drawing to a close in the time-honoured fashion with the historic triple-header organised by the *Gazzetta dello Sport* – Milan–Turin, the Tour of Piedmont and the Tour of Lombardy. Back from Colombia, on Boifava's advice, Marco agreed to ride Milan–Turin despite his long-standing ambivalence about one-day races, reasoning that it could at least serve as a useful warm-up ahead of the more prestigious Tour of Lombardy a few days later. During the race, as if to highlight his disinterest, Marco lurked at the back of the bunch and resisted any temptation to accelerate even on the Superga climb, traditionally where the race is decided. He did however hurl himself down the Pino Torinese descent, simply because swinging through curves at eighty kilometres per hour on a few millimetres of rubber is hard to beat for sheer thrill factor. Mindful of Pantani's descending skills, two riders moved into his slipstream, Francesco Secchiari and Davide Dall'Olio. The trio exited a sharp left-hand bend and could hardly believe it when they saw a car arriving from the opposite direction. It later emerged that local traffic police had waved the vehicle through thinking that the race was over. Despite braking hard, the three crashed into the vehicle with a thunderous force, were catapulted through the air and landed heavily on the tarmac. The race ambulance was already on its way to a hospital in central Turin with the victims of an earlier crash and a replacement was delayed by rush-hour traffic from the city and the dispersing race-goers. Finally, the paramedics arrived and the three riders were rushed to Turin for X-rays. The results showed a fracture to the tibia and fibula for Marco Pantani, a fractured pelvis for Francesco Secchiari, and a shattered femur for Davide Dall'Olio. To reduce Marco's fracture he needed a metal plate surgically inserted into his leg; Davide Boifava gave the go-ahead after consulting the Carrera team doctor Flavio Terragnoli. Little did he know it at this stage, but Pantani's discharge papers from the hospital in Turin contained information which was later used against him time and again in court cases throughout Italy. They highlighted huge fluctuations in Pantani's red blood cell count in the hours either side of his accident. According to magistrates this was evidence of the use of the banned drug EPO and they wanted to see him convicted of 'sporting fraud'.

The seriousness and nature of the injury left the race organisers and Turin police open to equally serious allegations of negligence. A decade on, Boifava is still incensed:

The local council and their insurers put their heads together so that they didn't have to spend a fortune. The two policemen who had let the car pass had been suspended and the council was using them to avoid having to pay tax – they were about to retire. Then the judge, Raffaele Guariniello, stuck his nose in. He sent men digging for dirt high and low, having made a series of allegations, including the claim, because of his high red-blood-cell count, that that one of the Carrera team doctors had sneaked into the hotel to inject Marco.

And yet, to me, the explanation was simple: he had been in Colombia for several days, at 3,000 metres above sea level, and then he had suffered a shock like that of the accident. I ask myself: why would anyone take EPO to finish 15 minutes off the pace – so far off the pace, in fact, that the police think that the race is finished and re-open the road? Where is the logic in that?

What I do know is that the *Gazzetta dello Sport* went big on Pantani that entire winter, trying to discourage Carrera from taking legal action. In the end the whole business did a gross disservice to all of the other riders and teams because, in the *Gazzetta*, all they talked about was Pantani, his recovery, when he might come back and so on. Guariniello kept searching until he finally managed to take Marco to court while, to my knowledge, Marco never got a penny from the Turin town council, even though that accident had cost him an entire season.

3

The Comeback and the Glory

Throughout Marco Pantani's stay in the Turin Central Hospital, his father, Paolo, kept his own vigil from a camper parked almost directly underneath the window of Marco's ward. Despite an infection (caused by the screws securing the metal plate in his leg) – which lead to a second operation – it wasn't long before father and son had returned to Cesenatico and Marco had begun his rehabilitation under the supervision of Fabrizio Borra. The physiotherapist would later become a key component of Pantani's support team in his most successful seasons, and a note Borra addressed to the rider shortly after his tragic death is a tribute to their friendship:

> Your determination when you were recovering from the accident in Milan–Turin blew me away. It seems like yesterday. Professor Terragnoli called me from Brescia and asked me if I wanted to take care of the rehabilitation of a certain Marco Pantani. At the time, I didn't work with cyclists – I came from motorcycling and I had started working in basketball – but I had heard of a promising youngster who had done great things at the Tour de France. At the same time, though, some friends in the medical profession had told me that the patient didn't have an easy nature and that he had less than amicable dealings with colleagues in the past. But with me, once some mutual trust had developed, I discovered a person who not only followed my instructions to the letter but encouraged me to stretch myself. To even hope to get you back to a competitive level, we

needed to leave the confines of traditional medicine, with all of the risks that this involved and that Professor Terragnoli kept reminding us of. But you were the first to tell me: 'Go on Fabrizio, if you think that this exercise will really help us, we'll divide the risk fifty-fifty.' Whenever I seemed worried you were the first to reassure me, despite the fact that it was your leg. Neither can I forget the way you spurred on the other patients who were coming to see me about other problems at that time, as if it was only them who were really ill and you were just passing.

How could I forget the time when a camera crew came to do a feature on your rehab? To enable you to immerse your leg in the water, I'd ordered a special sheath to cover the external brace from the United States; it had never been used before in Italy. The sheath had always worked perfectly, but that time you whispered to me that you thought water had got in. They had just told us that they wanted to film you getting out of the pool with the special sheath. You were a legend: you asked if you could get out of the water to go to the bathroom, you calmly emptied the sheath and from there we went straight to the massage table. You proudly showed the camera how the sheath had stayed perfectly watertight. I had to buy you a slap-up dinner for that.

Those six months left an indelible mark on my life. During that time, I know that I gave a lot but I also received so much. And after so many sacrifices, words couldn't describe the satisfaction of seeing you get back to where we had hoped, with your two legs perfectly balanced – so important in a sport like cycling where posture is at the centre of everything.

While Marco's long and productive relationship with Fabrizio Borra was just beginning at the start of 1996, his adventure with Davide Boifava's Carrera team was coming to an end. Boifava recaps:

Carrera was a giant company with a turnover of £300 million, but suddenly the whole thing collapsed and I no longer had the financial backing to carry on with the team. Luciano Pezzi had been wanting to get back into the sport for a while and we started talking about passing the whole team over to him. Although he was mostly interested in Pantani,

Marco would need a team built around him. Everyone who was under contract with Carrera moved across to Mercatone Uno, staff included, and my right-hand man Giuseppe Martinelli too. I, however, decided not to go as a matter of principle.

Because of Carrera's financial problems, I found myself needing £250,000 to finish the 1996 season. Luciano Pezzi, with whom I was negotiating the takeover of the team, helped me out: 'No worries, we'll give you the money then we'll come to an agreement.' That would have been fine had I not found out from Renato Di Rocco, the secretary of the Italian Cycling Federation, that rumours about Mercatone Uno bailing me out had been circulating for some time and they did my reputation no favours. At that point, I decided to forego the chance to manage the new team and an astronomical salary. I called Pantani and explained why I had refused. I said the same things to Martinelli: 'Dear Beppe, I'm giving you a rider and a team who will come back even stronger than before. You've been with me for a dozen years; now it is time for you to walk on your own two feet. If you need me you know where to find me, but you've got a very wise man alongside you in Pezzi. Don't worry.' After I'd made my little speech, Martinelli started crying. As for the £250,000 debt, I ended up making lots of sacrifices to pay it, but now I can walk with my head high knowing that I don't owe anyone anything.

Back in the saddle

During his long months of rehabilitation, while still relying on crutches to get around, Marco Pantani met Christina, a Danish student, in a nightclub. She had left Copenhagen to enrol at the School of Fine Arts in Ravenna and was working as a podium dancer to finance her studies. The first time Marco had reported to Borra's clinic it had been with her. Sporting a yellow and green Mohican, Christina didn't pass unnoticed.

For Marco, they had been long months full of sacrifices and tedious workouts, often under water, trying to restore muscle tone and re-educate the injured leg. Finally the crutches were thrown away and Marco was back in the saddle for the first, tentative outings on the bike under the strict guidance of Borra and Terragnoli. The call of the road was too tempting and – after a brief flirtation with the music business to sing the theme tune for that year's Giro d'Italia TV coverage – Pantani began to plot his return to racing. For the occasion, he wanted a minimum of fuss – none of the media circus which by now mobilised with his every move. The perfect opportunity presented itself at Cesenatico in a cyclo-tourist event called the 'Dino Ciaio' and organised by a group of Marco's friends. In the midst of bikes of every shape and colour, from mountain bikes and city bikes to the most high-tech racing machines, a girl dressed in a skin-hugging leotard and wig took her place at start line. Only at the end of the race, after the disguise had been shed, did the weekend warriors realise that the fast-dressing, fast-pedalling female had in fact been none other than Marco Pantani.

His return to competitive action was more orthodox. The date was 3 August, the race the GP Ceppagatti. Taking part was a feat in itself but by now Pantani was already thinking ahead to the following season. He was already in regular contact with Luciano Pezzi, who was busy preparing a new team to be built entirely around Pantani.

'Pezzi had given us carte blanche,' Giuseppe Martinelli remembers. 'There was a substantial budget and we had to put together a competitive team capable of supporting Marco at the Giro and the Tour. The first decision we made was to employ Roberto Pregnolato as masseur, seeing as Marco had already worked with him at Carrera. All of the decisions were rubber-stamped by Marco.'

The grey cat and the cry of the Alpe

The 1997 season got off to a promising start for Pantani, now sporting the yellow and blue colours of Mercatone Uno. He had trained well over the winter and continued his work with Fabrizio Borra. In the Spring, after his customary trip to Spain for some low-key early season races, he had ridden the second half of the Belgian Classics series, finishing well in both Flèche Wallonne and Liège-Bastogne-Liège. 'They are races you can win,' Alfredo Martini told Marco. But his mind was elsewhere – on

the Giro d'Italia, which that year was due to start against the romantic
backdrop of Venice.

His start at the Giro was less than ideal. Having lost a precious team-
mate, Simone Borgheresi, the victim of a bad fall in the San Marino
time trial, Marco lost ground to Pavel Tonkov, who was defending his
'96 Giro crown and whose stock was even higher now that he had
signed for the powerful Mapei team. The Russian underlined his
supremacy by outsprinting Frenchman Luc Leblanc and Pantani to win
on the Monte Terminillo. That evening, Pantani confided in Martinelli:
'Although I'm nowhere near my best, because a year out of the sport
takes its toll, I kept up with the others, even Tonkov who is stronger
than anyone at the moment. Let's wait for the big mountains and the
last week.'

In the event, his Giro would last only three more days. On the Valico
Chiunzi descent, the peloton was travelling at breakneck speeds when
the Swiss rider Felice Puttini collided with a cat. He was hurled across
the tarmac and took three riders with him; one of them was Marco
Pantani. The impact was hard and it took Marco several minutes to
remount his bike. His team-mates rallied around, encouraging him and
pushing him, to such an extent that the race jury later had to intervene
with fines. Having struggled to the finish-line, Pantani was rushed to
hospital for a series of checks. The diagnosis wasn't good: a torn thigh
muscle with internal bleeding inside the muscle. Riding on was out of
the question. Doctors told Pantani that he must observe a ten-day
period of complete rest.

In Pantani's absence, Ivan Gotti, another climber, would deny Tonkov
a second pink jersey thanks largely to a brilliant solo ride to Cervinia, the
ski resort perched on the Italian-facing flank of the Matterhorn. Pantani,
meanwhile, could only look ahead to the Tour de France, hoping rather
than believing that his latest setback wasn't the latest evidence of a
curse destined to follow him throughout his career.

The omens were good. As the Tour opened with a string of stages
marred by mass pile-ups, Pantani remained towards the back of the
peloton while Michele Bartoli, Gotti, Berzin and Rominger all crashed
out. Then, in the Pyrenees, Pantani offered glimpses of his brilliance

but finished third behind Richard Virenque and Laurent Brochard in a French Bastille Day bonanza. At Andorra the following day, he lost over a minute to Jan Ullrich, a young German prospect who a year earlier had finished second behind his team-mate and captain Bjarne Riis, and was now being touted as Indurain's heir. Almost unbeatable against the watch, Ullrich had proved his durability in the mountains, à la the great Spaniard.

A doubt was still eating away at Pantani: 'Will I be as good as before? Or have the accidents in Milan–Turin and Chiunzi caused irreparable damage?' He couldn't wait for the summit finish at Alpe d'Huez, the scene of a great triumph two years earlier. He knew that the Alpe would give him an answer, and so it arrived, emphatically, when he took off on the first hairpin of the mountain. No-one could follow him; his attack was devastating, sending the crowds lining the Alpe's famous 21 hairpin bends into ecstacy. He flew over the tarmac amid a swarm of motor-bikes, photographers and cameramen. He rode over the finish line with his arms spread wide and drowning out the crowd with his own celebratory roar. It was the end of a nightmare: Pantani was back. In fact, the stopwatch showed that he was stronger than before: he beat the record time he set on the Alpe in 1995, establishing a new mark of 37 minutes 35 seconds, which still stands today.

Unsurprisingly, after triumph came yet more adversity. At the Alpe, Pantani came down with bronchitis during the night. His breathing was badly impaired, and this allowed Ullrich and Virenque to return to centre stage on the second day in the Alps. Despite this Pantani needed only one day to reclaim his throne as the real king of the mountains – although it was Virenque who wore the polka-dot jersey. He broke away on the Col de Joux Plane, descending with his usual panache and going on to claim his second stage win. Marco knew that Ullrich and Virenque were out of reach on the overall standings, but he still dearly wanted to emulate his third place in 1994. Riis, who was by now reduced to the role of Ullrich's deputy, posed the biggest threat. The last mountains of the Tour, the less-than-terrifying Vosges, acted as the springboard for Pantani's final assault. It was one too many for Riis and, sure enough, Marco took a richly deserved third place.

On his way out of Paris, Pantani sent a parting message to Ullrich and Virenque: 'In a year's time, I'll be on top of the podium.' But before he turned his attention to the Tour, Marco wanted to keep a promise made to granddad Sotero as a child: 'One day, I'll win the Giro d'Italia.'

Triumph at the Giro

The 1998 Giro d'Italia was the 81st edition of the event. The race began in Nice with four favourites for victory: the Swiss Alex Zuelle, the Russian Pavel Tonkov, and the Italian climbing duo of Ivan Gotti and Marco Pantani. Zuelle was the most widely fancied, largely on the strength of his time trialling, and he duly prevailed in the prologue to claim the first pink jersey. An unlikely duel between Pantani and Michele Bartoli illuminated the opening stages: the latter, renowned for his prowess in one-day races, knew that he couldn't hope for overall victory in Milan but intended to enjoy a stint in the pink jersey on the way. Whenever the road began to rise, Pantani kicked but Bartoli kept hugging his wheel, leaving Zuelle as the only real beneficiary. Despite being caught up in a mass pile-up in sight of the finish line at Forte dei Marmi and losing his overall lead to Serghiy Gonchar, the Swiss remained the bookmaker's choice. Pantani and Bartoli continued to spar until Bartoli finally took the pink jersey on the eve of the first uphill finish on the race route at Lago Laceno. But in that lush, chocolate-box corner of southern Italy, which could easily be mistaken for a morsel of his native Switzerland, and on Pantani's preferred terrain, Zuelle regained command of the race. In fact, the bespectacled Festina rider left both Bartoli and Pantani reeling. As Pantani was forced to admit:

A rider who has won the Tour of Spain twice and has finished second in the Tour de France knows how to read a race. I used my instinct, him, his brain. I take some consolation from knowing that, if I can perform like that on this type of climb, which was only steep at the bottom, it means that I can do something special in the big mountains. On the other hand, I'm demoralised by the fact that Zuelle was the only one who benefited from my attack.

His confidence only slightly jolted, Pantani waited for the Dolomites to arrive, albeit with a scare on the way when he fell on the descent off the Passo di Zovo in the closing kilometres of the stage to Schio. Memories of his crash at Chiunzi twelve months earlier came flooding back. This time, there are no lasting effects, just a nasty fright. 'It was planned that I'd throw myself down that descent like a kamikaze, in spite of the slippery road, to put as much time as possible between myself and Zuelle,' he commented. Mission accomplished, because on the eve of the long time trial in Trieste, the final, windswept outpost before Italy becomes Croatia, the Mercatone Uno captain had reduced his deficit from Zuelle to just 22 seconds.

Twenty-four hours later all hopes of winning the Giro seemed to have evaporated again when he was caught by Zuelle, who set off three minutes after the Italian. The margin of defeat at the finish line was a mammoth three minutes 26 seconds, which meant that as the race entered the mountains, Pantani needed to recoup three minutes 48 seconds on Zuelle and one minute 46 seconds on Tonkov. It was a lot to ask, but Pantani always thrived on challenges like these.

In the first of three stages in the Dolomites, Pantani attacked with Giuseppe Guerini on the monstrous Fedaia pass and gained more ground on the Sella pass. At Selva di Val Gardena, while Guerini took the stage win, Marco pulled on the pink jersey after Zuelle had imploded on the Fedaia. Mum and Dad were there to share in the proudest day of his career so far. 'I would have liked my granddad, Sotero, to be here, too. He was one of my closest friends. He died in 1992, just before I won the amateur Giro d'Italia,' Marco said.

Romano Prodi, the Italian Prime Minister and a cycling fanatic, left one of many messages of congratulations. 'I'll see you soon,' he said, 'Maybe we'll even manage to go out for that famous ride of ours.'

Zuelle's threat had been banished, but Tonkov looked menacing. The Mapei rider even outsprinted Pantani at Alpe di Pampego to pocket some precious bonus seconds. It was on the next day, on the climb to Monte Campione, having appeared glued to Pantani's wheel, that the Russian surrendered. Inside the final three kilometres, Pantani delighted the *tifosi* with a desperate final attack. This time Tonkov was stuck to the road surface. After a brilliant stage victory, Pantani revealed: 'I said to myself: go on Marco, either you blow up or he will. He blew up, it turned out well for me.'

A time trial, which on paper boded well for Tonkov's chances of overturning his deficit of one minute 28 seconds, still stood between Marco and his boyhood dream. But Pantani went on to exceed all expectations to finish third behind time trial specialist Serghiy Gonchar and his team-mate Massimo Podenzana, increasing his advantage over Tonkov by five seconds. The performance raised eyebrows among the conspiracy theorists, who insinuated that Pantani's blood test sample had been illicitly swapped with that of team-mate Riccardo Forconi, who was thrown off the race on the morning of the time trial. The rumours received little or no coverage in the mainstream papers, which were too busy glorying in his success.

The final stage to Milan was no more than a lap of honour, an opportunity for the *tifosi* to hail their new god. In *the Corriere della Sera*, Pantani was compared to the last rider to enjoy that status in Italy, Fausto Coppi:

Pantani almost justified the irrationality of the fan in me. Coppi allied sublime climbing with the ability to grind away prodigiously on the flat; he used to win in the mountains and in time trials. Marco triumphed when the altitude graph reared up and he wowed us all in the solitary exercise against the clock, which had looked beyond his featherweight physique; he was able to use his opponents' sweat and facial features to gauge their suffering, and to devise a strategy accordingly.

The Italians' happiness was matched by Marco's own. But deep in his soul, there was also a note of sadness: Luciano Pezzi, the man who had wanted to bring him to Mercatone Uno, who custom built a team around him, who put faith in him when he was still hobbling around on crutches and might never have recovered, was seriously ill. Marco dedicated his Giro win to Pezzi, one of the wise old men of Italian cycling.

The apotheosis at the Tour

The days and weeks that followed the Giro were as breathless as the race itself: parties, award ceremonies, interviews, and invitations to appear on TV. After so much hard work and suffering, Marco was entitled to let his mind wander, especially now that Christina was almost ever-present at his side. In theory, there was a Tour de France to get ready for, but not even Martinelli, his devoted *directeur sportif*, had the courage to impose a strict regime of training. They should have been days of total relaxation, but grief meddled cruelly when Luciano Pezzi suffered a fatal heart attack. Pezzi had had the pleasure of seeing Marco parade in the pink jersey in Milan, but he wouldn't be around for the Tour. It was only out respect for Pezzi, a man who believed in Marco when other people's faith ran out, that Marco decided to compete in France. He skipped the Tour of Catalonia through illness but Martinelli soon dispatched Fontanelli, Barbero and Conti to Cesenatico to keep him company in training. His lack of race fitness would show in the first week of the Tour. At this stage Martinelli was suitably cautious. 'We are going to school,' he said. 'We are going to learn how we can win the Tour in 1999.'

Marco and his faithful troupe set out from Rome, bound for Dublin. In France, the football World Cup was nearing its climax. To avoid clashing with another international sporting showcase, the race organisers had decided to accept Ireland's lucrative offer to honour Sean Kelly and Stephen Roche by playing host to the first three days of the Tour.

Pantani now enjoyed star billing. He had won the Giro, every time he competed in the Tour he had left his mark in the Alpes and Pyrenees, and, above all, he promised to put up a fight against Ullrich, who looked in danger of establishing an Indurain-like hegemony over the Tour. Expectations were running high and some pundits even tipping Marco for the yellow jersey. Pantani, though, confused everyone when on the eve of the race, he declared: 'I came here so that I didn't have to watch the Tour on TV. Had I stayed at home watching the race, I would have started wondering what I could have done here. I didn't want to cause myself that headache, so I decided to come here on this fact-finding mission.'

The Tour was still in the blocks in Dublin when, in France, border guards performing spot checks on cars coming from Belgium stopped a Festina team car, the world's number one ranked team and the employer of Alex Zuelle and Richard Virenque. The driver was a masseur called Willy Voet. The car was full of doping products.

In Ireland, the team's manager Bruno Roussel denied all knowledge of the incident. The race organisers, the Société du Tour de France, could hardly do likewise since Voet's 'mobile pharmacy' was none other than a sponsored FIAT which they had provided. Nevertheless, they pointed out that Voet had been caught hundreds of miles from where the race was taking place and cordially invited Festina to explain themselves. Little did they know that within days the scandal would be threatening to bring down the race and everyone involved.

It was a rainy July Saturday when the action on the road began with a prologue time trial through the teeming streets of Dublin. Time trials were never Pantani's favourite discipline – he once threatened to ride armed with comics to alleviate the boredom – and he didn't even bother to inspect the course on the morning of the race. Instead, he stayed out of the rain by warming up on rollers. Only eight competitors recorded a slower time than him over the short, six-kilometre route, and Ullrich had already opened up a disproportionately wide margin of 43 seconds, even though he was beaten by Chris Boardman. The Englishman pipped the German by six seconds to take the stage and the first yellow jersey of the race. Hailing from just over the Irish Sea in Merseyside, Boardman was adopted as the de facto local hero. Many a pint of Guinness was raised in his honour before the Tour left Ireland.

Pantani didn't appear worried by his poor start. He also shrugged off criticism of his positioning at the back of the peloton, where he came away unscathed from a crash similar to the one which ended not only Boardman's stint in yellow but his race. 'If you have to fall, it will happen whether you are at the front, middle or back of the bunch. At the back, though, you have more time to avoid the bodies,' he said. What he didn't point out was that at the rear of the peloton, precious energy goes on closing gaps – short, sharp accelerations to keep up with the pace, which a rider can pay for when the mountains arrive.

The Tour landed in France, but there was nothing sweet about the return home. The investigation launched into Willy Voet and his already infamous Festina car continued apace. The quantity of doping products seized suggested that more than one team must be involved, raising suspicions of a trafficking ring; the team of investigators, marshalled by a magistrate in Lille, was working on several fronts. On the day of the Tour's crucial first time trial in Corrèze (after Mario Cipollini's sprint double at Chateauroux and Brive La Galliard), the Festina scandal finally erupted in all of its pyrotechnic, burlesque glory. The French police had raided the team's headquarters and found what they considered to be incriminating evidence. *Directeur sportif* Bruno Roussel, who police arrested along with team doctor Erik Ryckaert, caved in: 'It's true, we ran a system of organised doping within the team. The riders each put money into a kitty to buy doping products.' Faced with this, Tour director Jean-Marie Leblanc had no choice but to expel Festina and their riders, including Virenque, Zuelle, world champion Laurent Brochard, Laurent Dufaux, Christophe Moreau and Pascal Hervé. With hindsight, Virenque's tears, as he pleaded his innocence to journalists in a backwater Corrèze auberge, provided the enduring image of the Tour. Most fans still believed Virenque – with their banners protesting that 'Without Festina, there's no Tour' – but soon even *their* faith was crushed under a mass of evidence.

The mountains were approaching and every day Pantani felt stronger. He dumped his racing cap in favour of a pink bandana; in Pantani vernacular, the switch of headgear meant 'preparing for take-off'. The distracted, dawdling rider of the first week gave way to the usual stickler for precision who wouldn't think twice about asking his mechanic to adjust his saddle or handlebars by a single millimetre. The weather changed, too; most years, the July sun has the Pyrenees smouldering like giant, hot irons, but this time the riders were greeted by a cold, almost autumnal misty rain. Descending became treacherous. Francesco Casagrande and the yellow jersey Laurent Desbiens both crashed out.

The contenders played a waiting game until the Col du Peyresourde, when Pantani, who had complained of severe stomach pains that morning, threw away his bandana and went on the attack. Riders who saw him said later that 'he was like a cannon ball'. Nevertheless, he could only grapple back a few seconds from Ullrich, finishing second in Luchon behind Rodolfo Massi, a well-travelled Italian now riding for the French Casino team. The *tifosi* were relieved and delighted but Pantani soon bamboozled them again, telling Martinelli: 'You know, you're lucky. Had I won here, I'd have gone home.' Some, though, had sensed Ullrich's vulnerability, and Paolo Pantani and fan-club president Vittorio Savini were already on their way from Cesenatico with several coach-loads of Marco's most loyal supporters.

The race would as ever be decided in the second round of mountains, but before the Alpes there was a second summit finish in the Pyrenees, at Plateau de Beille. The sun had returned and with it Pantani's prospects improved. The final climb on that eleventh stage was long at 15.9 kilometres but, with an average gradient of 7.8 per cent, not prohibitively steep. Ullrich, still in yellow, got a puncture at the bottom of the Plateau. His team-mates stopped to wait. The German changed wheel and blazed off in pursuit of Pantani who made no attempt to capitalise: he had no desire to win by default, i.e. not just because Ullrich had been held up by mechanical problem. He waited for Ullrich to loom on his shoulder before beginning a slow torture which consisted of accelerating into every curve, slowing enough to allow a panting Ullrich to regain touch, then accelerating again. The Telekom rider was soon ground down. Pantani won the stage and reduced Ullrich's advantage on the overall standings to three minutes. Many now believed that Marco could overturn his deficit in the Alpes and complete an amazing Giro–Tour double. Ullrich's team scoffed: 'When Pantani has a three-minute advantage, then we will worry,' they said. 'We certainly aren't fretting now that he's three minutes *behind*.'

After such a trying start to the Tour, the rest day had never been more welcome. But in this Tour there was no respite. The nine members of Festina's Tour team had been detained in Lyons to be interrogated and drug-tested. Four admitted doping – the Swiss trio of Zuelle, Dufaux and Meier, and the reigning world champion, Laurent Brochard. Television channels beamed pictures all over the world of policemen foraging in team cars, storage lorries and riders' hotel rooms. The Dutch TVM team was also in the investigators' sights and, in the press, the coverage of the race barely registered among the number of pages dedicated to the scandal. Some commentators even wanted the race stopped. Then again, perhaps the Tour had found a new *raison d'être* in Marco Pantani, who could still enchant the hacks in his race-day press conference:

> When I attack, I try to psychologically destroy my rivals, who never know how far I can go. It's certainly hard to bear the responsibility of blowing the race apart every time, just as it's hard to tackle a mountain when you know the suffering that's around the corner. After I won the Giro, I could have stayed at home under my parasol, but then I thought that I can go home at any time. From the start in Dublin, I thought that I could win this Tour. To motivate yourself, sometimes you have to overestimate yourself. That's why I say now that I won't be happy with just any place on the podium in Paris.

The Tour was determined to brave its doping storm but the riders were now running for cover, having read and seen what had happened to the Festina riders. A hoax 'scoop' had muddied the reputation of the whole peloton (doping products were found in a rubbish bag attributed to a Tour team, but it transpired that they were put there by journalists working for a major TV channel). In Tarascon sur Arriège, the riders staged a sit-down protest in the middle of the road. A picture of a cross-legged, bandana-clad Pantani went around the globe. The riders wanted reassurances from the organisers and more respect for their work, and Pantani, now rechristened 'the Pirate' or 'il Pirata' by the Italian and French media, spoke out: 'We put ourselves through so much only for the media to talk about nothing but doping. The fans want to know our stories; the sheer number of people standing at the roadside is proof of that. I ask myself whether there's any point carrying on in these conditions.'

The Tour did carry on, as did Pantani, complaining all the while that the Tour was going out of its way to avoid the mountains. 'The crowds enjoy seeing riders climb mountains, but courses these days put races on a plate for time triallists,' he sniffed.

The Alpes couldn't come quickly enough, neither for Pantani nor the embattled organisers. The Festina scandal continued to dominate the race coverage. Mercifully, this changed, if only briefly, from the moment the peloton approached the harder, north face of the Col du Galibier, the first big Alpine ascent and the highest of the race. The Pyrenees had shown that Pantani revelled in the heat while others wilted, but on that morning Marco was greeted by slate skies and drizzle. The Galibier was still shrouded in mist when the peloton arrived several hours later. Four kilometres from the summit and with forty to go to the stage finish in Les Deux Alpes, Pantani cut through the fog with what looked like an action replay of his attack on the Perysourde and quickly began to eat up the advantage of a breakaway group which posed no threat on the overall standings. Pantani's belief that he could take the yellow jersey grew with every passing kilometre. He didn't panic when a stop to put on his rain jacket before tackling the descent cost him several seconds. He joined the remnants of the breakaway – compatriot Rodolfo Massi and three Spaniards – but quickly dropped the lot of them as the road began to rise again towards Les Deux Alpes. He didn't worry about what was happening behind, leaving Martinelli to find out via race radio that he was now the race leader on the road. Ullrich's challenge was perishing in the cold and the only question left was by what margin Pantani would take the yellow jersey. The answer was almost four minutes, leaving Bobby Julich, not Ullrich in second. The Tour's outgoing 'Kaiser' had in fact lost just under nine minutes on the stage and was now fourth overall, six minutes down on Pantani. The Tour had rarely seen such a dramatic turnaround. Pantani's Mercatone Uno team-mates were agog: on paper one of the weakest teams in the field, the race was now theirs to dictate all the way to Paris.

The next day there were five more mountain passes to overcome, including Marco's bogey climb, the Col de la Madeleine. It was here that Ullrich activated his plan to rescue his yellow jersey, his brutal attack unfastening everyone but Pantani. The German tried time and time again to shake off Pantani, but Marco's charity only extended to pretending to sprint but in reality gifting the German the stage victory on the line in Albertville. Both Ullrich and the fans applauded the sporting gesture, but Pantani's lead over Ullrich with five stages remaining was intact. Julich and the rest had lost ground.

There were more police searches, more interrogations. The crude attitude of the French *gendarmes* toward the riders who had spent their days toiling over mountain passes did the anti-doping cause little credit. The TVM team riders claimed that they had been 'treated like animals' – kept awake all night providing further urine and hair samples at a nearby hospital. Having pedalled like tourists for the first hour of stage 17, the peloton stopped completely while Laurent Jalabert and Bjarne Riis vented their frustrations at Jean Marie Leblanc. As the race leader, Pantani acted as the group's official spokesman and demanded 'that none of us are treated like the TVM riders.' Leblanc consented and promised to take the matter up with the French government. The Spanish teams still weren't satisfied and decided to abandon. 'With things as they are, I don't want to go all the way to Paris,' explained Jalabert, leader of the ONCE team and also, nominally, of the deserters. An Italian outfit, Riso Scotti, followed ONCE, Banesto and Vitalicio Seguros, all from Spain, out of the race. The whole Tour was now in danger of stopping; the detectives in Lille were making determined noises about finishing off not only the job but all drug trafficking in and around the professional scene. They were clearly not intimidated by almost a century of Tour history, as they proved when they threw 'King of the Mountains' Rodolfo Massi into an Aix Les Bains prison cell on suspicion of supplying drugs to other cyclists. A quick release after the allegations collapsed was no compensation for Massi having been robbed of the chance to take the polka-dot jersey to Paris. Only ninety riders now remained in the race. 'We have to arrive in Paris out of respect for Pantani. After what he has achieved, he deserves to do a lap of honour on the Champs-Elysées in the yellow jersey,' they choroused.

Pantani did make it to Paris, complete with polenta-yellow goatee beard, while the less follicly-challenged other members of the team and staff dyed their hair the same colour in honour of their captain. The Pirate took the final hurdle, the Le Creusot time trial, in his stride.

Entering the stage, Ullrich had haboured hopes of taking eight minutes and the yellow jersey off the Italian. Instead, over a 52-kilometre course, he recovered just two and a half minutes and could only cut Pantani's advantage to three minutes 21 seconds.

Standing on top of the podium on the Champs-Elysées, Pantani was joined by the last Italian to win the Tour, 1965 winner Felice Gimondi. The last Italian to triumph in the Giro d'Italia and Tour de France in the same season had been Italy's last *campionissimo*, Fausto Coppi, in 1949.

4

My Meeting with Marco Pantani

My first meeting with Marco Pantani took place in 1998. What follows is the story of a relationship which soon became a friendship, and which revealed the full depth of Marco Pantani's humanity.

Like everyone else in Italy, I had heard about Pantani's amazing exploits. News and praise of his Giro–Tour double reached even those, like me, who knew next to nothing about cycling. To tell the truth, I used to get bored watching races on the television and couldn't understand how the sport had the opposite effect on other people. But after Pantani's successes in Italy and especially France, whatever TV channel you cared to tune in to, on any news bulletin or current affairs programme, you saw Pantani. Or rather you saw something which looked as though it belonged in *Star Trek*, but had just staked a convincing claim for the title of the world's greatest endurance athlete.

I can remember how Max Biaggi, the star motorcyclist who I managed at the time – and whose jealousy was the only blot on an otherwise adorable character – started to worry that Pantani might put him in the shade. At that time, before Valentino Rossi matched and eventually eclipsed him, Max was the only cyclist or motorcyclist on the Italian sporting A-list. Perhaps unwittingly, he had given me an idea: I began to fantasise about managing both men – the world motorcycling champion and cycling's biggest name.

In the early summer of 1998, I took a trip to Riccione, just up the coast from Cesenatico, not to meet Pantani but to finalise arrangements for a convention I was due to host on behalf of a record company in September. I was lying by the swimming pool at my hotel when I received a phone call from Gianni Baldisserri, a close friend of Marco's. He said that Pantani was looking for a manager. Marco had met Alessia Tomba, the sister and PA of world-famous skier Alberto, and had asked her for advice on how to manage his image for marketing and PR purposes. Alessia had mentioned my name, explaining that I already took care of Max Biaggi. She also said that she could vouch for my honesty and professionalism.

I made an appointment for the following day, at the Bar dei Marinai ('The Sailors' Bar'), on the Porto canal in Cesenatico. I spent the next 24 hours agonising over how I would sell myself, how I would explain my methods to a sportsman whose profile was suddenly sky-high. I remember the problems I had come up against with Max, who invariably did the exact opposite of what we had agreed. Max cheerfully told me that a cyclist might be different. Moreover, judging by the handful of occasions I had seen him on TV, Pantani seemed like sweetness itself and therefore easy to manage. I just hoped that he hadn't let his hair grow: I was worried that I may not recognise him. Gianni Baldisserri was already waiting for me in the bar and, shortly afterwards, Pantani arrived dressed in an elegant grey suit – the sort of thing an Italian would normally wear to church. The suit was hanging off him. I had expected a giant and, instead, I found myself face to face with a waif. His personality was far more imposing. I would have been quite intimidated but I detected a certain twinkle in his eye which reassured me. I explained how I went about managing the image of a top athlete, my past experience, my favoured approach. I spoke for about an hour, after which, having listened attentively, Marco told me to do some research to find out how much his image was worth and then to draw up a plan. When this was ready, we'd meet again to discuss it. Andrea Agostini, another friend of Marco's, also joined us half way through the meeting. I didn't quite know in what capacity he was there, and he stayed silent throughout.

I set to work immediately. A call from Gianni was encouraging: Marco had been impressed, although Andrea had pointed out that there were no letters after the name on my business card. 'I look people in the eyes. I don't look at their business card,' had been Marco's reply. I duly completed the 'homework' and was asked to bring it to another meeting with Marco in a restaurant on the Porto canal. Course after course of seafood, and an equally steady flow of conversation, but almost no mention of what I had supposedly come to discuss. 'Big deals are always struck at the dinner table,' Pantani snapped, suggesting that he had already made his choice regardless of the contents of my study. The next step was for me to make an appointment with the owners of the Mercatone Uno supermarket chain, Romano Cenni and Luigi Valentini.

After the Giro–Tour double, Marco had received and rejected a seven-figure offer to join the Mapei team. The reasons for staying loyal to Mercatone Uno were both technical and sentimental, but it was still obvious that his current salary had to be revised. Increasing his profile meant raising Marco's salary but also negotiating the sale of his image rights. That day, I realised what kind of relationship Marco had with his sponsors. Marco considered Mercatone Uno a kind of family and he was worried that, by separating his private and sporting interests, he might break the bond. In the end we decided that Cenni and Valentini would pay Marco a sizeable salary but retain ownership of his image rights. My role would be to manage, advise and oversee.

With the ink on the contract still wet, Marco and Christina left for a holiday in the Seychelles. Shortly before boarding the plane, Marco called: 'I've received a lot of offers from other managers. I need time to think, to weigh them up, to decide whether I definitely want to offer you the job or pursue other avenues.' No sooner had he put the phone down than he seemed to vanish. His telephone was switched off – as it would be more often than not for the duration of the next five years. I'll never forget the next time he called and the message – typically provocative – he left on my voicemail: 'This is Marco Pantani. You complain about never being able to contact me, but what am I supposed to do if I call my manager and instead of hearing her voice I have to listen to her answering machine?' It was enough to confirm to me that he had made his choice, even if nothing had been formally agreed, not even verbally. All Marco said was: 'Now it's in your hands. I'm putting my faith in you... don't betray me!' And with that, our partnership began.

A fond relationship

In September, the record company convention I had helped to organise went ahead in Riccione. Every evening, a different member of the firm's artist portfolio performed. Knowing that I was now Pantani's manager, the directors of the record company asked me to invite Marco to a banquet in honour of Laura Pausini, arguably Italy's most famous female pop star and, like Marco, a native of the Romagna region. I was uncomfortable: we hadn't even started to work together and here I was already asking him a favour. But Marco had come back from the Seychelles refreshed and relaxed and accepted without hesitation. 'You know,' Marco explained, 'When I go on boat trips I always sing one of Pausini's songs – "Marco went away..." I'd like to meet her.'

When all of the guests, Laura Pausini included, had long since arrived at the restaurant on the outskirts of Riccione, a few kilometres down the Adriatic coast from Cesenatico, I was furiously pacing about the reception of my hotel because Marco was nowhere to be seen and – *plus ça change* – his mobile was switched off. I was about give up when I saw a vintage Mercedes approaching like a hiccuping tortoise, with Marco in the driver's seat repeatedly opening and closing the boot. He had brought along two close friends – Giumbo (pronounced 'Jumbo'), Christina's first Italian boyfriend, and Gianni. 'I don't know whether it is out of excitement at coming to see you, or because it needs air, but this car only goes forward if I open and close the boot,' Marco grinned.

Pausini was genuinely thrilled to meet Marco. I was quietly overjoyed at the buzz Marco's arrival had created, not that this stopped me asking him if everything was OK every few minutes and telling him that we could leave whenever he wanted. As it was, we spent several hours together in a completely relaxed setting. Later that night, I got a call from Giumbo which added to my satisfaction: 'You know, Manu, Marco says that there's real warmth between you two, and he feels so protected that he could never say no to you.' It was only the third or fourth time that I had seen Marco but I felt that same affection; in my eyes, Marco was like a little duckling who needed protecting. On one hand his charisma intimidated me, on the other I could his sense that he needed care and attention.

Professionally speaking, he was as meticulous as they come: just as the seatpost on his bike had to be millimetre perfect, so the way he was managed had to be perfect, too. But he also liked to delegate, which sometimes caused me problems. He would say that he trusted me and that he didn't necessarily need to know about everything I was doing for him. Or, as he often said in the last few months of his life: 'I don't have to tell other people what I want. If a person loves me, they understand me and if they look after me they do so without me having to ask.' In those first few months I realised that Marco was very careful, very difficult to read, and very subtle, but that this made me more determined not to make mistakes or to come up short of his expectations, even if this wasn't an easy task.

The first conflicts

The winter passed off largely without incident, what with the traditional round of pre-season meetings, the team presentation and the first races of the 1999 season. The first signs of friction started to appear when I took charge of Marco's endorsement deal with Citroën. Prior to my arrival, an agreement between Mercatone Uno and the car manufacturer had already been signed, covering both payment and what Citroën expected in return. A series of television adverts featuring Marco were to be filmed either side of the Giro d'Italia – hardly the ideal time for someone in intensive training for a three-week tour. On the days set aside for filming, after training in the afternoon, Marco was obliged to stay on the set until late in the evening and made no secret of his annoyance. One thing he didn't tire of was telling me that he should be concentrating on more important things: his job was to ride bikes. He had even passed up the chance to sing at the famous music festival in San Remo to honour his racing commitments. With the help of an acclaimed Italian songwriter, Marcello Pieri, Marco had written a song entitled '*In punta di piedi*' – 'On the tips of my toes'. Unfortunately, the San Remo festival clashed with the start of the racing season, so the world was denied – or perhaps spared – a sneak preview of the Pirate's singing and songwriting prowess.

There were several clauses in the Citroën contract which Marco considered unacceptable. This gave rise to the first disputes with Mercatone Uno – a result of the directors' understandable claims that they were entitled to a return on the investment they had made in Pantani. Marco was also critical of me: anything he did must be compatible with his core activity and it was my responsibility to ensure that none of the agreements struck encroached on cycling.

I tried to reason with Mercatone Uno that the ownership of image rights were undeniably important for their investment, but that it was essential to consider and meet Marco's demands as a rider. I advised them to be more careful when drawing up Marco's schedule of extra-curricular activities.

Marco also liked to do everything to the best of his ability and not just out of a sense of duty. Consequently, he immersed himself in the filming in the same way he would a training session or race. I tried to relax him but, over those few days, I realised that I had walked into a lion's den. Everywhere I turned, I saw envy: I wasn't a well-known name, I wasn't at the reins of one of the big PR agencies, and, what's more, I was a woman working in a world which still oozed prejudice. Whenever I seemed to forget this, Gianfranco Josti would remind me that up until the 1960s the rules of the Giro d'Italia forbade women to even work on the race. Not only was my job made difficult by being a woman, but I also had to act as Marco's filter. An example: before the historic Giro–Tour double, everyone had Marco's mobile number. Thereafter it became necessary to pick and choose who Marco had direct contact with. Otherwise Marco might as well change profession and retrain in public relations. There were hundreds of requests and it wasn't always possible to say yes to everyone. Marco also didn't want to let personal preferences intrude; he wanted to treat everyone in the same way. This 'policy', which I agreed with wholeheartedly, didn't go down well in some quarters of the media. I quickly became an unpopular figure. I was always the one who had to read the riot act to allow Marco to escape the public and press scrutiny and concentrate on his work. I think I can now affirm, on the basis of the experience I have built up over the years, that cycling is probably the sport where it is hardest to strike the balance between good PR and professional discipline, which Marco strived for in the years and months leading up to his death. I'm now convinced that the recipe for great sporting achievements is one with a long list of ingredients, of which solid relationships with friends and family are just one. All constructive energy has to be channelled towards reaching the kind of concentration you need to compete and win at the highest level. Sadly, as time went by, the absence or loss of some of these components helped to plunge Marco into the deepest and darkest abyss.

A cheerless Giro

As the 1999 Giro d'Italia drew near, Marco became practically inaccessible. He had forewarned me: despite considering the team a real family, he wanted everyone to stick to their role. Giuseppe Martinelli was to look after everything in the sporting department, Andrea Agostini was the team's appointed press officer, and I was, well, no-one as far as the team was concerned. Or, if you wanted to be sympathetic, you could say that I was an interested spectator whose brief it was to evaluate how much Pantani's image could bring to existing and prospective sponsors. I realised straight away, though, that in his case it was difficult to draw a distinction between sporting image and public image. I also felt that, in Marco, I was up against a brick wall. Had it not been for that glance we exchanged during our first meeting, which acted as a kind of Northern star for the duration of our relationship, I would have been completely lost. Marco warned me again: 'Look, at the Giro I'm not the man that you think you know at the moment. If I walk past and don't acknowledge you, don't take it badly. I'm in another world and I don't even register what's going on around me.' Marco was anxious that the public didn't think that fame had gone to his head; he wanted people to understand that if at certain times he wasn't accessible, didn't smile, didn't stop to sign autographs or to banter, it wasn't out of a sense of superiority. I had finally recognised this acute need for concentration and so – partly because I still felt like such an outsider on the cycling scene – told Marco that I would come to the start of the race, but then only to the stage ending in Cesenatico and a couple of stages towards the end of the race.

I made my way to Agrigento, the Sicilian town chosen to host the start of the '99 race, but had arranged to stay in a different hotel from the team. On the eve of the race I sat in the reception of the Mercatone hotel, watched riders, masseurs and *directeur sportifs* file by, then Marco finally appeared. He said: 'What are you doing here. Are you not coming to eat with us?' I still felt restless and deeply uncomfortable, so quickly made my excuses and left. I watched the first stage and, in the afternoon, asked Martinelli if I could go up to Marco's room while he was having his massage. The first words Marco said to me were: 'Have you seen all this crap?' He was referring to an incident that morning with a journalist from a satirical Italian television programme, *The Hyenas*, who had thrust a microphone under his nose and asked: 'Do you swear in front of the camera that you don't dope?' Marco had reacted angrily and Andrea Agostini, the press officer, didn't know how to deal with the situation. Marco then berated Agostini: 'These guys shouldn't even be allowed to get to me with their microphones, asking things like that! You have to stop them sooner! If someone has to raise their voice and send them away, that person shouldn't be me. But if no-one does it, then I have no choice but to say something.' Marco's popularity had now assumed such proportions that he needed a dozen bodyguards just to keep the fans at bay, never mind the tabloid press. I was beginning to understand what people meant when they talked about their passion for cycling.

I suggested to Marco that I should make myself scarce: this wasn't the time or the place for me or the very specialised nature of my work.

I told him he could call me at any time if the necessity arose, but I wouldn't bother him. We didn't speak again until the stage to Cesenatico. The only news I had from within the camp came from Martinelli, who at this point was still a rather distant figure.

Controversy breaks

The stately beauty of Agrigento's acropolis should have made a fine backdrop to the start of that Giro. Instead it was quickly overshadowed by an unsightly row between the Italian Cycling Federation (FCI) and the International Cycling Union (UCI).

Even before the previous summer's Festina scandal, drugs had long been a hot topic in cycling: just three years earlier, in 1996, the Italian narcotics police (NAS) had planned to swoop on the Giro as it returned to south-east Italy after starting in Athens in a diplomatic nod to the Olympics. The sting was foiled when the teams received a tip-off and dispatched their support vehicles back to Italy via Yugoslavia, leaving the NAS waiting at the Brindisi ferry port scratching their heads. The NAS would get their payback, with some interest, at the 2001 Giro.

No, in 1999, it wasn't the riders trying to outwit the police, but the testers who were squabbling among themselves. The Italian Olympic Committee (CONI), backed by the FCI, believed that it had found the best anti-doping weapon to date with its combined blood and urine tests, and intended to implement the tests at the Giro under the aegis of a campaign entitled 'I won't risk my health'. The riders refused to co-operate and, at the insistence of Mario Cipollini, Pantani took on the unofficial role of the rebels' spokesman:

> We have given our consent for blood tests because we want to rid the sport of the plague of doping. At the same time, we are athletes who pedal for hours at a time in the sun, the rain, the heat and the cold, and we simply can't allow any old person to extract our blood. If the CONI tests are essential, OK, let's sit down and discuss it. But at the moment they seem to overlap with the UCI protocol which we, at the moment, abide by.

Giancarlo Ceruti, the FCI president, was one of the most vocal advocates of the CONI tests. Davide Boifava, erstwhile manager of the Riso Scotti, recalls a conversation he had with Ceruti in the midst of what was fast becoming a minor scandal:

We were in the Marche region for the first time trial of the race. That evening, Ceruti said to me: 'Davide, tomorrow the FCI doctors are coming. Be sensible, now, and send all of your riders to take the tests.' I stopped him: 'President, you know very well that I can't force them, I can only advise them.' Then he pulled out his mobile phone, dialled a number and passed it to me. It was Dr Squinzi, the owner of the Mapei team but also of Vinavil, one of our co-sponsors. He said: 'Davide, you must make our riders take the FCI tests.' 'I'm sorry, Doctor,' I replied, 'but I have just told President Ceruti that I can only give them my advice, not threaten them.' Ceruti then left the hotel with a parting shot that I'll never forget: 'Soon,' he murmured, 'you'll see the fall of the Gods.' I called Pantani straight away. I told him what had happened and gave him my advice: 'Marco, do your own thing,' I said. 'That doesn't mean that you have to go against the rest of the peloton. Just take yourself out of the equation. Look, if you start fighting the authorities they'll destroy you. Listen to me: stop, let it go.'

When Pantani was faced with a problem, he invariably wanted to tackle it even if it didn't concern him directly. In this instance, as the race went on, he felt more and more isolated, leading to a heated mid-race exchange with Mapei's Andrea Tafi, who, following Squinzi's orders, had come down in the CONI camp.

The race was slow to take shape over the first ten days, Pantani's conquest of the pink jersey at the Gran Sasso d'Italia at the end of week one excepted. Twenty-four hours later, Frenchman Laurent Jalabert had regained the race lead in the time trial in Ancona.

The Giro carried on up the Adriatic coast to Cesenatico, where Pantani received the expected Messiah's reception. He just regretted that he had come up seconds short of his dream of returning home in the pink jersey, and that his friend Cipollini had been pipped to the stage victory by his sprinting heir apparent, Ivan Quaranta. The word on the Cesenatico streets was that the Pirate wanted to go home after the stage to see his family and spend the evening with his girlfriend. Rumours were also rife that Pantani could be the target of a random drugs test (not that 'random' meant that they were unexpected because one leading Italian newspaper had taken to revealing when they would take place with 24 hours' notice). The following morning, the men known in the sport as the 'vampires' duly reported for duty. Martinelli remembers:

> They tested Marco and three or four other members of the team. I sent Giannelli to collect the results of the tests, while journalists were swarming around the hotel because they had heard rumours that one rider's haematocrit was over the legal limit, and that that rider was Pantani. Total rubbish: Giannelli reassured me that everything was fine and that he had the results sheet in his hand. With hindsight, thinking back to that day and linking it to what was about to happen at Madonna di Campiglio, I can't help but wonder whether there was a strategy behind it all, a kind of murder mystery in which someone had to die. And, in the end, someone sure did get it.

The race resumed with Pantani salivating at the prospect of the mountains on their way. He took off on the Colle della Fauniera and plunged pink jersey holder Laurent Jalabert into crisis. Paolo Savoldelli, nicknamed 'The Hawk' by virtue of his descending skills, lived up to his reputation to swoop to victory in Borgo San Dalmazzo but, behind him, Pantani returned to the top of the general classification.

Twenty-four hours later, on stage 15 between Racconigi and Oropa in the extreme north-west of Italy, Pantani turned in what was – alongside his victories at Montecampione in the '98 Giro and at Les Deux Alpes in the Tour – undoubtedly one of the defining performances of his career. At the foot of the final climb to Oropa, Pantani's chain slipped and forced him to stop at the critical point of the stage. He lost precious seconds before fixing the problem – so many, in fact, that he was overtaken by around fifty riders. Once back in the saddle, Pantani dispensed with his bandana and sunglasses, one by one dropped the team-mates who had waited for him and began to hoover up the leaders. Jalabert, who he had dispossessed of the pink jersey the previous day, was the last man to be passed and commented eloquently at the finish-line that he 'had to move so that Pantani didn't flatten me'. On the back of this, Marco's second stage victory of the 1999 Giro, the *tifosi*'s hero-worship reached a new pitch, while record numbers tuned in at home. Pantani crossed the line without raising his arms. 'I didn't know if there was still someone ahead of me. I didn't want to make a fool of myself,' he said.

The Pantani road-show chugged along remorselessly. On the stage to Lumezzane, Marco did a passable impersonation of a sprinter and lost out narrowly to Jalabert. On more familiar terrain, at Alpe di Pampeago, he won by over a minute from local boy Gilberto Simoni. The next day brought yet another stunning victory at Madonna di Campiglio. The Pirate was now a bloodthirsty one – as insatiable as Eddy 'The Cannibal' Merckx thirty years before. In 48 hours, he was to be crowned the champion of the Giro for the second year straight. Unless of course destiny was to take him from the gates of heaven to the bowels of hell in just a tiny fraction of that time.

5

Madonna di Campiglio, Drama and Intrigue

One warm Friday in early June 1999 Italy was preparing, en masse, to celebrate Marco Pantani's second consecutive Giro triumph. That day's third-from-last stage was to finish in the plush Trentino ski resort of Madonna di Campiglio, and I was on the road early to avoid the weekend traffic. In the boot of my car was a large cardboard box which contained the special edition 'Pirate' jerseys which Marco's Mercatone Uno team-mates would wear in his honour on Sunday's final stage to Milan. The jerseys were the continuation of a theme I had begun at the pre-season team presentation that winter when I had the Mercatone Uno company conference hall decorated as an immense pirate ship and the riders decked out with the obligatory black eye-patches and bandanas. Although unorthodox, the concept had proved popular, so it seemed logical to carry it on here.

I watched the end of that stage with Fabrizio Borra in the hospitality village in Madonna di Campiglio. When Marco's bright pink jersey appeared over the brow of the mountain, all alone, Fabrizio and I looked at each other. 'He really is a phenomenon. Did he really have to do that today? He has the Giro in the bag, could he not save himself the trouble?' After the finish, I didn't see Marco, not even in the hotel. Martinelli had warned me that Marco was tense and therefore best avoided. I took the hint.

That evening, the organising committee of the Giro laid on a party at a local nightspot. I was invited and decided to make a brief appearance.

The Mercatone Uno doctor, Roberto Rempi, was also there along with Andrea Agostini and one or two mechanics and masseurs. I can remember thinking to myself: 'If they are all here on the night before a big mountain stage, it must mean that everything is under control.' It was getting late, so I thought better of going up to Marco's room to check for myself. He and I both knew that an early alarm-call from the blood testers was more than likely...

The following morning I was making my way to the start village when I bumped into Angelo Zomegnan, at the time a senior *Gazzetta dello Sport* journalist and now the Giro d'Italia race director. It immediately dawned on me that I could scarcely be less suitably dressed among men who already doubted my credentials: black high-heels, evening dress, and here I was face to face with the chief cycling correspondent of Italy's most influential sports paper. Antonello Orlando of Italian state radio broadcasters RAI took one look at me and drew his own conclusions about how much I had enjoyed the previous evening: 'Now this', he said, 'you have to explain.'

I didn't get the opportunity because within seconds my blushes had turned to full-blown horror. It was another RAI journalist, Davide de Zan, who broke the news. De Zan cut short a conversation on his mobile phone when he saw me. He looked me in the eyes, swallowed hard and told me that Marco had been ejected from the race for failing a haematocrit test. Running back in the direction of the Mercatone hotel, I passed Zomegnan again. 'Let's see how you deal with this one,' he grunted. Journalists and photographers had laid siege to the hotel and I had no idea how to react. I called Martinelli to tell him that, if he needed me, I would go upstairs straight away. He screamed at me to get up there at once. In the corridor, I found the entire team slumped on the floor, distraught, inconsolable. In his room, Martinelli wouldn't stop punching the walls and yelling that this sort of thing should never have happened.

I went to look for Andrea Agostini, who, together with Dr Rempi, had issued a statement to the press. He said that he had gone for the conspiracy-theory line and asked me what I thought. I replied honestly that, amid all this commotion, it might be easier to talk about conspiracies, but maybe it would have been better to say that we didn't know what had happened, that further tests would be carried out and that we would make further announcements in due course. Out of sight of the journalists and television cameras, despair and disbelief filled the second floor of the Hotel Touring like noxious gases. No-one was more disbelieving than Marco's team-mates.

Nobody had the courage to set foot in his room, number 27. I knocked and went in. Marco was sat down on the edge of a chest of drawers, back against the wall. He smiled and it occurred to me that he was afraid he had let me down. He said: 'Manu, you see what's happened?' 'Don't worry,' I said, 'let's stay calm, we'll see if we can find out what is really going on.' I had absolutely no concept of what repercussions that failed blood test could have.

I wondered where Marco's father was. Aware that he was following the Giro in his camper van, I tried to imagine what a parent could be feeling at a time like this, so close to his son but unable to reach out to him. Pretending to stay calm, I went to look for Paolo. He was cooped up in the camper van, his head in his hands, tears running down his face and his eyes fixed on the floor. I told him that Marco needed him. We made our way back to Marco's room and we found him holding up his right arm covered in blood: in a fit of rage, he had put his fist through a pane of glass. Paolo ran towards him and started administering first aid, removing the splinters from his flesh and trying to cover up the wounds.

Later, much later, remembering those moments, Marco would tell me: 'You know, when I saw my dad come into the room at Madonna di Campiglio, it was like going back to when I was a kid, when I would get up to some sort of mischief and he would come to tell me off. I said to myself: "Now he's going to give me two good slaps". That was why I suffered more in that precise moment than at any other time, because I knew that I had let him down.'

This wasn't the first time that Marco had talked to me about his relationship with his parents and how it often played on his ever-restless mind. He was anxious for his father, in particular, to be proud of him.

'You know, I always wanted to prove to my dad that I was the number one, that I wasn't a joke.'

From the moment he decided to ride a bike, Marco made a secret pact with himself that he would never be a burden to his parents. On the contrary, he would strive to offer them some recompense for the hard times they'd been through and the financial constraints they had lived under. It was no surprise that when he came crashing to earth and brought his parents with him at Madonna di Campiglio, his sense of disappointment and humiliation proved insurmountable.

In the corridors of the hotel, chaos still reigned. Andrea told me that arrangements were being made to smuggle Marco out of the back of the building, through the kitchens and straight into a car well clear of the crowd of journalists. I thought that this was wrong and said so: Marco shouldn't be 'escaping' like the criminal that some people were already making him out to be. It was put to me that my point was OK in theory, but who in practice would dare tell Marco that he should walk out through the main door and straight into a scrum of pressmen? I said that I would. For the second time, I knocked on his door, went in and began to make my point:

Marco, I was the last one to arrive so maybe I am the last person who should have the right to talk. However, as I see it, the Pirate leaves with his head held high through the main door – he doesn't sneak out of the side entrance. Don't let the emotion of it all obscure or rush your judgement. If they ask questions, you just answer: 'I'm sorry about what has happened. I'll try to get to the bottom of this even though there's no time left – the Giro is carrying on without me. That said, I am truly surprised by all of this; at the moment I can neither explain nor justify what is happening.' That's my advice.

He looked hard at me and said that I was right. I remember that we walked the length of the corridor to the lift with our arms linked: the terror on his face reminded me of that vulnerability which had struck and so charmed me during our first meeting. He was on another planet, speechless. Like a child waiting for orders from a parent. Then, two police officers acting on behalf of local magistrates arrived and asked Pantani if he wanted them to take away some samples. If he made the request, the blood could be used as evidence to support the claim of a plot against him. Instinctively, Marco said yes. I thought about it for a second then added, on Marco's behalf, that if Dr Giardina, the appointed magistrate, wanted to confiscate and test the samples, he could, but that we didn't intend to make any formal request.

No sooner had we set one foot out of the hotel than we were engulfed by a swarm of mics, dictaphones and cameras. Marco made a statement which I have since read and re-read countless times:

> There are plenty of things we could say, but I would be wasting my breath... After a lesson like this, reluctantly, I have to say that if this happens to a sportsman like me you have to wonder... I had the pink jersey, I have been tested twice, the last time with a haematocrit of 46, and now I wake up to this unpleasant surprise. It's all very strange. To lift myself up from a blow like this... I did it after serious accidents, I've always got back up, but I can't do it this time. Not again. Now I just ask for a little bit of respect. I'm thinking of my fans, I feel sorry for them and for cycling.

Lots of questions, no answers

One of the key figures in the Madonna di Campiglio cause célèbre was undoubtedly Giuseppe Martinelli, the Mercatone Uno *directeur sportif* whose association with Pantani dated back to their Carrera days. Here is Martinelli's version of events:

> The first thing I would like to point out is that we were perfectly calm that day, especially me. I wasn't Pantani's doctor, I wasn't his coach: I was Pantani's *directeur sportif* and, up to that point, we must have been doing a decent job because, from a tactical point of view, Marco agreed with every one of our decisions. We were expecting the UCI testers to visit that morning. In fact, the previous evening, I had spoken to the owners of the hotel to make sure that someone was up and about at the crack of dawn. They

performed the test in my room because it was near Marco's, and also took a sample from Paolo Savoldelli, who had come with his team doctor Carlo Guardascione. What happened and why Marco's sample came back with that high blood count, I swear I don't know. I have asked myself and still ask myself: but why would I have risked losing the Giro d'Italia? Forget about Pantani for a second, why would we throw away the Giro by doing something risky? We already had the race won! I say that Marco could have raced on a mountain bike or in trainers that day, because he was so strong, so superior, that no-one could have beaten him.

I know that some stirrers talked about a 'refill of EPO' a few days from the finish, ordered by me, against Marco's will. First problem with that: no-one could impose something on Marco if he said no; secondly, just saying the word 'refill' turns my stomach. All of this palaver came from one newspaper article. They wrote that Marco wanted to drop everyone on the Gavia and Mortirolo the next day and ride alone into the finish in Aprica, as he had done years before, when the *tifosi* had first fallen in love with him. All lies. We hadn't decided on any tactic for the next day because there hadn't been any time. The night before, Marco had stayed behind after dinner to talk to Candido Cannavò, the director of the *Gazzetta dello Sport*. He had gone to bed at around half past eleven. In the morning, the testers arrived at quarter past seven and after a quarter of an hour they sent someone to tell me that Marco was over the limit. When would we have had the time to talk about the tactics for the race? The question that puzzles me more, though, and that I still haven't figured out, is how they analysed the sample so quickly. Now it takes them well in excess of an hour. If the tests were so reliable back then how come they have since changed the method?

Of course, that day and in the days, weeks and months that followed, everyone looked for someone to blame. Personally, I'd rather not say, 'I have nothing to feel guilty about', because that would imply that others do. I do, however, feel compelled to say that something didn't work that day, but it certainly wasn't something in Marco Pantani's body or in the Mercatone Uno team. I can't answer the many questions I still get asked and which I ask myself, because I don't have an answer. Today, with the benefit of years of hindsight, if I had gone wrong somewhere, why shouldn't I admit it now?

Almost as much as his incomparable climbing, Marco's aggression and will to win – even compared to 1998 – had been a feature of his performances in the Giro. Martinelli accounts for this apparent change in Pantani:

> He felt laden with responsibility and his solution was to show his strength on the bike. He clearly put noses out of joint. It is an Italian national pastime: whenever someone is successful we always try to knock them down. I remember how, at the end of '98 and beginning of '99, whenever we were in the car, we would talk about the usual, banal things, and I would say to him: 'Marco, just tell me: what is it that you've done in your life which makes people worship you like they do?' He perhaps didn't even realise what Marco Pantani really meant in the public's eyes, to everyone from the child to the old-age pensioner. Everyone who rode their bike was Marco Pantani. People turned on their TV sets to see Marco Pantani. We would stop at a petrol station to fill up and straight away there would be a crowd around the car. I have worked with other stars – I still do today – but what happened with him will never be repeated.

In the days following Pantani's exit from the Giro, with explanations still elusive, the conspiracy theorists continued to make hay. One group remembered Pantani's rejection of Mapei's huge contract offer the previous summer, linked it to the mid-race disagreement with Tafi over the FCI blood tests, and then extrapolated. Faulty logic according to Martinelli:

> I had nothing to do with Marco saying no to Mapei. In any case Dr Squinzi would never have employed me. In fact, I was never approached by or had a meeting with either Squinzi or one of his representatives. Marco went to speak to him alone and I only found out that he had rejected the offer a fortnight later. He said no for two reasons: firstly, because he was very attached to the people who had shown faith in him when he was still hopping around on crutches, and by that I mean Luciano Pezzi and Romano Cenni; secondly, because we had built up a team which he would never have left. They weren't supermen, they didn't have the same

pedigree as Mapei's riders, but the group was so united that he would
never have betrayed it. Let's not forget, Pantani never betrayed anyone.

The next account is that of Roberto Rempi, the Mercatone Uno team
doctor at the 1999 Giro:

I saw Marco after his stage win at Madonna di Campiglio. He was on the
massage table. He felt so good that I didn't need to do anything. After
dinner, before the boys fell asleep, I did my usual rounds of the rooms.
I spoke to Marco, warning him that a blood test the next morning was
inevitable, but that all his measurements were within the legal boundaries.
I then wished him good night and decided to let off some steam after
three stressful weeks by going to the end-of-race party in town. What
happened the following morning still keeps me awake at night: a change
in temperature from the start of the stage to the end, stress accumulated
overnight, defective conservation of the blood after extraction, insufficient
rehydration after the stage...? One final point: in the morning, having
taken Marco to the test, I wasn't present when the blood was extracted,
as I had been at Cesenatico. I had gone to collect Marco Velo, one of
Pantani's team mates, from his room.

To shed further light on the events of that fateful Saturday 5 June,
here is an illuminating extract from the open letter which Fabrizio Borra
wrote to Marco Pantani after his death:

We spent whole days trying to understand what was happening, from
that terrible morning in Madonna di Campiglio onwards. People started
talking about doping straight away, while in reality you had failed a
'health' test. It bears repeating for the benefit of those who don't know
the details of your case: Marco Pantani never tested positive in an anti-
doping control. Those tests and the 'I won't risk my health' campaign
were born out of the need to safeguard the riders' health: without the
means to conclusively detect certain products, it had been decided that if
an athlete's haematocrit went above fifty, he must observe a fortnight's
rest period before undergoing repeat tests. No sanction would be

incurred, since it was the riders themselves who had decided to submit to the rule, recognising that certain substances were undetectable, for example EPO.

But let's go back to that day because, while on the one hand I never agreed with the conspiracy theory cooked up by Mercatone Uno's lawyer in that dreadful press conference a few days after the incident – and I could never be hypocritical enough to say that medicine has no role in sport – I acknowledge that something strange happened that day.

It's worthwhile remembering that it was the penultimate stage of the race, that you were leading by over six minutes, and that everyone knew that the top ten riders on general classification would be tested that morning. I remember being in your room the previous evening; you took a sleeping tablet then told me that you had decided to give Enrico Zaina some freedom the next day, as a reward for the help he had given you up to that point. Also, some quarters of the media were starting to turn on you, accusing you of monopolising the Giro.

At that time, I was still new to cycling and, in my naivety, asked you whether you could afford to relax about the tests the next morning. You didn't hesitate: 'Of course, everything's fine, what do you take me for, an idiot? The Giro's in the bag. Let's go and double-check, just to make sure. I'll show you.' The reading was 48.6 per cent. 'You see? Everything's as it should be.'

The following morning, things started turning odd when the testers arrived. They seemed strange, nervy. They knocked impatiently on your door, telling you that they wanted to come in immediately. They took your blood and the way they asked you to check the name on the sample was particularly arrogant: 'You see that this is your sample, am I right?' They must have asked you three or four times. A very strange attitude indeed, even though you didn't think anything of it because at the time you had nothing to fear. You were even more relaxed at breakfast, when the team doctors double-checked after the blood had been taken and obtained the same result as the previous night.

Another conundrum: you and I are sitting at the breakfast table when we start to see journalists running in the direction of the hotel. We wonder what all the commotion is about. When it later becomes clear, this question gives way to another: how did they get their mitts on the news before the person concerned was officially informed?

Then rumours about someone in the team being over the limit began to filter through. You had gone up to your room to get changed when the doctor and Andrea notified me that it was you, Marco. A sudden chill descended on the corridor: someone would have to tell you, but no-one was brave enough to even enter your room. Roberto, the doctor, was on the telephone to Martinelli, despairing, and at that point I plucked up the courage to come in. That moment, that image, will remain fixed in my memory until the day I die. I sat on the end of the bed, where you were lying down. You said: 'What is it? You're not going to tell me that I'm the one over the limit, are you?' When I replied in the affirmative, your voice became quiet: 'It's not possible. Someone has robbed me. Why?' You stared at the floor and didn't say a word for a quarter of an hour. The next words that came out of your mouth were: 'It's over, Fabri, this time it's really over.'

Another thing that struck me as peculiar: why did they deny the request to check that reading by taking another sample, seeing that their result didn't tally with ours. Admittedly, the regulations didn't make any allowance for it, but we all agreed that before destroying the career of an athlete of your stature it was better to be absolutely sure. We found out that our doubts were justified when we had your blood re-tested at a UCI-accredited laboratory in Imola later that day and it was under the limit.

For the purposes of my own research, I later consulted some of Italy's leading scientists, who made me aware of how difficult it was to measure a person's haematocrit in a laboratory. Imagine then, how unreliable a test could be on a sample extracted in a hotel room then analysed in a different hotel. I also discovered that a huge number of factors can cause variations in a person's haematocrit: if you take the blood when the rider is standing or lying down, if he is relaxed or tense, if he is dehydrated. The fact that the method was completely changed the following year, precisely on account of all of these variables, reflected the previous test's limited reliability.

And then the vindictiveness of the media's coverage of the incident. It was designed to destroy you, with no mitigation. You got a death sentence without even standing trial. For example, they talked about a positive B-test when, in fact, the real B-test is the check which they do on another brand new sample stored in another container. In your case, though, they were talking about a verification of the same blood sample. Obviously, the result wasn't going to change.

No-one ever raised the possibility that a mistake might have been made, perhaps not intentionally, even accidentally, something to do with the anti-coagulant in the sample, for example. Or if the sample was left exposed to the air for too long, or mishandled. No-one doubted that you were guilty. But, then, if the method which caught you was accurate, why change it?

The journey from Madonna di Campiglio to Imola

Marco Pantani left Madonna di Campiglio in a Mercatone Uno team car driven by Beppe Martinelli and escorted by a police vehicle. At Imola, the team organised for Marco to take another blood test. The reading was below the fifty per cent threshold, prompting Mercatone Uno co-owner Romano Cenni to issue the following statement that evening:

This morning, the Giro d'Italia champion elect underwent a blood test which indicated that his haematocrit was above the legal limit according to the acting UCI-accredited laboratory. The matter couldn't end there. Without wishing to undermine the credibility of the UCI, early this afternoon Marco Pantani took an identical test in another UCI-accredited laboratory. The result: his red blood cell count was within the authorised limit. A paradox. At this point, we would kindly ask the UCI to cross-check the procedures of the two accredited laboratories, identifying their respective responsibilities.

As we left Campiglio, we had arranged to meet in Imola, at the team's headquarters, where I found Marco sitting outside. He was disconsolate. He kept massaging his head with his hands, almost as though it was a crystal ball about to reveal a miracle solution.

He hardly spoke, but words weren't necessary: his body language was articulate enough. He seemed dazed. It certainly wasn't the demeanour of someone who had transgressed or been caught *in flagrante*. He kept repeating: 'Someone has to explain to me what's happened, because I'm sure that I haven't cheated. My conscience is clear on that score.'

At that moment, the focal point of his anxiety was the Giro d'Italia that he hadn't won. He had no inkling of the torment which was about to suck him in, almost devouring him completely. Plus, another worry started to gnaw away at him: 'Who knows what people will think of me now. I've let everyone down. They have to know that I am the one who has been cheated, not the cheat. But they'll think that it's all true, that I have stolen my success; they'll start to doubt all of the sacrifices I've made up to this point. That, I can't bear.'

He became obsessed with finding a direct means of communication to ensure that what he said wasn't manipulated. I remember the telephone conversations we had over the next few days, when he was barricaded in a house surrounded by dozens of journalists, photographers and cameramen. They had every angle covered and had even managed to hide long-range microphones in the bushes of the neighbouring houses. Every time someone opened a window or someone went out into the garden, they were dazzled by hundreds of flashes.

The invasion of his privacy, the thought of being spied upon, was one of the hardest things for Marco to tolerate; the very notion that there might be someone on the other side of the gates listening to his every conversation with his parents, his friends or Christina, drove him to distraction. In the months and years to come, when the effects of the cocaine had cranked up the intensity of every thought and emotion, he was haunted by a recurring nightmare: being shut away in his room, besieged by spies. At the time, I communicated with Marco via the telephone while his friends – both true and phoney – paid regular visits to his house. This didn't help, what with everyone believing him or herself to be the sole proprietor of the answer to Marco's problems. I soon realised that we had to find a way to escape from that impasse, the suffocation chamber that his home had become.

I proposed that he do a single-subject interview with a journalist who made him feel at ease, who let him open his heart without the cross-examination he might be subjected to at a press conference. Marco wanted the people at home to draw their own conclusions. As usual, he relied on his instinct to suggest a provisional list of candidates to conduct the interview, not considering, for example, whether they were right or left-leaning – an important factor in an Italian media system dominated by political interests – or were from private or state television. Whatever the choice, someone was bound to feel snubbed, so we decided to go with Marco's idea of opting for someone from the state-owned RAI stable. Unsurprisingly, Mediaset, Silvio Berlusconi's private network which at that time owned the rights to broadcast Giro d'Italia, reacted angrily. We therefore decided to also organise a press conference at Monte del Re, the Mercatone Uno management complex. I contacted Gianni Minà, Marco's journalist of choice, who said that he would look for a production company for the interview with Marco.

It was agreed that a *Marco Pantani Talks* special would be put out immediately after the press conference. That same evening, however, someone leaked a recording of the interview with Minà to the *Repubblica* newspaper. The scoop infuriated the other Italian dailies, as one would expect, and guaranteed Marco a frosty reception at Monte del Re. We had had a very hard time persuading Marco to do the press conference but he had eventually consented under pressure from Mercatone Uno. I remember that his choice of clothes wasn't the most appropriate that day: a horizontally striped T-shirt which made him look like a convict. But no-one could ever have guessed that he had truly entered his own mental prison and that he would be there for the rest of his days.

The trial of Monte del Re

The Monte del Re press conference was organised by Mercatone Uno and co-ordinated by Andrea Agostini. Andrea had been Marco's friend since childhood, and they remained close even when their paths diverged, Andrea's towards university and Marco's towards a cycling career. At Madonna di Campiglio, clearly swayed by Marco's initial reaction, Agostini had immediately espoused the notion that Pantani was the victim of a malicious plot. The two lawyers hired by Mercatone Uno, Guazzaloca and Insolera, had taken this idea as their baseline, announcing to the press that they had requested DNA tests to prove that Pantani's blood sample hadn't been switched.

This completely shifted Marco's angle of attack. Earlier, Fabrizio Borra and I had suggested a very precise strategy: plant the idea in people's mind that something may have gone wrong with the way the test was carried out at Madonna di Campiglio. There happened to be an international haematologists convention taking place in Florence that June. Fabrizio had managed to come away with a statement signed by several leading specialists to the effect that a person's haematocrit level was subject to numerous variations and that therefore the reading in itself wasn't significant. With no other concrete facts at our disposal, it was the only route we could go down without running the risk of being proven wrong.

The outcome of that press conference was not especially positive: two schools of thought continued to prevail – the minority who believed Marco innocent and the majority who reckoned him guilty. And they almost unanimously invoked the same thing: a confession from Marco. The upshot was that Marco's relationship with the press deteriorated irrevocably. Marco particularly began to mistrust those journalists who until a few days earlier had hallowed his every move and extolled his every virtue. In the months that followed Marco re-read the front-page *Gazzetta dello Sport* editorial that appeared on Sunday 6 June and carried the bi-line of the paper's director, Candido Cannavò. Its title was 'Betrayal all around him'.

Among the many damaging aspects of this episode, the one that aggrieves me the most is the ferocious sense of betrayal, human and sporting. I don't know where it comes from, I don't know what share of the blame belongs to Marco Pantani, or how much he is the victim of some shameless provocation on the part of his entourage. However, whatever the truth, it is an act of betrayal...

A shockingly botched lab test? Paradoxically, I would be pleased if it was, even though the weight of an injustice would be added to that of the current trauma. But it's just not feasible, not with such a tried and tested method, the evidence and the proof which back up these elementary but reliable International Cycling Union (UCI) tests... Even proceeding with caution, we begin to see the outline of a misdemeanour. In cycling, duplicity and hypocrisy reign: not getting caught, being a snake in the grass are praiseworthy exercises. There is no real desire to eliminate the poison and come down on the wrongdoers...

I think about Pantani's gang, his powerful team, Mercatone Uno's family atmosphere. They have received universal praise... However, this entourage, this exemplary group, with its managers, its doctors, its envied coaches, didn't manage to protect Italian sport's greatest asset from a dirty error, from an evil temptation, from a collective weakness. This is the very germ of the crime. The same thing happened thirty years ago with Merckx. In 1988, Ben Johnson was chased out of the Seoul Olympics the day after breaking the 100 metre world record. The demon called doping may change its appearance, but it doesn't give up. I don't think that Pantani will retire, but neither cycling nor his messianic status can continue as they were. But it's him, with his charisma, his charm, his wisdom and his pain who must lead the revolt: not against occult powers but against the hypocrisy and the deceit of an environment which has dragged him into an inferno.

Marco said to me: 'You see, Manu, he has labelled me a doper even though I wasn't. The evening before Madonna di Campiglio, he had me believing that he was a faithful admirer, the next day I was a traitor. And he didn't even consider the possibility that something may not have worked in the test.'

Pantani was even more rancorous towards Angelo Zomegnan, the editor of the *Gazzetta*'s cycling pages. Cannavò himself had phoned Marco to announce that Zomegnan would visit him at home – off limits for all journalists – officially in his capacity as representative of the Giro organisers, but really as a friend, to discuss his 'rehabilitation' as a cyclist. After the Monte del Re press conference, Marco had returned with

Zomegnan to Cesenatico, where, in Marco's lounge, they had discussed the pressing issues in relaxed mood. The following day, the *Gazzetta* dedicated a full page to a special report entitled 'Our correspondent in Pantani's den'. The quotes were faithful to what Marco had said in the press conference – naturally – because Marco's story had only one version. But the fact that Zomegnan had come in the guise of a representative of the Giro organisers and purportedly as a friend had enraged Marco: 'Manu, there's no point trying to tell me otherwise: I can't trust anyone. I don't want any more contact with certain journalists.'

Skipping the Tour

After the hullabaloo which accompanied the press conference had died down, Marco resumed a life which bore some resemblance to normality, albeit only that – a resemblance. The more time passed, the more the attitude of Marco's fellow riders puzzled him. Not a single telephone call, not one rider had made an effort to lend him moral support. He had come to the conclusion that the rationale of his peers was 'They want to make out that Pantani, who won so much, is the only one who doped? Let's just let them believe that. Then, finally, they might start talking about us clean riders as well as Pantani the star.'

As far as I can judge, at Madonna di Campiglio, Marco paid on the one hand for the jealousy of the riders who he had overshadowed, and on the other for acting as spokesperson for the dissenters against the Italian Federation tests and in favour of those of the UCI. The fact that it was a UCI test that he failed, then, made him doubly guilty in the eyes of the masses, if not of everyone. He had got it into his head that the cycling world couldn't wait for something to happen to him – something much more serious than the usual crash – to get him out from under its feet. This was the thought which hurt him most. Increasingly, his logic became: 'It's true that when I was at races, I was the only one they interviewed, that the crowd cheered for me more than anyone else, and that it was my autograph they all wanted. But how many people did I attract to cycling? And how much exposure did the other riders, the other teams get as a result? It may be a pure coincidence, but, since I haven't been around, RAI has scratched more than one race from its schedules. When I was around, they even showed the Vuelta Valenciana (a Spanish stage race). Now, unless someone finds it on the internet, no-one in Italy knows the Valenciana exists any more.'

As the days and weeks went by, new, partial or possible explanations began to crystallise in Marco's mind. In his father and his manager, he had a sympathetic audience. One line of reasoning went that a Giro d'Italia mountain stage had millions of Italians glued to their television sets, taking considerable sheen off viewing figures for the Italian national team's football matches or a Formula One grand prix. However, a traditionally working-class sport such as cycling doesn't fill the State's coffers like other sports. There are no gate receipts at a cycle race.

Pantani, though, had raised the profile of this ancient, poor man's pursuit above that of many other sports, and we wondered whether herein could lie the reason for the system emptying all of its fury on Marco. Post-Madonna di Campiglio, Marco had made some very thinly veiled and cutting remarks about why cycling had been targeted while football and Formula One were comparatively unregulated. Tonina and Paolo told me that, days later, Marco received registered-delivery letters from representatives of both sports suggesting that he retract what he had said. Perhaps he said too much? Perhaps someone was frightened by the fact that such a national treasure, who could exert such a pull over the Italian people, would rather stay faithful to his own convictions than to what the system dictated. But this is a question that we will never be able to answer with any certainty.

What I am sure of is that Marco wasn't in favour of doping. Quite the opposite, he wanted to fight it. He always said: 'If only a system which could detect doping substances infallibly could be found, I would be the first to give it my backing. The fact is that the current rules are ambiguous and aren't equal for everyone, which means that they get manipulated according to how someone decides he wants the merry-go-round to turn.' This, in a nutshell, was the injustice that Marco perceived and which would continue to grind him down until his very last day.

In the days immediately after the Giro, Marco's friends made it their aim to convince Marco to prepare for the Tour de France. It was immediately clear, however, after a discussion with Martinelli, that their efforts would be in vain. According to Marco's version of events, his *directeur sportif* had told him in no uncertain terms that the trip to France was too dangerous, that he would be shot at from all sides. Supposing he didn't come away with a good result, it was easy to imagine how the journalists would react: '...So this is what happens to Marco Pantani when he doesn't use drugs.' In other words, Martinelli took away any motivation that Marco might have had. The alternative Pantani chose was to take full advantage of summer on the Romagna Riviera and that was the last I heard of him for several weeks. Beppe Martinelli recounts a very different series of events:

First of all, I want to say one thing: in the car, going from Madonna di Campiglio to Imola, we both cried for a hundred kilometres. And it was very rare to see Marco cry. The only thing he kept saying was: 'Martino, don't nag me, because, I'm not going to ride again. I know, you'll do everything to try to persuade me otherwise, but I'm not riding again.' I replied: 'Don't worry. We'll go home now and you'll see that tomorrow or the day after tomorrow, you'll be out on your bike and it'll all pass. You'll see: we'll go to the Tour and we'll win again.' But he didn't want to know: 'You carry on doing your job but don't worry about me because I'm not riding again.' The next day we spoke again and he seemed to have changed his mind saying: 'Martino, today I did the same number of kilometres I should have done in the penultimate stage of the Giro and tomorrow I'll do the last stage. Then we'll go to the Tour and, you'll see, we'll cut them to pieces.' On the Tuesday, we met in Cesenatico, at his house, and that's where he said to me: 'Maybe I'm not ready to go to France'. Maybe this, maybe that, so I insisted: 'In my opinion, you have to start racing'. I can't remember whether Marco's dad was there; I do know that there were people there who I have erased from my memory because I'm sure that it was them who persuaded him not to go to France in the end. As they saw it, he had to make them pay, he had to make cycling pay for what it had done to him, because cycling needed him and not vice versa. I, on the other hand, was convinced that the only way to respond was on the road. Several of us agreed, from the owner of Mercatone Uno, Cenni, to his team-mates. But we didn't get through to him because Marco was always immovable once he had made a decision. I was probably overruled; there were people (his friends) whose opinion counted more than mine and who had got deeper inside his head than I did. I only ever did my job as *directeur sportif*: I never went out on the town or clubbing with Marco Pantani, I was never even invited. I was his *directeur sportif*, not his friend, nor his confidant. In Pantani's eyes I represented cycling and at that moment cycling had forgotten he existed.

Whenever he considered something a matter of principle, Marco was monumentally stubborn. Luigi Valentini, Romano Cenni's partner at the helm of Mercatone Uno, visited him at home during that period. In an effort to persuade him to return to racing, Valentini explained to Marco that he would have to learn to accept that he had been robbed at Madonna di Campiglio, and that he should react immediately and stop tongues wagging with his results. But this was a road Marco Pantani had no intention of going down. Around the same time, Valentini and Pantani travelled in the same helicopter to the opening of a Mercatone Uno store in Trento in the extreme north of Italy. I lost count of the number of times that Marco told me about how Valentini's words had left him sobbing during that journey: 'Behave like a man,' Valentini kept telling him. Marco felt offended, but he knew that Valentini was right.

That was Marco. Whenever I tackled him head on, he would bristle like a hedgehog, offended, annoyed. But then he would say: 'Manu, you really had balls. I need people like you who tell it like it is to my face; people who aren't influenced by my fame. That's the only way I ever feel that I'm not being made a fool of. At the end of the day the ones who say that I am always right aren't sincere people.'

I held regular meetings with Valentini and Cenni to decide how to go about rebuilding bridges with the *Gazzetta dello Sport*. Marco had to understand that withdrawing into himself would only make things worse. But forgetting or at least accepting what had happened and letting the consequences wash over him wasn't Marco's style, and neither was it mine. Marco had been incensed by Cannavò's editorial. He expected the *Gazzetta* to understand, to give him the chance to find out once and for all whether that day had been some horrid mistake. Marco knew that he had respected the rules laid down by his sport, so calmly accepting his sentence was out of the question. Most of all he felt suffocated because he sensed that no-one believed him.

I decided to act and to ask Cenni and Valentini to come with me to Milan for a reconciliatory meeting with Cannavò. I, too, wanted to know why the paper and, by association the race, had adopted such a tough, obdurate stance. Bringing the two big cheeses to Milan wasn't an easy task, all the more so because Valentini didn't 'believe' in the mountain coming to Muhammed. For instance, when Albacom renewed their contract to co-sponsor the team in 2000 – in marketing terms, Madonna di Campiglio was widely viewed as a hiccup, and Pantani's endorsement was still highly prized – Valentini asked me if I knew Albacom's annual turnover. When I gave an accurate answer, he snapped back that Mercatone Uno's was bigger and that, consequently, they should come to him and not vice-versa. I don't know how, but I persuaded him to break the habit of a lifetime and accompany me to Milan.

That day, Cannavò beckoned us all into his office then sent for Zomegnan. Apparently, Zomegnan often took offence when he wasn't let in on matters like these and Cannavò seemed frightened of precisely that. Cenni was similarly submissive, asking Cannavò where we had gone wrong and assuring him that we would follow his advice on how to atone. Obviously, here, Cenni was referring to how Mercatone Uno had dealt with the incident and still didn't so much as entertain the thought that Marco might have transgressed. Cenni had never erred from the conviction that Marco had fallen victim to a malicious plot.

I can clearly remember Cannavò saying that what he had written in that 7 June editorial had not come from the heart. In short, he advised the Mercatone Uno bosses to follow a line of acceptance and to admit that they had made a mistake. If they did as he said, everything would slowly return to how it had once been. When I later gave Marco a brief summary of the meeting, he was speechless: he couldn't fathom what we were supposed to admit. At the end of the discussion, Cenni and

Valentini returned to their respective offices. Cenni believed that missing two hours of work was a crime, and Marco identified with his commitment; in Marco's eyes, Cenni was living proof that behind every achievement there was a sacrifice. In the meantime, after the meeting, I stayed behind with Cannavò. We went out for a coffee. I had barely put the cup to my mouth when he asked: 'So who put you here?' I looked at him, stunned, and replied: 'I don't know how it works with you guys, but let me assure you that it's more straightforward than you think. Marco hired me because he was looking for an honest manager who would represent his image exclusively, someone who could devote themselves too him fully. He didn't want to be one of many clients in an international agency. It's that simple: no mystery, no ulterior motive.' In certain businesses, simplicity can seem amazing and even disturbing...

6

The Beginning of the Nightmare

I began to suspect that something was amiss at the end of July. I was due to meet Marco because Albacom wanted him to appear on their stand at a trade fair in Rimini. I have already mentioned the fact that the events of Madonna di Campiglio had not significantly dented Marco's appeal to sponsors. In fact, Citroën had seen its sales increase by 25 per cent on the back of the adverts broadcast during the Giro, and was now keen to feature him in a further campaign. The owner had even tried to console Marco by giving him a car and reassuring him that he was still number one in the company's eyes. They still believed in him.

That evening, I had arranged to meet Marco at his house at seven, but he was nowhere to be seen. He wasn't home and his parents didn't know what had happened to him. I later discovered that he was over at Giumbo's place. Marco was positive that he had been seeing Christina again and had searched the entire house for proof. It had ended in a fight and the first signs that Marco's confidence in his best friends – or so-called best friends – was slipping. In truth, his relationship with Christina had begun to deteriorate – as it turned out irremediably – precisely when he needed it to hold him up. Marco needed a woman with a capital 'W', but Christina's circumstances dictated that she wasn't able to fulfil that role.

A red hot summer

At that time, Christina worked in the snack bar alongside Tonina and was there to welcome Marco whenever he returned home between races. When he was away, they had no contact because Marco would leave his mobile phone at home. While Tonina and Paolo were on the edge of their seats in front of the television, she would be at the beach. Christina certainly didn't share her boyfriend's love of cycling, not least because it took Marco away from her: 'Make a choice! It's me or it's the bike!' she would implore. The image I have of Christina in the immediate aftermath of Madonna di Campiglio is one of an ornament on the mantelpiece: yes, she was in the house but her presence was completely passive. It almost seemed as though she was underestimating Marco's suffering, or that she didn't quite comprehend what had happened. The idea that she didn't understand, her coldness and her distance drove Marco crazy. Their arguments became a routine occurrence with an equally routine ending: Marco going out alone with his friends. Christina had a very different mindset to Marco. She had run away from home at a very young age, leaving behind a stressful family life and paying her way by working as a podium dancer in nightclubs. Marco had taken one look at her punk-rocker's hairstyle and clothes and was intrigued. More than this, though, he sensed that she needed protection.

Marco always tried to be a father figure to her, to show her the attention and affection that he heaped upon people who needed them. But the way he did it was always very gracious and discreet. This was one of his hallmarks; he knew that certain so-called friends would go with him to nightclubs to bask in his notoriety, because he always paid, or because the owner of the club was sure to slip anyone who brought in such a famous customer a hefty tip. Marco reasoned 'without him, these boys might struggle to even get by, and I can help them indirectly here'. Similarly, in Christina he thought that he had found a girl who would put herself in his hands and who would give him the warmth and the attention he craved. He would be disappointed. With hindsight, I even believe that her disengagement in the days which followed

Madonna di Campiglio helped to accelerate the spiral of despair in which Marco was now caught.

Marco became suspicious of everyone; he seemed more and more convinced that people wanted to exploit him. He wasn't far wide of the mark. And it wasn't just sponsors. An example: a young, aspiring female singer who he had dated for a while claimed that she was pregnant with his baby and was demanding £30,000 to keep quiet. Once the necessary clinical tests had been done and enquiries made, it emerged several weeks later that it had all been a charade.

At almost exactly the same time, Marco decided to confront Christina, who he suspected was cheating on him. He was now an open book from Christina's point of view, while she remained an enigma to him. She didn't open up to him and skirted around his questions. Marco was at his wit's end. I recently read and re-read some of the notes Marco left behind and some of Christina's letters. The recurring theme is the lack of communication. He had made mistakes with her, admitted that he had neglected her and, with brutal honesty, laid himself bare. She, on the other hand, at least according to Marco, continued to lie. One day, in the car, I said: 'Marco, you can't always rush things and want to solve all of your problems straight away. Let's stay calm and take them one at a time.' But this approach was anathema to him. In this sense, he was very similar to his mother Tonina. His come-back was: 'You know that's the way I am – I always want to get to the very bottom of things. I dig, dig and when I get to a certain depth I don't know what's going on any more and I get totally confused. Then the fear of emptiness hits me and I descend into chaos.' This character trait would later be exaggerated by the excessive use of cocaine, which numbed him to his own sensations, beating him into a corner, into a blind alley from which he would never escape.

To try to unwind, Marco decided to take Christina on holiday. They set off in a camper van for their own tour of Italy. It should have represented a fresh start for their relationship, but it turned out to be the beginning of the end.

The secret meeting

Against this backdrop of uncertainty in his private life, Marco was also undecided about whether to retire or continue racing. First of all, he wanted to set the record straight. We all tried to make him realise that results on the road were the best response he could give, but he was stubborn. He couldn't bear the thought of going back to racing still labelled as a doper, through the side door. There needed to be a shake-up, some signal from the top, not necessarily from Marco's sponsors or Cenni or Valentini. Fabrizio Borra seized the initiative and organised a meeting in Rome with Gianni Petrucci and Raffaele Pagnozzi, respectively the president and the secretary of the Italian Olympic Committee (CONI). Marco suspected that CONI, and especially its antidoping disciplinary committee, had wanted him out of the Giro because he had dared to criticise the manner in which they had 'superimposed' their blood tests. Deep down, he was sure that CONI anti-doping crusader Sandro Donati and his men had chosen him as their sacrificial lamb to prove the effectiveness of their campaign. There could be no doubt that Pantani's name would earn more publicity for their cause than a journeyman plucked at random from the peloton.

Petrucci's thesis was simple: there was no grudge against Pantani on CONI's part, although several different blocs coexisted within the organisation, of which Donati's hardliners were among the most influential.

It was in everyone's interest to protect a national treasure like Marco Pantani, whom CONI wanted to see return to cycling with his head held high. Moreover, that year's world championships were due to take place in the neighbouring Italian cities of Treviso and Verona, and Pantani's presence would be a major fillip for the event. A few days after the CONI meeting Italian Prime Minister Massimo D'Alema officially honoured Marco for his contribution to Italian sport. In July, the world championship organisers had already given him a vote of confidence by inviting him to a press conference in Treviso and telling him that they would be happy to see him compete. 'I'll prove on the road that I'm strong, stronger than before. I'm targeting the world championships,' Marco told the media.

The day of that press conference, Italian Cycling Federation (FCI) president Giancarlo Ceruti sat alongside Pantani. Ceruti was attending the press conference on behalf of CONI. Within comfortable earshot of Mercatone Uno boss Romano Cenni, Ceruti had turned to Marco and expounded the view that he, too, thought that they had wanted him out. After that brief encounter, Marco wanted to know what Ceruti had meant and invited the FCI president to his house for a face-to-face meeting which ended up lasting several hours. Marco thought that, in Ceruti, he had found the brains behind the conspiracy. Every once in a while, Tonina and Manola, Marco's sister, came in and out and overheard snatches of the conversation. Ceruti's basic message to Marco was that he should move on, because he was alone against the world. If he admitted that he had made a mistake, everything would resolve itself and no-one would persecute him any more. Marco replied that, no, he couldn't accept it, because he knew that the truth was a different one.

Withdrawal from the Worlds

With the world championship now at the forefront of his mind, Marco had embarked upon a brutal training regime that August. So brutal, in fact, that when, on the eve of the Giro del Lazio, Marco announced that he had given up all hope of riding the Worlds, Beppe Martinelli explained:

> It took Marco forty days to get over the body blow he received at Madonna di Campiglio, having been on the verge of quitting the sport. He has asked himself questions about everything and everyone. Then he got back on the bike. In fact, I'd say that he positively threw himself at it with that determination only he knows. That's when the problems with his right knee, his healthy knee, started. For three weeks he lived with the discomfort and tried not to attach too much importance to it. He told me that it had given him a bit of trouble at the Giro but that it was a pain that came and went, either at the start of a training session or at the end. The

physiotherapist said that it was a muscular problem; we assumed that Marco had pushed himself too much after such a long lay-off. We all thought that it would pass with training. The injury was behind our decision to pull out of the Tour of Spain because Marco wanted to be on top form and didn't want to risk not being ready for the Worlds.

Why, Martinelli was asked, had the problem been kept secret from the press? 'Can you imagine the reaction? The aim was to get Marco to Verona in perfect condition. Realising that he wasn't improving, and after consulting a specialist, we ordered Marco to rest. Having done that, he was examined in Brescia. The results showed that his patella was off its axis by a few millimetres and that he would need to undertake a long rehabilitation programme to rectify it. Fabrizio Borra, Marco's regular physiotherapist, is overseeing everything.' Marco's *annus horribilis* thus drew to a suitably anticlimactic end. It could have been much worse as, on 19 November, Marco was involved in the latest in a lengthening string of car accidents. Fortunately, as usual, he emerged unscathed.

A woman in the ranks

Without the bike to occupy him, at the end of that 1999 summer Marco had allowed his life to drift into a state of mild chaos. He went out every night and fought with Christina almost constantly. One day, on the telephone, I told him to get his act together and concentrate on his work. I then called his father Paolo to see where we stood and to decide what we should do. At the time, I still didn't feel close to his parents, despite the fact that they thought highly of me because they could see that Marco trusted me.

Madonna di Campiglio was still haunting him. His latest hang-up was how the team's staff had been incapable of dealing with the situation. As a result, he wanted more control over what happened in the team, not only from the point of view of his image but also on the road. Marco felt that the team had become arrogant because it could count on his charismatic personality. He was also critical of Martinelli for having been unable – in his eyes – to massage relations with other teams, the inevitable consequence of which had been a groundswell of ill-feeling against Mercatone Uno. According to Marco, the other teams had then exploited his misfortune at Madonna di Campiglio.

Having received conflicting messages from people in the cycling and car businesses, Marco had even begun to suspect that his promotional deal with Citroën might have put enough noses out of joint to leave him exposed to a revenge attack. He knew that the *Gazzetta dello Sport* belonged to the RCS group, the organisers of the Giro d'Italia. And RCS, in turn, had a long-standing connection with Turin car giant FIAT, Citroën's leading competitor. Franco Cornacchia, the Mercatone Uno financial director who had negotiated Marco's Citroën deal, had been voted out of the Association of Italian Cycling Teams precisely because of his agreement with the French company. Every team except Mercatone Uno, in fact, used FIAT team vehicles.

Marco's lateral thinking was immaculate. For my part, all that I could add is that the negotiations over payment and the terms of the contract hadn't been the smoothest. I pointed this out on several occasions, angering Mercatone Uno in the process. Citroën had an annual advertising budget of fifty billion lire (around £17 million) and Marco had become 'Mr Citroën'. He was now more readily associated with their cars than with the Mercatone Uno brand. However, Marco's contract wasn't renewed simply because Citroën didn't believe that the potential gains justified the risk of further damage to their image. It wasn't that Citroën had wanted rid of Pantani – I've already drawn attention to the fact that they had planned to film more adverts even after Madonna di Campiglio – but that the two parties, us and them, couldn't agree financial terms. I tried to explain this several times to Cenni and Valentini, but without success. Instead, they reproached me for having made Mercatone Uno pay too much to renew their contract with Marco.

Over the next five years, they never quite forgave me for that. Every time I went to Mercatone Uno HQ on business relating to Marco, I would be accused of having forced them to pay an exorbitant amount to add a further three years to Marco's contract after the 1998 Giro–Tour double. They never hesitated to tell Marco himself that I talked a lot but didn't bring in sponsors. I don't want to dwell on this topic: the accuracy of my estimates on how much money Mercatone Uno made by tying themselves to Pantani was confirmed by Cenni, who stated on the record that his company had gained more from Pantani than he had received from them. I'm not interested in one-upmanship and I'm not trying to justify myself. Marco and I both knew how things really were. On our long car journeys together, smiling mischievously, Marco would sometimes burst into song: 'If we are together, there must be a reason...'

I certainly wouldn't be intimidated. If Marco wanted answers on something from Mercatone Uno, I would endure as many meetings or negotiations as it took. During that autumn of 1999, Marco began to hatch a plan to have me employed in the team, to make him feel more protected. Something had clicked in his head: he wanted to start racing again, but only on his own terms. He told me about his plan: 'You're the only person I trust, so I want you to come into the team as general manager. Let's go to Cenni and Valentini and put it to them: if you want me to start racing again, Ronchi has to be in charge of the team.'

Marco's ultimatum was finally accepted despite almost universal scepticism. I had no experience in the sport and, as if that wasn't enough, no woman had ever fulfilled that role in cycling. When Marco outlined his proposed reshuffle, Cenni turned a colour resembling purple and retorted that I knew nothing about cycling. But Marco was adamant: there was nothing *to* know and he would explain to me what was important. He wanted people with experience outside of the cycling world, which, in his view, needed new ideas and new blood. Eventually a compromise was reached: Mercatone Uno appointed me to assist the team, but Felice Gimondi, the former Tour and multiple Giro winner, would be made president of the team.

Marco was less than enthusiastic about Gimondi's involvement. He would have preferred Alfredo Martini, the former Italian team national coach, with whom had he struck up an excellent relationship. But he couldn't have the final say on everything so left this decision to Cenni and friends. Cenni told me to help Felice to communicate with Marco, and said that Gimondi could take on Luciano Pezzi's mantle as Marco's 'guru' – a role I shouldn't entertain any thoughts of taking on given my lack of experience. I can acknowledge my own limitations and, not only for Marco's good, I would never have tried to impose myself as his only advisor. In fact, I did my utmost to bring Marco and Felice closer together. It wasn't easy, as there was an enormous gulf between them; in fact, between Gimondi's diplomacy and Marco's raw impulsiveness and pride, there was an ocean.

As for the management structure of the team, in practical terms little had really changed: Martinelli was still the manager of the team with Alessandro Giannelli and Orlando Maini alongside him as *directeur sportifs*. Lower down the hierarchy the mercurial masseur Roberto Pregnolato had been kept on – the bosses at Mercatone Uno had wanted him out, but nothing was done about it – and there were no changes among the mechanics. The team had let Roberto Conti leave and signed the highly rated Spaniard, Igor Astarloa. Press officer Andrea Agostini was eased out and Emilio Magni replaced Roberto Rempi as team doctor. Agostini was incensed: from day one, he hadn't taken kindly to me and now, having been released from the team, he became even more hostile. He was fearful that, with his job, the friendship that he had built up with Marco since their school days and first cycle races together would also go. Every day, he would turn up on Marco's doorstep, accusing him of not having used his influence to save his position. Marco would then call me, bewildered:

Manu, I've already got enough problems of my own. Does it seem fair to you that now I have to feel guilty for what's happened to Ago? He's saying bad things about you, which, frankly, I find disrespectful towards me! I've always helped him: he wanted to race and I took him with me; he wanted to be a journalist and I got him a job at Mercatone Uno in the most important year of my career. If he showed that he wasn't up to the task what can I do about it? If Mercatone Uno doesn't want him any more, I can't always fight against the whole world to save my neighbour. I always help everyone, but now it's me that needs help.

Marco's thoughtfulness could be extraordinary. If he found out that a rider was having trouble finding a contract, he would lobby for them to get taken on by Mercatone Uno. He always used to say that he didn't need talented riders, just people who knew how to sacrifice themselves for him. 'You have a special gift for sacrifice,' he would tell them. 'If they have to devote themselves to me, I have to be the first to help them when they need me. I can't do it on the bike because it's not my job, so I do it in life instead.'

That was Pantani. I think that one of the things which made him suffer the most was a lack of gratitude towards him. He was always willing to go out on a limb to defend a team-mate. Just one example: when, in 2003, Davide Boifava (who had by then moved from Carrera to Mercatone Uno) announced that he was going to release Ermanno Brignoli, Marco was so outraged that he threatened to retire from cycling if Boifava didn't reverse the decision.

Back in court

In the meantime, Marco's legal headaches had begun. The Turin public prosecutor Raffaele Guariniello had started proceedings against Marco on a possible charge of sporting fraud, having requested the seizure of the clinical files pertaining to Marco's fall in the 1995 Milan–Turin. Mercatone Uno had already commissioned the lawyers Guazzaloca and Insolera to represent Marco in the Trento enquiry launched by magistrate Bruno Giardina into the events of Madonna di Campiglio, and now asked them to do the same in Turin. To tell the truth, Marco wasn't particularly enamoured with Mercatone Uno's choice of lawyers. After the Imola press conference, he had sensed that they lacked specialist skills and knowledge in the sporting field and lost confidence in them. Out of respect, he didn't want to question Cenni's wisdom, but neither would he give Guazzaloca and Insolera his wholehearted backing. Cenni maintained that they were the best around. The best, yes, but in *their* specialist field. They had no experience of cases based on allegations of doping in sport. I called in Mr Santoni from the Rossotto practice in Torino as a reinforcement. As well as being my own personal lawyer, Santoni knew the Turin legal scene. Unsurprisingly, Mercatone Uno were furious and contrived to keep Santoni at arm's length by having the case moved to Forli, several hundred kilometres away.

Pantani's first court summons would not be his last. Far from it. He was ordered to appear before Guariniello in Turin at the beginning of November. Insolera demanded that I organise for him to meet Marco. How could he work on the enquiry, he said, if he could never speak to Marco? In this sense, Marco was an infuriating man to work with. Tracking him down could be a nightmare and I would inevitably have to rely on my instinct. He particularly disliked talking to the lawyers, especially Insolera. I finally managed to arrange a meeting in Bologna shortly before the hearing in Turin.

I can remember that day like it was yesterday. I made my way to Cesentico to pick up Marco. I was extremely agitated, as I always was when I was on my way to meet him. I always had to be full of energy with a full array of answers at the ready. At the same time, I had to remain cool and compassionate. I arrived at Marco's villa and rung the doorbell. Marco's Dad opened and I glimpsed Tonina in the background. They looked haunted. I stepped inside, smiled: 'Are we ready then?' I could see Marco's silhouette approaching from the corridor which leads to the bedrooms. His face was drawn and unshaven. No-one dared look me in the eye. Perhaps Tonina was trying to tell me something with her body language, but I didn't pick up on it. I considered it normal to see glum faces in such a difficult period. Marco reluctantly left the house and said that we had to talk. He said a gruff goodbye to his parents, then, having slammed the car door, slumped into the passenger seat.

'Marco, what's up? You seem strange... Come on, we'll spend some time together, you'll get it off your chest and you'll see that there's a solution to everything.' Silence. 'No, Manu, there's no solution to this.' Naturally, I thought that he was talking about Madonna di Campiglio and Guariniello's investigation. I tried to cheer him up: 'Now, we'll go to see the lawyers, to please Insolera, then we'll go for dinner and chat about whatever it is.' He replied: 'We're not going anywhere. Something awful has happened. You can't begin to understand. There's no way to solve this. Take us to Christina's flat and I'll explain.' More silence, interminable this time. A million different worse-case scenarios crossed my mind – all but the one that he would reveal a few minutes later.

Marco opened the door to Christina's flat, a studio. It was a mess, with several days' worth of dirty plates piled up on every available surface and cans of tuna lying open. Christina was painting, hence the noxious smell and canvasses strewn all over the flat. You had to watch where you put your feet to avoid tripping over. The bed was unmade. You couldn't even see yourself in the bathroom mirror it was so dirty. 'You see how messy Christina is? I am a bit, too, but she beats me hands down,' grunted Marco.

He began pacing the room, nervously passing his hands back and forth over his head. 'Sit down!' he commanded. 'You know, my best friend...' He interrupted himself. 'Well, I'll get straight to the point...' He took a deep breath and then blurted out: 'There's no point in carrying on, Manu, I'm finished. I'm a junkie. That's it, I'm afraid...' At first, I thought that it was a confession about Madonna di Campiglio. There was nothing else *to* think. Marco hated cigarettes. He hated drugs and was completely intolerant of them. He used to enjoy himself in nightclubs, admittedly, but he didn't have any bad habits. I was foxed. 'Someone gave me cocaine,' Marco picked up, 'Now I'm a junkie and I can't get out of this on my own. My mum and dad know everything. Don't take me home, please, my parents are too worried. I don't want to make them ill. I need to think: take me with you.'

I couldn't feel my legs. I didn't know what to say. I didn't even know what cocaine was. Or rather, I knew what I had heard from other people or the media. That's all. I looked to Marco, wrapped my arms around him. He began to cry floods of tears. I steeled myself. 'No, my friend. You're not getting rid of me that easily. Now I'll take care of this. Stay with me and we'll make it out of this. I'll help you.' Marco looked at me apprehensively, then smiled as though finally liberated. He had been afraid that I would judge him. He had been afraid that I would abandon him. He began to loosen up a little and told me enough for me to under-stand how it had started: someone had told him that it would do him good. Marco was always very tough on himself and had clearly wanted to confess to punish himself for having bowed to the temptation.

I went to get some fresh air. I felt as though I was suffocating. I had to talk to someone, now. But who? My fiancée, Paolo, who I was due to marry a few months later, was the obvious candidate. I called him and tried to explain. He said: 'Now you can't drop him. I'm with you all the way, Manu.' After that telephone call, I felt even stronger, more determined. We went to the Dolce Vita hotel in Cesenatico, which had become my base and control centre for all Pantani-related matters that hot summer. I booked a room and told the owner that Marco and I would go straight up because we had work to do. I was conscious of the fact that I sounded eager to justify my disappearing into a hotel room with Marco Pantani. I was scared of being judged. In Cesenatico, gossip travelled fast, and at Mercatone Uno and on the cycling circuit in general everyone already thought that something was going on between Marco and I.

In the room, Marco relaxed a little and asked me to call his parents to reassure them. I spoke to his father: 'Paolo, I know everything. Marco's with me now. I won't leave him on his own. Don't worry. It'll all be fine.' Marco looked at me and said: 'You speak so well, you say all the right things. You're really good, you know. Together, we'll do this.' We stayed up the whole night, talking. The following morning I was due to go to the Mercatone Uno offices. I had been called in for a meeting about the team's contract with bike manufacturer Bianchi. My heart and my mind had already started to put up protective barriers. The nerves made my heart beat fast. I was scared. Marco had asked me keep his secret. I had to help him; I certainly couldn't shout from the rooftops about a problem regarding his private life. He had put his trust in me. It was easy to say, but how could you keep personal and private separate where Pantani was concerned?

I tried to be strong. Marco needed a strong woman. I couldn't run away. I told myself that I had to do everything to pull him out of the mire. His health depended on it, and his health was all I cared about from that point on. The rest was incidental. In the meantime I had to fulfil the role I had been given to the best of my ability. But the cocaine problem had to be tackled and overcome. For him to have the psychological strength to summon all of his courage, Marco had to be treated like Marco Pantani, not someone who was mentally ill. I knew that I shouldn't spoil him and that, from then on, all professional decisions had to respond to the needs of the star athlete and the team but also, and above all, to those of a man who felt that he had lost his dignity.

I returned to Cesenatico late that afternoon. Marco had slept all day. When he woke up, he was a different person. The effects of the cocaine had passed. We went to Milan. Our car journeys were a unique experience. He would constantly torment me with jibes like: 'You're so slow that I'd get us there quicker on my bike.' We would stop off in service stations and Marco would stock up on sweets and popcorn. I had a weakness for those gobstoppers from the one-arm-bandit type dispensers. Marco used to tease me because I could easily wolf down twenty in ten minutes. We arrived in Milan, at my house in Via Sofocle, a short walk from my office in Corso Magenta. Marco was afraid of having to face Paolo, my husband to be. He was shy and not used to being in other people's houses, but it didn't take him long to find his bearings.

That evening we went to bed early. At two o'clock the next morning the telephone rung. Paolo's grandmother, Irma, had died. We rushed to Cimamulera, the village where Irma lived, on the road that leads to Macugnago. I reassured Marco that we would be back in a few hours. Paolo was distraught because Granny Irma had been like a mother to him. The funeral was arranged for the same day that I was supposed to go with Marco to Turin for the hearing, which posed a problem. As usual, Paolo understood: 'Manu, you have a commitment and you've got to respect it. Irma would have understood. Go ahead and don't worry.'

We got back to Milan at around six in the morning. Marco was awake. His eyes were wild and they terrified me. Maybe he still had some coke with him. I don't know. Fortunately, as the hours went by, he seemed to return to his normal self.

We set off for Turin on a journey devoted to talking about his problem. 'You know, there's no point in running away from Cesenatico. If I want to, I'll pick up the telephone and they'll deliver the cocaine to wherever I want it. You wouldn't believe the level of organisation behind it.' I began to sense what a long and arduous battle lay ahead, but I didn't let myself be intimidated and replied sharply: 'I'll give you all the organisation you need. You don't know who you're dealing with. I won't give up, my boy.' He squeezed my hand and murmured: 'I know...'

The hearing with Guariniello lasted a matter of minutes. He and Marco didn't even look each other in the eye, and Marco exercised his right not to respond to the judge's questions. We went for coffee and Marco asked what I wanted to do now. 'To be honest, I'd really like to go to Paolo's grandmother's funeral, since we got away pretty quickly, but you're here so we'll do what we have to do.' 'Let's go to the funeral,' Marco replied, 'but I'll stay in the car because I don't want to divert people's attention away from Paolo's grandma. It would be a nice thing to do.' I was amazed and at the same time moved by his thoughtfulness, and by the deep respect that he was showing. They were qualities which Marco struggled to express, but which were irresistible when he did reveal them. We arrived at Cimamulera just in time. It was snowing. Marco was wearing a blue fleece. We had practically fled Cesenatico and Marco had brought almost no luggage. When Paolo saw us, he burst into tears. Sure enough, the entire congregation saw and recognised Marco, much to his embarrassment. Everyone wanted autographs but he just wanted to stay out of sight. He didn't want to be recognised. He was ashamed.

We returned to Milan immediately after the service. A journalist from the satirical TV show *Striscia La Notizia* was waiting for us on the pavement outside my office, ready to present Marco with the 'Golden Tapir' award – roughly Italy's equivalent of Noel Edmonds' Gotcha Oscar – on account of his meeting with Guariniello. Marco accepted the dubious distinction in good heart, laughing at his own expense. We had dinner in Milan then Marco decided that he should go back to Cesenatico to talk to his parents. First, he wanted me to contact them: that way, they would calm down and not be tempted to keep him under 24-hour surveillance. Marco's parents are wonderful people, to say the least. They idolised their son, but didn't spoil him or always bow to his demands. Paolo's bravery was worthy of the highest praise. Marco marvelled at Tonina's ability to combine strength with tenderness, and the two had a unique relationship. They only had to exchange glances to know what each other was thinking.

Marco's sister, Manola, seldom saw him. Marco never wanted to bother her because she was raising two children in circumstances that were far from ideal after the break-up of her marriage. Tonina and Paolo also withheld some of the gorier details about Marco's life. Manola's life, they reasoned, was already complicated enough, what with work and her children. Manola would often stop by at the villa, even though she hesitated to ring the doorbell for fear of invading Marco's privacy. When she plucked up the courage to visit him, she'd make him his favourite fruit tart. Sometimes, she would start to clean the villa as an excuse to stay with him, but he would tell her off: 'I don't want to see you on your hands and knees cleaning: go home to your kids.' That was his hint that he wanted to be left alone.

Before we reached Cesenatico, we stopped off at Forlì, the town around forty kilometres directly inland from Marco's home town. Marco wanted to go out with a friend, a girl, as revenge for something that Christina had done. I dropped him off where he had asked, but I realised that he had hoodwinked me when I heard a man's voice crackle out of the intercom: 'Are you alone?' I waited for him and that night, after we had booked into a hotel in Forlì, he admitted that he had lied to me, that he had given in to the temptation. He apologised, almost cowering. He kept telling me not to leave him. He gripped my hand. He was frightened of everything. Inside, I was crying. I realised then that it wouldn't be easy to lift him out of this vortex which had a name: cocaine. We went back to Cesenatico the next day and discussed the situation with Marco's parents. Paolo suggested that I move to be near Marco and not to let him out of my sight.

Off to Cesenatico

For a few days, I felt uncomfortable in that vast but soulless villa. It was tastefully decorated but reflected none of Marco's personality, as the architect had done everything. All Christina wanted to do was leave everything in a mess and Tonina spent her time cleaning and washing up after her. Marco asked me to go next-door to his parents' apartment to explain that we wanted to be left alone and that we would cook and buy food for ourselves. They understood and seemed relieved.

Our days merged into seamless monotony. Every morning, after an almost invariably sleepless night, I would prepare breakfast. Jokingly, we called each other 'George and Mildred'. Marco was tickled by how I would lay the table because he was used to eating on his feet and without cutlery and napkins, except when Tonina invited Marco and Christina to dinner in an attempt to break down some of the barriers put up by Christina. Every day, by mid-afternoon, I might finally convince Marco to go out on his bike. Marco's dad helped enormously with this, even donning his cycling gear and keeping Marco company on his training rides and offering endless encouragement to him. It was cold that winter and the first few days, Marco came back a few minutes after he had left, shivering. Sometimes, he would go out for longer, but Paolo said that I should check his cyclo-computer to make sure that he hadn't stopped off at Christina's apartment, currently empty after Christina had returned to Copenhagen following yet another row with Marco. Most of the time I would cook lunch but sometimes Marco would teach me how to make one of his specialities, like ravioli in broth or sophisticated fish dishes. I realised how much Marco needed a woman who loved him unconditionally, a good homemaker, someone from whose affection he could draw strength, love and courage.

Our afternoons would be mundane and repetitive with trips to the local supermarket and endless visits to Christina's apartment, where we would stop outside and gaze up at her window to check for any sign that she was back. Often, Marco would go up to the flat, convinced that he had seen her shadow. Nothing. Christina wasn't there, so Marco had to be content with the next best thing – endlessly talking about her, yearning for her to return: 'Manu, do you think that Christina is the woman of my life? I'm in love. If she dumps me I'm finished.' I never took the liberty of passing judgement on their relationship. I didn't want to interfere. I did, however, tell him that there was something peculiar about her, and that the way she had lived her life certainly couldn't have made her stronger than him. It was therefore unlikely, I said, that she could help him to solve his problem. Also, Christina was very selfish and, as the notes Tonina and

I found lying around the house revealed, she found it hard to cope with Marco's imposing personality. She was almost jealous of his fame but she was also ashamed of having allowed it to cross her mind that she could reap the financial rewards of dating someone so famous. Granted, on occasions she could charm the birds out of the trees, but Tonina would often say to me: 'When I look at her, she seems like an angel, but then she turns nasty and selfish. She tries to pit Marco against his family and she shouldn't because we have loved her like our own daughter and we're not invasive people. My son needs to feel loved but, by trying to drive a wedge between us, she just hurts him.'

Every evening Marco and I would make an executive decision about where to eat. A different restaurant every day. We were both crazy about ravioli in broth. We would stay just long enough to slurp up the last few drops, then it was back home, down to the basement, fire on, a film on the TV and a long night ahead of us. Paintings hung from almost every wall in Marco's basement. When I pointed out that they were all signed by him, Marco admitted that painting was another of his passions. Typically, no-one on the cycling scene knew about this, which confirmed once again that he bared only selected parts of his soul to the outside world. With hindsight, the subject matters of his paintings seemed to me to be deeply significant: suns obscured by the clouds, shattered men's skulls, flowers and seeds as signs of new life.

At around one o'clock I would go to bed. I slept in the small guest bedroom next to Marco's room, leaving the door half-open. A few minutes would go by before I could hear Marco pacing up and down the landing. He would peer through the darkness to see if I was awake, then ask: 'Manu, are you sleeping?' I would tell him that I was trying, upon which he would go back to his room and call Christina on his mobile phone. He suspected that she was cheating on him with Micael Rocchi, a car salesman from Cesena. Night-times were synonymous with fear for Marco. He thought that the house was full of bugging devices and he looked for them everywhere. Sometimes, he would take me by the hand and we would scour the garden for hidden microphones with a torch. He could hear footsteps on the roof. He dismantled everything to look for video cameras. At that time, he wasn't using cocaine, I was sure of it. But the turmoil in his head didn't let up, with Madonna di Campiglio and Christina his dual obsessions. Occasionally, I would find him sitting down on his bed, staring at a photograph of granddad Sotero, talking to him, asking him for advice. In Marco's eyes, Sotero was class and wisdom personified. It was that wisdom in other people which became an object of Marco's futile pursuit after the death of Luciano Pezzi.

We spent entire evenings discussing morals and relationships, how to respect one's parents, the superficiality and the hypocrisy of modern society. With me, he never entered into the specifics of what had happened at Madonna di Campiglio. He merely underlined that he had been harshly treated and how this was hurting him. We talked about everything besides cycling.

The amount of time that I was spending with Marco provided salacious grist for the rumour mill. It's fair to say that this was one of Marco's milder preoccupations. 'Work is work, personal or sexual relationships are personal or sexual relationships. I'm sure that I would like to be with a woman like you: I'm certain that it would be the making of me. But you represent 70 per cent; I need that 30 per cent which comes from intimacy.' And it was always a short leap to link the conversation to Christina: 'She's cold. She judges me, runs away from me when I need her. And stubborn as I am, I always try to put her to the test.' He was right: when he was healthy, she never left his side, she had money and everything else that she wanted. When he relapsed – and sometimes he did it on purpose, to test her commitment – Christina withdrew her affection, telling him that he was an idiot and storming off to a nightclub with her friends. It became a vicious circle, a continuous struggle.

Later, I would find a note from Marco dating back to that period, which clearly illustrated Marco's resentment:

There's a person very close to me who is making me do drugs but it's impossible to work out how to get away. Some people want to ruin me: they think that they've got it all worked out, how to hurt me, but I am and always will be clean. The person I love most is manipulating me.

The no-show at the Giro d'Italia presentation

The presentation of the 2000 Giro d'Italia was to be held in Milan at the beginning of December. To celebrate the millennium, the race would begin in Rome after a special blessing for all of the riders from Pope John Paul II. I tried to persuade Marco to attend the presentation. Just as, at Madonna di Campiglio, I had told him to leave the hotel with his head held high, now I insisted that he face his demons and reconnect himself with the cycling world. But Marco wouldn't have any of it:

> I just know that Cannavò will make me out to be the victim just so that the *Gazzetta* can 'redeem' me of my sins in that highfalutin way of theirs: they'll wheel me in front of the cameras and start pitying me. Well, let me tell you, I refuse to be pitied by a person who was talking about involving me in charity work the night before I my failed test at Madonna di Campiglio, then depicted me as a monster the next day.

I let it lie for a few minutes then insisted until he was so exhausted that he finally said yes. But the night before the presentation, Marco, clearly resenting how I had twisted his arm, said that he had changed his mind: 'I'm not coming tomorrow. It's out of the question.' Having learned to read his reactions, I didn't protest, safe in the knowledge that the following morning we'd be in the car on our way to Milan: 'Let's sleep on it. We'll talk tomorrow morning,' I said.

At three in the morning I heard knocking on my door. It was Marco. He looked a mess. 'We're going nowhere, understood?' I always wondered and still wonder today how he managed to get his hands on the cocaine he'd clearly consumed that night, as at that time I wasn't letting him out of my sight. He had been right: the supply chain he used was so well organised that he could make a single telephone call and the merchandise would appear, as if by magic, on his doorstep or in some hiding place in the garden. He was also unwell that night, with a high temperature, and to try to relax him I made him a camomile tea.

In the morning I warned his parents: 'Marco's through there, in bed, with a temperature. I think he's been snorting coke. He's asleep and he's determined not to go to Milan. I was up all night trying to persuade him, but there was no way.' Reluctantly, I then picked up the telephone to call the *Gazzetta* journalist Angelo Zomegnan to tell him that Marco wasn't well and wouldn't be leaving Cesenatico. Angelo passed me over to Cannavò. I will never forget the tone with which the ensuing conversation was conducted.

I had barely even begun to explain when Cannavò cut in and grunted words to the effect that pro cyclists are used to riding their bikes even when they have a temperature of forty degrees. If Marco didn't want to come, we should literally throw him into the car and bring him to Milan. We spoiled him too much. We weren't capable of managing him. Pantani had been flagged up as the star attraction and the whole evening had been organised around him.

I burst into tears – both as an outlet of the stress accumulated in over a month spent with Marco and the umpteen sleepless nights, and because I realised that a no-show by Marco would only open another hornets nest of gossip and innuendo. But also because it was dawning that I would have to keep telling lies, albeit for a good reason, every time cocaine had its wicked way with Marco and his attempts at resistance.

I felt sad, most of all. Marco was patently sick, yet all Cannavò could care about was his blasted show. I asked myself: did Cannavò make all this fuss about Marco because he wanted to help him return, as he claimed, or was his presentation an exercise in self-glorification with not the slightest regard for other people's suffering?

Marco's father, Paolo, was standing nearby, watching my emotions spill over and finally snatched the telephone out of my hands: 'Mr Cannavò, I am Marco's father. Do you have any children? If you do, you should respect our suffering at the moment or at least respect us as people. Thank you, goodbye.' Within minutes, Cannavò called back to tell me that he was only doing it for Marco, because if he didn't show up people would start talking about Pantani as a victim who didn't have the courage to show his face. I promptly replied that this also depended on him: if he simply said that Pantani wasn't able to attend because he were sick, no-one would cry foul. And that's how it turned out, notwithstanding a bitter outburst by the team's new president,

Felice Gimondi, about bad PR. Over the weeks and months that followed, Felice would often make it clear to me that if Marco continued in the same vein, he would step down because he had no intention of losing face in the cycling world.

That afternoon, as I recall, Marco had woken up at four o'clock. I had shown him the Giro route and asked him for his verdict because the papers wanted a quote from him in their vox pops. He replied with a caustic: 'It's a Giro tailor-made for Savoldelli, who in June got through the tests because his haematocrit was 49.9 per cent and ended up finishing second behind Gotti.' Marco only had to look at the route map to feel like he was already out of the race for the pink jersey.

Marco's anxiety and dejection are clearly delineated in yet more scrawled notes which Tonina found in his villa after his death, and which date back to November 1999. Here are the faithful transcriptions of those notes, complete with grammatical errors:

I've felt like a loser ever since Madonna di Campiglio. There's only sadness and pain. I didn't deserve this. Are there junkies in sport? 'No' you have to feel like they say only if you go into everyday life. You fools: how can you be journalists if you inflict stupid punishments. I alone have learned from all of you how to take drugs, not to win but to lose. Go and look in schools in offices and in bars then you'll find material to write about a real and alarming problem. But with me it's easier to talk nonsense. Shame on you I've lost the woman I loved and lots of friends because of your lack of professionalism. You journalists should love your work like the athletes do. But you envy their success and their money. If only there was some justice for the people who pay unjustly!

I know that my letter is a dog's dinner. But it's an outburst and I had to take drugs but if Berlusconi wants to govern I think that he should do something. It's inadmissible that the magistrates can do whatever they want, there are serious problems in this country. And they just target fame.

All this effort to change but I'm not well and everyone is all over me trying to help and they only make me feel incapable. I wanted you Christina but for a while you're sweet and affectionate, then you fly off the handle with me it seems as though you do it on purpose to test me but I am always thinking of you and you can't love me any more.

I am so afraid of what's going to happen to you. You seem naïve, but I've been useless to you for a while no. I can only give you some money some and things to clothe Gualtieri [the psychologist who was treating Christina] he seems good to me but you need to get yourself back on track, you know men are cunning and sometimes unscrupulous and you mustn't get taken for a ride. I'm sure that you're a good girl, I want Christina to understand that it isn't easy to hear so many accusations. I feel a bit lonely. I haven't been home for ages, and now I feel like I don't have any roots because I feel the desire to be ill, perhaps that way I'll think about you less!?

Here is the second of those letters:

At times like these I start believing in our father. My spelling is probably all over the place and there are mistakes and it's always been a weakness (I hope you understand). There are times when out of weakness or because of bad or just misguided friends you make mistakes. And I don't want to blame anyone but I just want to say that I have succumbed to the disgusting problem of drugs, but only because to an extent my woman and to an extent my friends made me think that it would give me back my will. No, I isolated myself the slave of a problem which doesn't make you strong but the slave of pain and I apologise to everyone. But above all to the people who believed that Pantani is great and who believe that I was honest in my goals like my rivals and I'm sure that the same rivals will admit that there were short-cuts which made a difference in fact everyone did what they could which the law of equality dictated.

I feel guilty for other things and want to hurt myself and become a real junkie. My family has been exceptional and I want to denounce myself to everyone so that they know that you can ruin yourself on your own lots of people have taken advantage of me even a woman who threatened that she wanted money because I had got her pregnant, I only asked her to tell me what she wanted and she made me anxious I was able to tell her everything, and I knew that I could lose her, but she had been treating me unfaithfully for some time, but I thought that, if I did the same as her she would understand (I copied her stupidly) but with time I have stopped wanting to punish her, to reason better, and she, smart as she is, deceived me. She even expressed her esteem for me when I was out of the way...

But I was simply blocked and a bit absent. She was so sneaky having tried to deny ever using any drugs she confessed that she had a great capacity for using those same drugs, and with the help of a few common friends they gave me the d...! And then I got addicted. But even if it's hard I want to give up.

I faced up to my responsibility saying that as she wanted to keep it, to go ahead with my alleged son, I didn't want to become a killer by giving her the money she was asking for after I clearly wanted proof to be certain of my possible fatherhood, and after causing a real racket she came to me with an aborted child, threatening me, that's inhumane I only hope that even if it was a big responsibility on my part she just did it for the money. I hope that my woman has sinned against me sometimes, but then I have against her, too.

Marco finally gets help

In that period I was torn over whether tell Romano Cenni about Marco's predicament, and it was Marco who finally solved my dilemma by confessing in person. I phoned him one evening and he said that he made clear to Cenni that he had used cocaine, that he had major problems with Christina and that he was keeping bad company in his private life. Cenni suggested that I look up Steve Benedettini, a motivational psychologist he'd dealt with for personal and company reasons. I picked up the phone immediately and when Steve told me that he was on holiday in Trentino, in the north of Italy, I jumped into the car and drove to meet him. With all that Cenni was doing for Marco, I felt it my duty to act on his recommendation, although I knew that bringing the matter up with Marco would be immensely difficult. Marco hated psychologists, not least because Christina consulted one and he was convinced that it was the psychologist who turned her against him. Nevertheless, with the help of Tonina and Paolo, I managed to persuade Marco to come with me to Milan to meet Steve a few days later. Marco arrived with his parents wearing a black hat, a long overcoat in black leather and a facial expression perfectly co-ordinated with his mood. 'Is nothing sacred any more? Look what I have to do: even go to a psychologist. I'll make *him* go crazy. You'll see: after ten minutes of talking to me he'll be the one needing treatment.'

After a preliminary assessment, it was decided Marco would undertake a programme of treatment consisting of weekly sessions, although no sooner had we stepped out of the psychologist's office than Macro stressed that he had only accepted to placate his parents and to stop them bugging him. We returned to Cesenatico and I stayed with him for a while longer. After a few days, he came to wake me at seven in the morning, already dressed. 'Manu, I've decided. Call Bologna airport and book me a ticket for Copenhagen. I'm going to look for Christina. I have to clear things up. I have to work it out. Just don't say anything to my parents.' Marco's parents were already furious with the way that Christina had apparently dumped Marco and fled Italy. They had welcomed her into their home when Marco had met her, put aside any prejudices they may have had about her clothes, hairstyle and job and accepted their son's choice. They had given her a home, a family, love and affection. Tonina knew that Marco needed a different type of woman, but she would always say: 'I can't choose for Marco. If he loves this girl then I'll learn to love her, too.' She was as good as her word. But when a mother and father see their son suffer desperately for a woman, it's no wonder that they suffer too. Also, at the time when she had left Italy, there was no doubt that Marco needed Christina more than she needed him.

Marco's decision sent me into a panic. I knew that I couldn't keep him under lock and key at home, but I tried to dissuade him, reminding him that he didn't even have Christina's telephone number or her address. He wouldn't let this deter him. At the airport, just as we were about to get out of the car, Marco's telephone rang. He answered and his face lit up: 'Cri! I'm coming to see you...'

My heart was in my mouth and it remained there for three days. Marco was very sweet – he called me every three hours to keep me up to date and to tell me that everything was fine. His parents knew nothing about his trip to Denmark until he got back and I agreed with Marco that telling them would only add to their anxiety. Marco emerged from the baggage reclaim clutching a teddy bear dressed in a red and white horizontally striped jersey and pirate's skull cap – my present from Denmark. He reassured me that everything had been cleared up with Christina and said that I must now help him to make his parents accept her; he understood their attitude, but he wanted to find a way of living together which was acceptable for everyone. In the meantime Christina came back to Italy, while I returned to Milan with plenty to think about.

That Christmas eve I was at my parents' house on Lago Maggiore, the westernmost of Italy's three major lakes – Maggiore, Como and Garda – when my mobile rung. It was Marco. Despite the bond that had formed between us, every time I saw the name 'Panta' appear on the display my hands started sweating, usually because I was frightened that something had happened to him. The calls that came from him were usually about accidents or other problems. This time, though, he was sending me a wonderful Christmas present: 'It's Panta... I'll be forever grateful. Christina is back and my parents understand. There's a lovely atmosphere. On the first of January we'll make a fresh start, definitely.'

7

The 'Substance'

Marco Pantani could be forgiven for hoping that 1 January 2000 would not only signal the advent of a new millennium, but also a bridge between his pre- and post-Madonna di Campiglio life and career, conveniently passing over the wretched event itself. It was with the same hope that Giuseppe Martinelli went about organising the traditional warm weather training camp in the Canary Islands for the beginning of January. Martinelli duly reported to Marco's house in Cesenatico a few days later, expecting to drive his protegé to Bologna airport, only to find Marco bed-ridden. It seemed that the enthusiasm Marco had shown a few days earlier had raised false hopes, or perhaps it was Marco who had thought that he could give up taking cocaine whenever the mood took him. It simply couldn't be that easy. I don't think that Martinelli knew about the problem at this stage. What I can say for sure is that Giuseppe bundled Marco into the car, dragged him through the departure lounge then, minutes later, called me in a state of horror and disbelief. He said that as soon as he had seen Marco he had been petrified. As for Marco's cocaine problem, he said that he had suspected something, but he had no idea it had already escalated to the point that he had to be almost carried onto a plane. Martinelli knew all about cocaine because he had already known and helped one addict, and he probably picked up on and recognised Marco's symptoms without anyone having to explain what was causing them.

Roberto Pregnolato was the delegated organiser of the trip. Together with Marco, regular training partners Marco Velo, Enrico Zaina, Ermanno Brignoli and Fabio Fontanelli were also in the party. The first few days passed off without major incident, although strong winds had forced the riders to cut short their training sessions. I joined the party on 13 January, Marco's birthday. I remember stopping to buy him a Swatch, which I knew he would like. Marco met me in the hotel reception, a mite embarrassed by the gift because, he said, he wasn't used to either giving or receiving them. Tonina and I will never forget one of the last things we heard Marco say when, having bought several Rolex watches for friends, he explained his largesse by saying: 'I only give presents to enemies, not to friends…' I breathed a sigh of relief, since he had rarely if ever given me presents. That night, my first in the Canaries, we had dinner in a restaurant serving local specialities then went back to the hotel. I went to bed early, assuming that after a hard day of training the others would be doing likewise.

I discovered that I had been naive when I was woken suddenly in the early hours by Enrico Zaina banging hard on my door. I was still half-asleep when an ashen-faced Zaina opened the door, held up a small, see-through plastic bag full of white powder and asked me whether I knew anything about it. I leapt out of bed and asked where Marco was. Zaina admitted that the previous evening, he and the other members of the team had felt like partying, but it hadn't even crossed his mind that Marco could have this problem. This was why he had wanted to speak to me so urgently that morning and hadn't been able to wait until breakfast. I quickly got dressed and ran to Marco's room. Martinelli had beaten me to it and was already giving Marco a harsh dressing down when I arrived. Giuseppe grabbed the drugs and threw them down the toilet. Marco claimed that they had all decided to make a night of it except Velo, who had gone to bed early. Then the others had done the dirty on him, spouting off about his habit and humiliating him in front of everyone. It was one of those furious rows in which things are said which aren't necessarily meant, but suffice it to say that by the time it was over, Martinelli wanted to take the first plane back to Italy.

Marco and I were now alone in his room. He was spread out on the bed, crying, his face hidden under the sheets, burning with shame at having betrayed my trust. 'I've let you down, I've let you down, but then so did they behave badly towards me.' Some time later I would do my own research into the psychological and behavioural effects of cocaine abuse and discover that Marco's attempts to justify himself and look for an alibi every time he relapsed fitted the typical symptomatic profile. He was also ashamed of using the word cocaine and preferred to use the euphemism 'substance' or similar expressions. When he told you about his addiction, Marco wanted to be viewed as a normal, intelligent human being: when he was wrong he expected that to be acknowledged just as he expected to receive credit whenever he was right. I've found out that when dealing with cocaine users, it's a common mistake for people to distrust everything the addict is saying, assuming that it's all lies and excuses. The effect is counterproductive, especially when the subject has a personality like Marco's: doubt them and they become defiant, often ending up humiliating and hurting themselves.

I can remember stroking his head, trying to console him: 'It's not that you've let me down, Marco. We know that it's going to be a long process, that you can't kick this overnight. The most important thing is that you don't tell me lies. Your team-mates wanting to party and then getting a fright because they saw that you'd gone over the top is one thing, but I'm not interested in establishing whether it was Zaina's fault or not.' I tried to get through to him that I didn't want him to always shift the attention onto other people, something he often did to avoid facing up to his problem. Maybe his team-mates had messed up, but all I cared about was that he got better. I wasn't bothered about finding out whether Zaina was telling the truth or deciding whether Martinelli had been unfair or not. Marco couldn't hold back the tears. He held me tight and said: 'Please, help me, stay close to me, please don't you judge me as well, because cock-ups like these do me no good at all. The way I am, I'm not capable of reacting; they trigger this defence mechanism which only makes things worse.'

He wanted to be left alone. Martinelli was in reception, still shaken and drained by the argument. His mood was not helped by the fact that he was taking some of what Marco had said personally – a common mistake when dealing with drug users. Pregnolato, in contrast, was justifying everything that Marco did or said, one aim of which was to turn him against the other members of the team and staff. I think that this was one of the biggest weaknesses of Marco's entourage. They all wanted to make a name for themselves and when he criticised someone they all backed him to try to carve themselves a place in his affections and satisfy his whims. Marco knew it and played on this vanity, one upshot of which was that there was none of the cohesion and comradeship you would have expected in the team. Being critical, you might say that Marco was only reaping what he had sown when he would then voice his dissatisfaction with the lack of team sprit at Mercatone Uno. What is certain is that greater harmony within the team would certainly have aided Marco's attempts to rebuild his career after 1999.

I stayed in the Canaries for another two days. Mercifully, there were no repeats of Zaina's early morning alarm call or anything remotely similar. The months which followed before Marco's return to racing weren't a happy time, principally because the fear of Marco relapsing again was ever-present. While those around him now seemed to have buried the memory of Madonna di Campiglio, it was still playing wicked games with Marco's mind. He still had unanswered questions and his headaches were compounded by his impending trial for sporting fraud relating to the 1995 Milan–Turin and his relationship with Christina, which had taken another turn for the worse. Cocaine was exacerbating, not helping to resolve his problems. I'm sure that he relapsed several times that winter and in the spring of 2000 when I wasn't with him in Cesenatico. I would guess that it happened every time Marco saw a race looming, when fear would force his hand – fear of testing himself, fear of not being the rider he was, fear of being judged. His pride and his will to win drove him back to racing but that also meant being under constant observation. The fear which haunted him most was that of other people's readiness to judge him and make comparisons with the recent past, when he was still a winner.

A difficult return

Marco began his comeback with a series of races in Spain linked by a common theme: his failure to finish. He was plagued by injuries, from his knee to his back to an assortment of other muscle strains.

His biggest Achilles heel, though, were the relapses which cancelled out the hundreds of kilometres ridden in training, therefore ruling him out of contention in races and sharpening his already acute sense of humiliation. Unfortunately, we couldn't go public with Marco's problem and were forced to suffer in silence as journalists and armchair experts attributed his lack of success to the fact that he could no longer dope.

As if we didn't have enough on our minds, the spectre of Guariniello was looming large again. The lawyers had managed to have the case moved to Forlì and the first hearings were now taking place. Marco was accused of having committed sporting fraud in the 1995 Milan–Turin, the race in which a terrible fall had left his career hanging in the balance and in different circumstances may have cost him his life. 'You do realise, Manu, that I abandoned that race, so I don't see how I could have "cheated" in order to win,' he would say. 'What's more, I almost died and this lot go digging up my clinical files and disputing my haematocrit levels when I had been given a blood transfusion. You can't carry on like that. I'll go crazy!' His indignation seemed justified. I paid regular visits to Insolera to see how we stood and received nothing but reassurances. If I remember rightly, there were several different clinical files because the original had been lost and they all quoted different haematocrit levels… The lack of reliable evidence was one major weakness in the case for the prosecution, while another even more flagrant one was the fact that the law was inapplicable because in 1995 the alleged offence didn't constitute a crime.

The hearings continued and the outlook of the lawyers became progressively less optimistic. The presiding judge, a Ms Del Bianco, seemed to be against Pantani. Rumour had it that Guariniello had resented seeing the case moved away from Turin and out of his control and had pulled strings in Forlì. Apparently, Del Bianco had worked with Guariniello in the past and had been given the case to finish off the job he had started, i.e. to make life equally hard for Pantani. There was no way of finding out whether this was just gossip or whether the theory had any basis in fact.

On 11 December of that year I was in the courtroom for the decisive hearing. It was the first time I had attended a courtroom trial. I was nervous. I was also highly pessimistic, though I couldn't quite pinpoint why. I had asked Fabrizio Borra to come with me and we sat in on the hearing, together with a large press corps. Insolera's speech was so long-winded that, after exchanging impatient looks with the experts representing the prosecution, the judge asked him to keep it brief because she didn't have much time and she had things to do! I was stunned. The courtroom was silent and tense. Then, the public prosecutor stood up and asked for Pantani to be acquitted due to a lack of proof. We breathed a sigh of relief and looked at each other and some of the journalists, as if to say: 'this time we've done it!' But the illusion lasted only a few minutes. Del Bianco came back into the auditorium and announced her verdict: Pantani was GUILTY. My gaze remained fixed on the motto displayed above the judge's chair: 'Justice is equal for everyone!' That day I realised that what I had thought was a universal truth may be no more than wishful thinking.

We left the courtroom, distraught and disbelieving. Professor Benzi, an expert who had testified on behalf of the prosecution, was celebrating in front of the TV cameras. The consummate opportunist: a few days after the sentence, Benzi tried to contact Marco to offer his services as a personal coach. He claimed to be the only person who could take Marco back to the top.

Now I had to work out how to break the bad news to Marco, who hadn't attended the hearing. On the way back to Cesenatico, I stopped off to pick up Martinelli in Riccione – a resort town around forty kilometres down the Adriatic coast from Cesenatico – where a training camp intended to encourage team-bonding around Marco and ease his sense of isolation was to start that day. Marco had decided that he would rather hear the news at home, then he would make his way to the nearby hotel to join up with his team-mates. I called to forewarn him as Martinelli and I were on the way to pick him up at home: 'It didn't go quite as we expected… But, you'll see, we'll appeal and solve this bloody mess!' He cut me off. We arrived at the villa. The front door was open and Marco's head was bowed and his face hidden under the rim of a baseball cap. He picked up his suitcase and wheeled it disconsolately towards the car. He got in without saying a word and slammed the door. He slouched on the seat and yanked the cap even further over his eyes. All he said was that he wanted new lawyers.

We arrived at the hotel and Marco's spirits lifted in response to a sympathetic reception from his team-mates. Several journalists were waiting at the hotel in the hope of getting a fiery reaction to his guilty verdict, and Marco didn't disappoint: 'I hope that Guariniello has children... and that he experiences what me and my family are experiencing now!' He was disgusted at how the affair had been handled. After every previous hearing, the press had always reported the prosecution's version of events and never that of the defence. Everything had been embellished to reflect badly on him. The trial had been conducted through the press more than in the courtroom and the papers had given Marco no right of reply. I remember an incident which illustrates how the press has to generate news at any cost, even if it means manipulating the facts. In court, judge Del Bianco asked the principal of the Turin general hospital if he was able to affirm categorically that, in his absence, no-one could have gone to the hospital to inject Pantani with EPO. The question was phrased very strategically and the witness was intimidated, as well as being set the difficult task of remembering something which had happened five years earlier. The principal said that he couldn't be absolutely sure. The following day the newspapers opened their sports pages with the headline 'Pantani even took EPO in hospital', or subtle variations on the theme. Large swathes of the public neither required nor received any further explanation. Unfortunately, when the person in question is finally acquitted, the news is reported in a tiny corner of the back page.

In Italy, there is no presumption of innocence, only of guilt. The pawns in this unjust system can end up being destroyed, which is what happened to Marco. After the trial, RAI TV journalist Davide De Zan ventured his opinion that Marco's lawyers hadn't been up to scratch. De Zan and Marco's friend, the former rider Davide Cassani, suggested that I get in touch with Francesco Cecconi, reputed to be Italy's best sports lawyer. I discussed it with Marco and decided to consult Cecconi immediately. Marco's only reservation was that Cenni might feel that, by rejecting Insolera and Guazzaloca, we were rejecting his generosity, but

I said that I would mediate and take the flack for both of us. The most important thing was that Marco felt protected and that new brainpower was brought in: we wanted to find out whether we had lost because our case had been poorly presented or whether there was so much ill will towards him that no lawyer could have obtained a better result. Cecconi went on to win the appeal on 24 October 2002 and Marco was absolved because the offence didn't constitute a crime.

Marco stayed in the hotel in Riccione with his team-mates for a few more days before the training camp was cut short with Marco making the usual noises about preferring to train alone. To an extent it was true: he loved training in total solitude because he felt it allowed him to enter into an almost mystical union with his bike; he let his mind wander and he felt free. He only trained with team-mates in the build-up to big races, to carry out final checks on his fitness. On this occasion, however, the request had a ulterior motive... Marco couldn't wait to isolate himself and seek refuge in that evil white substance.

Midway through March, I went to see him in Cesenatico to voice my concerns: I told him that we had to consult a doctor, and that the team's own medical staff should be informed. In any case, rumours and suspicions were already circulating. Although I was strongly recommending it, whether to not to own up to his habit was to be entirely and exclusively up to Marco. He shouldn't have felt ashamed, yet he did need to be comforted and helped more than pitied. He needed to surround himself with determined people who were more interested in actions than in pontificating. Most of all, though, he needed to be honest about his problem, if not with the public then at least with himself, which is precisely what he refused to do.

Several months after Marco died, I would be asked to explain why we hadn't gone public immediately. I replied that, sure, I could have made capital out of Marco's personal problem to prove my credentials to those who suggested that I wasn't capable of managing Pantani's relationships with his entourage. I could have argued that all of his difficulties in dealing with the press and bonding with his team-mates were caused by cocaine. I could have taken these easy options, but by revealing Marco's weakness I would have exposed him to the harshest criticism.

I knew his character well and I knew that this would have finished him off. You could perhaps describe it as a professional secret, a kind of discretion used to shield a fragile man, but this is isn't the same as denying the obvious or turning a blind eye. It means giving someone the breathing space they need to be able to face up to the problems they have with relating to their external environment. This was the route that I went down, privately sounding out numerous medical professionals and never yielding to the temptation to ad lib. Marco's sessions with Benedettini, while no doubt healthy, certainly weren't likely to significantly improve matters. Realising this, I persuaded Marco to call Emilio Magni, the team's head doctor at the time, and soon Magni came to meet a terrified Marco at home in Cesenatico. Marco imagined that if everyone in the team became aware of his problem he would feel judged and pitied, which perhaps explained his initial trepidation with Magni. Later he found the courage to open up and was relieved at the doctor's reaction. Magni didn't appear shocked and neither did he judge: he was clear-sighted and compassionate, even suggesting that Marco come to live with him and his family for a while. Magni's house had a converted attic where Marco could sleep and, Magni said, by spending time together they could work out how to tackle the problem. Out of shyness, Marco declined, and, in any case, we all agreed that temporary solutions were no longer what was needed: Marco was under constant pressure and he was unlikely to be able to compete seriously if first he hadn't cleared his thoughts about how to move forward.

At around the same time, Tonina gave me a self-portrait of Marco which vividly captured his state of mind after the events of Madonna di Campiglio. It's an alarming drawing, which depicts Marco on a bike with an oversized front wheel and tiny rear wheel. Marco has wings and a dagger plunged into his back, level with his heart, which has been ripped out. There is a giant boulder dangling from a noose tied around his neck. As I interpret it, Marco had depicted himself as a eagle with a dagger through his back and whose heart had been ripped out. The bicycle was his heart: at that time, riding it had become an enormous, unbearable burden.

The comeback trail

After so many sleepless nights of endless brainstorming with Marco, I came to the conclusion that something had to be done – anything it took – to resolve the crisis.

'Marco, why don't we write an open letter in which we state clearly that without passion, without enthusiasm and without motivation you can't race. And that you neither want to delude nor betray anyone, and that above all you want to be honest with yourself, so you're taking time out to reflect. Whoever wants to wait for you can, and whoever doesn't, well, never mind.'

The tension building around Marco was palpable. Many thought he should be left alone and allowed to make a calm decision, but not a day went by without somebody calling to ask: 'So, is he racing or not? Why is he going so badly? Why is he abandoning races?' Someone as sensitive as Marco couldn't handle all of these pressures. I took it upon myself to draft a letter and make him sign it, telling him that I would send it out and inform Mercatone Uno. At first Marco seemed to approve, but in the middle of the night he came to wake me swearing that the next day he would be back on his bike and that there would be no more hiccups. It was a promise I'd heard too many times, so I replied that I would take charge: if we didn't make that step, there would be no other way out. We would publish that letter and Marco would feel a weight off his back. Also, we would finally know who was going to stick around and who would flinch and desert him.

The following day, a meeting was called: Cenni, Ghiselli, the managing director of Mercatone Uno, and Gimondi, in his capacity as president of the team, were all present. The word cocaine wasn't uttered; it was simply established that Marco was depressed and therefore wasn't able to compete. Marco himself was itching to defuse the mounting pressure on him. For my part, I said to Cenni that if he was disappointed in me as the team manager, he ought to tell me, and I would be ready to resign, but that I wouldn't abandon Marco. Cenni told me to carry on as team manager and not to worry. It was obvious that Marco had caught everyone napping and that his decision to temporarily opt out of all competition was fraying nerves at corporate HQ, but at the same time Cenni acknowledged that there was no alternative.

When the press reported the news, Marco felt that an albatross had been lifted from around his neck. Shortly afterwards, we went for a drive together and he turned to me and whispered: 'Manù, you have to promise something. I'm going to set up camp in Saturnia and I'm going to start training for the Giro d'Italia, but no-one is to know. A few days before the Giro, if I feel ready I'll do it, if not I won't. But you mustn't tell anyone, not even Cenni, because if you do you'll trigger those expectations which only end up making me paranoid.'

I managed to keep the secret from everyone bar my fiancé and we swiftly made arrangements for the training camp in Saturnia, dispatching the masseur Roberto Pregnolato and one of Marco's training partners, Ermanno Brignoli. At the same time, Marco continued to attend weekly therapy sessions with Benedettini, which gave him the opportunity to let off steam, at least theoretically. But Marco had little faith in the talking technique and only persevered to appease Cenni, who had recommended Benedettini because he thought that, with Steve, Marco could find a way to lift himself out of the mire. Cenni was deeply concerned about Marco, but he also had genuine faith in him and was anxiously awaiting his comeback. I appreciated Cenni's good intentions and determination to help Marco, but unfortunately the results were disappointing. Marco always found a way of contradicting the therapist or putting him on the back foot. And standing up to Marco wasn't easy: almost every doctor who had dealings with him ended up resigned to the difficulty of treating him after their initial enthusiasm had burned out.

Perhaps against the odds, the secret training camp went well and Marco didn't relapse in Saturnia. Pregnolato drove behind Marco on training rides which doubled as moveable karaoke sessions, with Pregnolato's stereo volume cranked up and the pair singing along to Italian pop star Gigi D'Alessio as they ate up the kilometres. After a month of serious training, another court summons arrived, this time requesting that Marco go to Ferrara for questioning as an informed party in the doping trial of Italian Professor Francesco Conconi. It always required courage to break news like this to Marco. Sure enough Marco was beside himself: he couldn't understand why he had to go to court as part of an investigation that had nothing to do with him. I tried to explain to him that, whatever he thought about it, it was his civilian duty to co-operate and that he shouldn't make too much of a drama out of it. I finally convinced him: we would go to see the judge in Ferrara for what would hopefully be a brief and amicable chat, then we would head home and start training again.

The interrogation in Ferrara lasted around two hours. I waited outside the courtroom and could hear Marco growling that he was unhappy with how his statement was being recorded. After his grilling from the magistrate, Marco and I were due to meet up with Gimondi. There were ten days to go before the start of the Giro d'Italia and it was time to inform the team that Marco had decided to race. While Marco was in Saturnia, his conversations with Martinelli and other members of the team and its staff had become less and less frequent. In the meantime, Martinelli had clearly begun to draw up his battle plan for the Giro: in the absence of the team's talisman, Pantani, it was likely that, by the end of April, he was already grooming the emergent Stefano Garzelli and the consistent Enrico Zaina for the role of joint-leaders. It therefore seemed only fair to announce Marco's decision to the team in good time, and Pantani duly informed Gimondi, who he told explicitly not to inform the press: he planned to appear in Rome on 13 May with no prior warning, no doubt creating the story of the race even before the Giro had started.

8

Back with a Whimper

Despite Gimondi's reassurances, somehow the news of Pantani's surprise return was leaked and the following day the *Gazzetta dello Sport* reported that Pantani was practically certain to ride the Giro. Understandably, nowhere did the news create more excitement than at Mercatone Uno HQ, where no-one had been aware of Marco's training binge in Saturnia. A Giro without Pantani would have been an anti-climax for everyone; the news that he was to take part had neutral observers smiling and his fans jumping for joy, regardless of whether he was in form or not.

In fact, there was widespread scepticism about Marco's physical fitness and his capacity to ride a Giro d'Italia without an adequate base of winter training. Marco had no intention of making gun-toting promises of pink jerseys, stage victories or sensational attacks in the mountains, but knowing his pride and determination I expected him to set himself impossible goals. Deep down, he even secretly thought that he could win. Marco was the antithesis of cycling's latest generation of stage-racing stars – the Indurains and Armstrongs whose success was inevitably the result of almost forensic planning and calculation; Marco followed his instinct and belonged to that rare subset of lavishly gifted sportsmen who marry sport with art. That year, at the risk of being ridiculed, he wanted to defy the received knowledge which suggested that, in cycling, it was impossible to win the Giro without the correct preparation and training. Marco knew that only by pulling off this challenge and doing it emphatically could he regain credibility and restore his lost dignity. I knew that he wouldn't settle for just a stage win or a token attack. He felt like a winner, someone who had scaled the heights and by winning the Giro and Tour in the same year had secured a place in the century-old annals of cycling. Marco wasn't a man of half measures; anything short of sensational was never enough.

Although the news of his participation in the Giro was greeted with huge excitement, because of his lack of preparation, no seasoned commentator was prepared to bet on him even notching up a mere stage victory. We arrived in Rome for the papal blessing at the Vatican. Marco was impeccably turned out and very emotional about meeting Pope John Paul II. He couldn't wait. Later, on leaving the Vatican, he told me that when the Pope had looked him in the eyes it was like a wave of peace, wisdom and serenity washing over him. It couldn't have been a more auspicious prelude to Marco's return to racing.

The lonely Giro

The first part of the Giro was reasonably positive. Pantani's unexpected comeback had, as expected, mobilised the interest of both public and media. They still wondered how he would keep pace with the other well-trained, well-prepared riders. Most sympathisers realised that Pantani was intent on performing well, but at the same time were mindful that he shouldn't be burdened with too many responsibilities or expectations. However, as I have already said, it was in his nature to set himself targets beyond his reach. He had come back into the team, been reinstated as captain, and therefore wanted a team united around him. Unfortunately, that's not what he got. He felt as though he was gate-crashing someone else's party, upsetting the plans which Martinelli had already based around other riders. Marco felt out of the loop, and how could he not be: he was the one who had said that he wouldn't ride, so he certainly couldn't expect Martinelli to keep his plans on hold while he waited for a last-minute decision, without knowing, moreover, in what kind of condition Marco would have turned up in Rome.

On this count, Martinelli's attitude and that of the team was quite legitimate. But it's also true that, from a psychological point of view, they didn't improve Marco's chances of making a successful return. During that Giro, I was able to observe Marco's relationship with the team from the outside, objectively I suppose. I watched his eyes and his body language and saw them glaze over with frustration when he didn't like what he was hearing. It was sad to see him left on the margins of camaraderie, which cements bonds within any given team, and in this case one which had helped him achieve the Giro–Tour double in 1998. When Marco joined the others at the breakfast or dinner table, silence would suddenly descend and the banter only picked up where it had left off when he skulked off to his room. Similarly, Marco was systematically kept away from tactical meetings. He would phone me in my room and say: 'You see? I don't count any more: they only talk and discuss things when I'm not around. It suits them because I'm Marco Pantani and, even if I'm not up to winning the Giro at the moment, I'm the captain and I have to bear all of the responsibility and the tension.'

He felt used and at the same time 'unloved' by his team. I think it's important to stress this. Often I was criticised for 'cosseting' Marco, which I presume implied that I would bow to his every demand and agree with whatever he said. I can categorically refute this. If my definition is more or less accurate, then 'cosseting' certainly wasn't the kind of attention Marco needed. On this very subject, I can remember Marco telling me the year before he died:

You saw, I used to be better than the rest because I can go over the pain threshold like you wouldn't believe. I grit my teeth and I'm at one with my bike, in a kind mystical connection. When that happens, I need to feel surrounded by warmth and feel that my team-mates believe in me, trust me, give their soul for me. I have a hunter's mentality, my instinct tells me to attack, to do whatever it takes to catch my prey, which is the finish line for me. When, however, I don't feel protected, when I'm at the start of a race and I don't feel as though all of my team-mates are supporting me, or when in a race I realise that my team-mates are close to me only because they have to be and not because their heart is in it – maybe they know about my problem and have lost faith in me – then, in that situation, surrounded by that hypocrisy, I feel like the prey and not the hunter. Then I bristle like a hedgehog, stay at the back of the bunch and there's no trigger in my head.

This was why Marco had started that Giro sincerely hoping that he would be able to say: 'Ok, I want to surprise everyone. I'm coming back into the peloton and I want to see the team's plans overhauled and everyone giving their all to put me in the right frame of mind to aim for the jackpot, even win the Giro d'Italia.' In the event, the atmosphere in the team immediately turned sour, right from the first mountain stage which included the San Pellegrino in Alpe and Abetone climbs. I watched that stage from Martinelli's team car. I was a ball of tension, my hands were sweating and I feared that Marco was heading for his umpteenth humiliation. He and those around him had made Herculean efforts to prepare him for the Giro, psychologically, physically and logistically: keeping the sponsors sweet, trying not to raise false hopes, but at the same time instil the necessary belief in Marco. Under any circumstances it would have being a trying time, but it was also punctuated by court hearings and meetings with lawyers and judges which certainly didn't help to maintain Marco's already precarious equilibrium. I was frightened that we were about to witness a debacle, a new nadir: it wasn't the likelihood of Marco not winning which preoccupied me, but the possibility that failure would give him the perfect excuse to seek solace in cocaine. I was still hoping for a miracle, but rationally I knew that Marco wouldn't be able to treat us to one of his trademark exploits. In fact, as early as the penultimate climb to San Pellegrino in Alpe he was dropped while Francesco Casagrande took off towards a stage victory. I asked Martinelli what was happening. He replied that Marco didn't have good legs, that he couldn't follow. I overheard Stefano Garzelli's voice coming through Martinelli's earpiece. He was asking whether now was the time to attack.

My memories of those precise, hectic moments are too foggy for me to be able to say whether Martinelli gave Garzelli the green light, but it's highly likely in view of how the race was panning out. All I know is that Garzelli ended up accelerating and finishing behind Casagrande and that Enrico Zaina quit the Giro at the end of the stage. We later found out that Zaina's abandonment was an act of rebellion against Martinelli who, said the rider, had stopped him from riding his own race. Zaina also turned on Marco, who initially didn't take too much notice but later saw the incident as symptomatic of the poor atmosphere in the team. In his heart of hearts Marco understood Zaina's motives and his anger towards Martinelli, whose relationship with Pantani was now deteriorating by the day. My role was to take the heat out of some of the hostility, because it certainly wasn't the time to attribute blame, which is exactly what Roberto Pregnolato was trying to do. Rather than trying to reduce the tension between Martinelli and the riders, he invariably ended up increasing it. When a masseur is working with a rider, he knows that the massage table is a place where, because they are very relaxed, riders are particularly susceptible to having ideas planted in their head. But, I repeat, it was the least appropriate time to start attributing blame and responsibility to this member of the team or the other. Instead, everyone should have been concentrating on how to resolve the situation. This is Martinelli's assessment of Zaina's shock withdrawal:

> On the Abetone stage, the team's strategy was for everyone to stay close to Marco. Only Garzelli had been given carte blanche, but on one condition: either he finished in the leading group or he, too, would stay at Marco's side. I stopped Zaina when he wanted to attack but he didn't want to know. 'Ok, stop Garzelli as well, then,' he screamed at me when I pulled up alongside him in the car. 'Leave Garzelli where he is: remember that I'm Mercatone Uno's *directeur sportif*, not Pantani's, so you have to do what I say.' He took offence and he quit as a protest gesture towards me. Bear in mind that Zaina had been signed for a specific purpose – to stay close to Pantani. That's why he was earning four hundred million lire (£130,000) a year, while Garzelli was an up-and-coming rider.

The negative outcome of the stage probably convinced Marco that victory in the Giro was an impossible dream. Despite this, I don't remember him wanting to abandon the race at any time. Except maybe once, a few stages into the race, when he came to my room, sat cross-legged on the floor and told me that he wanted to go home because no-one believed in him. It was one of his usual tirades, admittedly, but it was also easy to sympathise. Witnessing what happened at that Giro, you couldn't say that he was wrong. I think that Martinelli always acted in good faith, that he really was fond of Marco, and his behaviour certainly didn't strike me as dishonest. However – and this was that group's biggest weakness – the team was sadly lacking when it came to mind management, and this would become apparent time and time again before the end of the Giro.

Marco saw so much animosity around him that he even began to suspect that someone was sabotaging his bike before the start of the stages. At Saluzzo, the morning after a Garzelli stage victory which had taken him to within striking distance of race leader Francesco Casagrande, Marco emerged from his room muttering that he wanted to leave the race and go home. 'Have you seen, Manuela? Now they're sabotaging my bike. I reckon I'll do thirty kilometres today then go home.' I thought to myself: 'Just you wait – this is the day when Marco gets nasty, gets determined and does something special.'

I was right: that day Marco not only put Garzelli in a position to win the Giro but he also gave the entire field a lesson in selflessness and sportsmanship. The 177-kilometre nineteenth stage was to take place over the 22-kilometre long Colle dell'Agnello and the shorter but steeper Col d'Izoard before finishing in Briançon. On the legendary Izoard, Pantani accelerated repeatedly to shake off Casagrande and Gilberto Simoni but then slowed when he saw Garzelli also struggling. Marco the master then turned servant, dropping back to the team car to collect water bottles for his team-mate. In the end he could have won the stage but stayed with Garzelli until the climb up to the finish line in the old citadel of Briançon. Only then did he break clear, too late to deny Paolo Lanfranchi the stage victory, but in good time to secure second place on the stage – a minor personal triumph which had also kept Garzelli within 25 seconds of Casagrande on general classification. I can remember rushing to the team's hotel, desperate to hug Pantani and hold him tight. We were sharing our first real victory together, albeit only a moral one. I went into his room and found him singing while shaving in front of the mirror. He embraced me, covering me with shaving foam, truly happy. We began the celebrations by gorging ourselves on a basket of cherries and strawberries, then I said: 'Now we have to go down. There's a press conference, there are journalists to attend to, so don't tell me you don't want to talk to them, because this is such a great day. I'm proud of you.' 'Yeah, we did it together,' he smiled. 'You know, today I wanted to show that a captain needs his *domestiques* but when a *domestique* needs his captain, the captain must be the first one to prove that he's capable of lending a hand.'

Apparently inspired by Marco's contribution, Garzelli duly snatched the pink jersey away from Casagrande in the following day's mountain time trial to Sestrière and went on to claim his first Giro victory at the age of 26. Marco was a little jealous, not least because the sponsors were swarming around Garzelli like bees around a honey pot. For such a headstrong champion, who had contributed so much to that team, it wasn't easy to accept defeat. Marco's envy wasn't malicious – just evidence of his competitive spirit and his desire to be the best. So many times in interviews, even when he was a junior, Marco had said: 'I'll never accept being number two.' Now, two years after winning the Giro and one year after dominating it for nineteen stages, Marco had finished the race in a lowly 28th place, almost an hour down on Garzelli, but the single day's racing to Briançon suggested that an upturn in his fortunes was finally nigh.

Sadly, the enthusiasm didn't last long. On the evening after the race finished in Milan, the team gathered to toast Garzelli's victory in the Giro. I was also invited, though tried to remain as discreet as possible. Gimondi, as the president of the team, gave a speech to thank the entire team: he said that it had been a difficult year, that everyone had made a lot of sacrifices and that we should applaud Garzelli for winning in spite of the fact that the team had sacrificed itself for Pantani, who wasn't fit enough to ride the Giro.

I saw Marco's bald pate glow like a beacon, as it always did – almost comically – when he was angry: this frankly wasn't what one would have expected Gimondi to say. I felt slightly offended. Without being arrogant, I thought that I had done a good job as the team's manager and that the victory had been the fruit of teamwork and also our efforts to bring Pantani back for the Giro. Granted, Gimondi and Pantani weren't the best of friends, but ultimately we were bringing home the

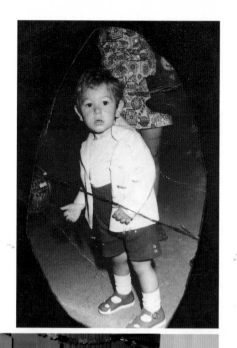

Right: Marco Pantani recalled, 'To say that as a boy I was a little rascal is an oversimplification; I was a real pest, a hothead, difficult to manage and always up to trouble.'

Below: Marco with his sister, Manola, on her confirmation day.

Above: Aged twelve, Marco receives a prize for the 1982 season, at the beginning of his cycling career. Beside him stands Nicola Amaducci, Fausto Coppi's *directeur sportif*.

Above: Marco at the start of an amateur Giro d'Italia; his first victory came in 1992, the year in which he moved into professional cycling.

Below: A great picture of Marco beside the Porto canal in Cesenatico, a place he was particularly fond of.

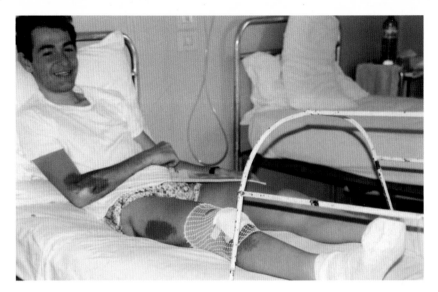

Above: Marco had his first serious fall in 1986: in the Sant'Arcangelo descent near his home, he was struck by an oncoming car and came close to dying from a ruptured spleen.

Below: Top physiotherapist Fabrizio Borra treats Marco after his terrible fall in the 1995 Milan–Turin. A great friend, Borra stuck by Marco not only during his years of triumph, but also the depths of his cocaine addiction and his difficult return to the big races after the events of Madonna di Campiglio.

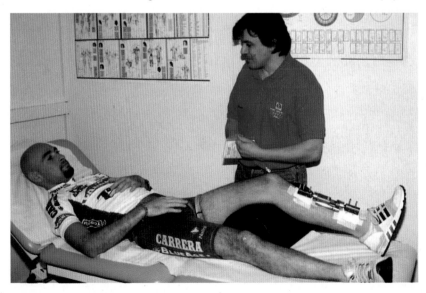

Above: One of Marco's crazy 'Uncle Fester' get-ups.

Below: Marco with Gianni Morandi at the start of a football match between the Italian national singers and an 'All Star' team (including Pantani). Marco was involved in charity work but he performed it discreetly: he maintained that good work should be done quietly.

Marco beside
Miguel Indurain
during the 1995
world championships
in Duitama, Colombia.
He won third place,
behind Abraham
Olano and Indurain.

Top: The crowd goes wild for 'the Pirate's' lonely run on the bends that lead to Alpe d'Huez during the 1994 Tour de France, his first Tour, in which he came third behind Indurain and Piotr Ugrumov.

Centre: During the 1998 Tour de France.

Above: With the Giro's pink jersey that Pantani – and millions of fans – had long dreamed of.

© Roberto Bettini

Left: The Pirate's climbing prowess – not even the lashing rain seemed to tire him.

Below: In the Briançon stage of the 2000 Tour, Lance Armstrong in the yellow jersey tires of holding out against the mighty Pantani.

© Boutroux

Left: Marco enjoying a hunting trip, one of his main passions outside of cycling.

The dramatic announcement of Marco Pantani's death on the front cover of the *Gazzetta dello Sport*.

top prize and I felt that everyone had made a contribution. I would have expected at least a thank-you both for me and for Marco. But in the end none of this mattered: what I was looking for wasn't so much recognition as to succeed in creating that human environment around Marco which he needed to get back to his old self. This intention was misinterpreted by a lot of people in cycling and particularly by Mercatone Uno as my desire to 'mother' him, cosset and spoil him. But if I resisted doing that for five years alongside a personality like Pantani it's because I had the strength to tell him what I thought to make him realise when he was wrong. Pantani – I repeat – didn't need a door mat or people who worshipped him and always agreed with him, not least because people like this could last no more than a year with him. For my part, I can acknowledge that I may have made mistakes with Pantani. I had been brought in to manage the image of a top rider from a marketing point of view, yet within eighteen months I had found myself in the position of manager of a sports team and Marco's personal confidante, suddenly occupied with many aspects of his private life. I could have opted out, but no-one else was willing to take on such an unorthodox manager's role.

That year, I often wrote to Marco about the problems that my job presented and the excess responsibilities I was forced to bear; I often told him that I would gladly have given up my position as team manager had someone wanted to replace me. I myself acknowledged that my managerial expertise needed to be allied to that of someone with specific experience in the sport. However, in the cycling world I always found myself facing insurmountable barriers or total incompetence when it came to man management. My 'psychological tactic' of staying close to Marco was dismissed out of hand: I was acting like his mum and I knew nothing about cycling, so I should be left at home.

After Gimondi's speech, I left what should have been a joyous evening of celebrations with a bitter taste in my mouth. Marco called ten minutes later from his car, dumbfounded by what he had heard and urging me to go straight to Cenni to explain how we felt, otherwise he would quit cycling. He was furious, and at first this quietly excited me because I thought that he had finally forgotten Madonna di Campiglio and his legal worries and that he was now focusing on the team. Marco's anger was a good sign: it seemed to signify a determination to get his career back on track. I duly spoke to Cenni, but with the problems that Marco had created in the first six months of the year still fresh in his memory, he reacted badly and said that he didn't want to know about Marco's complaints. Cenni told me that I should have tried to becalm Marco and better explain Gimondi's role. Marco's only preoccupation should be with getting results, because only results would silence his critics.

The man who wouldn't lie down

Marco spent the month of June preparing for the Tour de France. He was edgy but at the same time highly focused: he knew that he had been getting stronger every day at the Giro and he wanted to do well at the Tour. His anxiety came not least from the knowledge that, while at the Giro his surprise return had generated largely favourable publicity, now he was worried that people expected results, and probably himself more than anyone.

The big favourite for victory was Lance Armstrong, who had left not only cycling but the entire sporting world open-mouthed by winning the 1999 Tour. Having beaten testicular cancer, the Texan had returned to the sport transformed as an athlete and evidently stronger than before the illness, when he had already become the youngest world champion in the sport's history in Oslo in 1993. However, twelve months earlier neither Jan Ullrich nor Pantani had been in the field at the Tour, so everyone was curious to see how Armstrong would fare against two past winners of cycling's most prestigious event.

The first few flat stages were largely incident-free: as usual, Marco dawdled at the pack of the group, forcing to his team-mates to chase and waste precious energy every time there was a fall or crosswinds split the bunch, and leaving him in 86th position overall on the eve of the first day in the Pyrenees. That stage, the tenth of the race, was to serve up a summit finish at Hautacam, the mountain overlooking Lourdes, after the gruelling ascents of the Col de Marie-Blanque and Col de l'Aubisque. As soon as the road began to rear up the final rise to Hautacam, with the leading contenders still all closely bunched, Marco threw off his bandana and kicked hard. Armstrong was alert to the danger, caught him, rode alongside for a few metres, then powered away. Marco's legs suddenly turned to lead as Armstrong disappeared into the mist and others swept past him. Once again, not only had Marco's pride been badly injured, it had happened in his own kingdom, in the mountains.

Fortunately, two days later he came back brilliantly on the second summit finish to Mont Ventoux. That day I was waiting at the top of the mountain known as the Giant of Provence, whose lack of vegetation lends it the appearance of an immense lunar crater, and which was made infamous by the death of Tom Simpson on its upper slopes in the 1967 Tour. Another feature of the mountain, the mistral wind which buffets its north side, was so strong that day that I couldn't lift my mobile phone to my ear for fear that it would blow away. I was huddled up in my jacket, propped up against the railings alongside the finish line. I saw Marco's head emerge over the brow of the mountain in front of Armstrong's, his features gripped in a rictus of pain, but edging just ahead of the American to take the stage victory. The sense of liberation was overwhelming and I couldn't hold back the tears. Pregnolato got annoyed and snapped that I mustn't let Marco see me cry because he didn't like compassion. The comment hurt me, but it didn't matter, because to me it was a landmark moment in both mine and Marco's career: I had witnessed Pantani's first victory since Madonna di Campiglio.

I soon found out that Marco wasn't so enamoured, judging that the win had cost him too much suffering for his liking. To add to the sense of anticlimax, Armstrong, who was riding in the yellow jersey, was immediately at pains to clarify that he had let Pantani win. On principle, Marco thought that if Armstrong had really let him win, he could have kept it too himself, and in any case, *he* was absolutely convinced that it had been an authentic and deserved victory. He had worked out that Armstrong was vulnerable psychologically. I remember how Marco used to be able to intimidate other riders at the start of a race just with the look in his eye: his greatness lay therein, in knowing how to compete not only on the road but above all in the mind.

The Tour headed towards the Alps to be greeted by a large travelling army of supporters from Italy and particularly Marco's terra firma on the Adriatic coast. Marco's parents had also made the journey north in their camper van, although Marco didn't want his family and closest friends to be seen with him before and after races, preferring them to follow the race in among his fan club members, who were becoming more and more numerous and vociferous. On the afternoon of stage 15 to the Alpine resort of Courchevel, however, Tonina wanted to see her son at all costs: dressed all in red, she took up a prominent position on a hairpin on the final climb. When Marco passed, he saw her and launched one of his famous attacks, creating a vacuum behind him. He went on to win the stage – one of the most prestigious in that year's Tour and featuring the ascents of the Cols du Galibier and Madeleine – and leave Armstrong trailing almost a minute behind. On general classification he had now moved up to sixth place, nine minutes adrift of Armstrong's yellow jersey.

Christina was also in Courchevel that day and was thrilled for Marco, but that same evening, Marco seemed to withdraw into himself, perhaps because things still weren't going well with Christina. He told me that he didn't want to do a press conference the next day, the Tour's rest day. I should keep the journalists away because he felt tired and weak and wanted to relax. The next morning, however, Angelo Zomegnan, the *Gazzetta dello Sport* reporter, bumped into Marco at the team hotel and told him that he had talked to me and that I had agreed to a meeting with the Italian journalists covering the Tour. In reality, I had simply told him that Marco didn't feel like doing a press conference, but if he changed his mind I would alert him and all of the other Italian journalists. Marco found me on the hotel stairs where he proceeded to give me an angry lecture: 'If I told you that I don't want to talk to anyone, you explain to me why you go and tell Zomegnan that you're happy for him to interview me.' Suddenly, there was real friction between us, and as if that wasn't enough, I was criticised for the umpteenth time by the journalists, who considered me incapable of managing Marco's media relations. He ended up giving just a few soundbites to the Italian television news and refusing to satisfy any request from the written press.

The stage after the rest day, stage 16, was to take the peloton over four more Alpine passes on the way to Morzine. I knew that Martinelli and the team had premeditated for Marco to attack almost from the starting gun. Marco wanted to turn the Tour on its head and, with nine minutes to recoup on Armstrong but only one more mountain stage at his disposal, this was his last chance to do it. On the first climb, the Col de Saisies, he had attacked with the Spaniard Fernando Escartin and Frenchman Pascal Hervé on his wheel. In the peloton, Armstrong seemed to maintain his composure, if only because Marco's long-range strategy seemed wildly ambitious with the summit of the Col de Saisies some 120 kilometres from the finish-line. After Pantani's win at Courchevel, the Texan had criticised him in his rest-day press conference, reverting to Pantani's old and unflattering nickname 'Elefantino'. 'On Mont Ventoux, I made a mistake. I should have won that day because I was the strongest, just as Pantani was at Courchevel. I let him win because he had ridden really well on that climb and I knew what he had been through. I was wrong to be generous, though.'

Pantani stayed ahead of the field for around eighty kilometres but then was struck down by stomach pains which effectively ended his dreams of capsizing the general classification. Swept up by peloton, he eventually crossed the finish line over ten minutes behind the contenders for the yellow jersey and stage winner Richard Virenque and plummeted to fourteenth on the overall standings. That evening journalists laid siege to the hotel, anxious to know whether Marco would race on or go home. Doctor Magni delayed the decision until, at around eleven o'clock that night, he called me to confirm that Marco was too sick and that he would go home. Also, one of the side effects of the intestinal problems Marco was suffering from was a fluctuation in certain blood parameters and there was surely no point running the risk of more nasty surprises should he be blood-tested the following day. That evening I tried to contact the journalists, but many had turned their mobile phones off or were unreachable. Meanwhile, Martinelli informed the president of the race jury and the race organisers, the Société du Tour de France. To make sure that everyone received the news, I called the Italian press agency ANSA: all of the news desks of the main Italian papers would be brought up to date.

The following morning, the press pack gave me an even frostier reception than usual. Again, Zomegnan and the *Gazzetta* were furious with me. They wanted to know why – in what they had already dubbed 'the night of many mysteries' – I had informed all of the news desks in Italy before the journalists working on the race. This time I was deeply offended. I was beginning to feel that I could do nothing right in their eyes. Overruling Marco's protests, we staged a press conference in the hotel reception, which was also covered by Italian television. Zomegnan acted like a private investigator: instead of asking Marco questions about his health and about how it felt to abandon the Tour, his interest homed in on what Marco had eaten for breakfast, in light of the problems which had forced him out of the race. His attitude irritated Marco intensely. Pantani was left wondering why, wherever he was concerned, the journalists always jumped to negative conclusions and why, when he was trying to stave off allegations and innuendo, the press interpreted this as him moaning and hiding behind a persecution complex.

That morning Marco was very tense. Not even I knew how to approach him. We sat down together at the breakfast table and I asked him: 'So, what time are we leaving?', to which he snapped back: 'What do you mean, what time are we going? At what time am *I* going: this isn't the battle of Caporetto, you know [a famous First World War battle in which around 300,000 Italians lost their lives]. You're the team manager, you have to stay here to do your duty. I'm going home on my own.' I replied: 'I intended to go with you then come straight back here. I don't think you should go back with just Pregnolato. Don't forget that I'm also *your* manager.' I wasn't about to be bullied into submission because I was worried that, after this set-back, Marco could be a danger to himself. I immediately called Fabrizio Borra, who had joined us in the Alps, and told him that I didn't want to leave Marco alone with Pregnolato. It felt awkward, but Macro and I never left each other after an argument without clearing the air, so I went up to his room. 'Is there something wrong?' I asked him. 'Just remember that you shouldn't speak to me like that. I don't think that I'm a fool for telling you that I want to take you back home. Have it your way, though: I'll stay here and you go. Borra's going to come with you and Pregnolato, it's not a problem. I'll say it again, though: I don't think that I should be spoken to like that.' He justified his reaction by saying that he was very tense and that I always wanted to dot the Is and cross the Ts on everything; I shouldn't take any notice of some things that he said and, when he had calmed down, everything would work itself out for the better.

I was only half-satisfied, especially when, shortly afterwards, I overheard Pregnolato telling Martinelli in the corridor that Borra should unload his suitcases from the car because Marco didn't want him either. Borra took it badly and trouped off to hire a car in which he then drove back to Forlì. Marco and Pregnolato set off from Morzine towards the end of the morning and I found out via the TV news that he had only arrived home in Cesenatico at seven o'clock that evening. One look at his face as the camera showed him getting out of Pregnolato's car and I knew that they must have 'stopped off' somewhere on the way. Marco looked exactly how I didn't want to see him.

After that day, Marco completely disappeared off my radar. Having returned from the Tour, I tried to track him down in Cesenatico. July and August proved to be difficult months. Pantani was miffed at his failure to win the Tour and coming back to Cesenatico posed the usual problems. Consequently, I decided to arrange a meeting with him at home with the intention of discussing solely professional matters.

The aim of the meeting was to determine what would be our next move. I was very worried about Marco: I knew that without something to work towards, an immediate objective, he would become dangerously demotivated, and he was also far from satisfied with how things were going in the team. That day we spoke at considerable length and he agreed that we needed to make Cenni understand that he needed more attention. A complete rethink and reconstruction was in order. He said that he was moving to Saturnia for a while to rest and try to patch things up with Christina. For my part, I would initiate talks with Martinelli and

Gimondi to work out how we would review our approach for the following season and avoid repeating the previous year's mistakes. The only snag was that Mercatone Uno wasn't particularly interested in what I had to say at that time. In fact, I was beginning to sense that a chasm had opened up between us despite the fact that Marco and I had been open with Cenni about how disappointed we had been with Gimondi's attitude at the end of the Giro. Their bugbear with me was the same as always: I didn't bring in sponsors and I spoiled Marco. Gimondi's hard-line tactics were doubtless better received. Perhaps not everyone could see that there was almost no rapport between Marco and Gimondi and that Gimondi rarely showed his face even at training camps and races. When we really needed him, he took care to make himself scarce.

The 2000 Olympics and my wedding

At the end of the 2000 summer and after his premature exit from the Tour de France, Marco began his preparation for the Olympics in Sydney. The Italian coach, Antonio Fusi, had asked him whether he fancied taking part in Australia at the Tour and Marco replied that he did. But the omens certainly weren't good. Ever since Madonna di Campiglio, at least in the media's eyes, Pantani had been living under a cloud of allegations which were patently at odds with the Olympic ideals of moral virtue and sportsmanship, so it goes without saying that Marco's call-up to the Italian team raised eyebrows. He then reported to Rome to submit himself to the Italian Olympic Committee (CONI) testing protocol and again his results raised suspicions. Although his haematocrit level was under the 50 per cent limit, it varied according to where the blood sample was analysed: in one lab, it returned a reading of 42 per cent, in another a value of 46 per cent. The insinuations made by the press and the general cynicism about Pantani had to be seen to be believed and almost persuaded Marco to withdraw from the squad. Then, on the eve of the Games, a bitter war broke out between CONI and their own scientific and anti-doping commission. The secretary of this commission, Pasquale Bellotti, had sent CONI a confidential letter in which he drew their attention to a 10 per cent variation in one rider's haematocrit. The 'confidential letter' soon leaked into the public domain, prompting Marco to make an official complaint to the government minister of confidential information about the clear violation of privacy which had led to the publication of data regarding health. For once, Felice Gimondi, the Mercatone Uno team president, leapt to Marco's defence:

> As I have received no notification about the 'leading athlete with worrying haematocrit levels', I can only deduce that it doesn't concern my rider but someone else. The authorities either say what they have to say, quoting names and surnames, or they shut up. They made the rules and according to their parameters Marco Pantani is perfectly in line. If they then decide that their rules need changing, they should have thought about that earlier, without causing all this commotion.

The stance taken by the Italian Professional Rider's Association via its president and spokesperson Enrico Ingrillì was even tougher: 'This is a paradox: not even by passing the tests laid down by CONI can a rider kill the bad faith of those who inexplicably want to sully the reputation of Italian athletes and particularly cyclists.'

The day before the Giro del Lazio, his final dress rehearsal before leaving for Sydney, Marco addressed the media through gritted teeth:

> If I wasn't upset by the virulent scandal-mongering of the last few days I'd be a very sad man. I don't think that what I've received is the most logical treatment for someone who's duty it is to represent Italy in the world's most prestigious sporting event. Had I known before that there would be this feeding frenzy around me, then perhaps I wouldn't have made myself available for selection. Looking back on what's happened, I have the distinct impression that someone is trying to destabilise sport and cycling in particular. Any Tom, Dick or Harry sets himself up as an expert and starts doling out sentences without knowing the facts. Why have they got something against Pantani? Maybe because I'm a bit too popular. So it's easy to cling to Pantani, either to side with or against him. That way, you're

guaranteed publicity. I decided to go to Sydney, taking all of the necessary tests and more: I took four in ten days. And my results are OK because I am OK. I'm not even thinking about staying at home. I do, however, think that someone is playing a shameful game to try to rock the boat.

In the end it was only his patriotic pride which prevented Marco from carrying through his threat to withdraw from the Olympics. But to the very last – in fact, the day before the Italian team was due to fly out to Sydney – it was hard to shake the suspicion that someone else wished that he wasn't on the plane. He received a delivery of his official Italian team uniform and accessories, among which was luggage bearing the label DAVIDE REBELLIN. Rebellin just happened to be the first reserve for the Italian team and the rider who Marco's critics wanted to see drafted in at his expense. I kept that name tag to prove that this time it wasn't simply a question of Marco being paranoid. Even when he had arrived in Sydney, the atmosphere around him remained poisonous. One of the Italian team's track riders who had spent many years competing on the road, Silvio Martinelli, welcomed him onboard with this message:

He must bear in mind that while he's here the cyclists will be in the line of fire. If he was caught [doping], it would cause shocking damage to the reputation of the entire sport… Marco Pantani has lost and is still losing an opportunity to contribute to the war on unethical sport. He has adopted and is continuing to adopt a stance which I don't understand. Why does no-one have the courage to admit, 'I made a mistake'? I'm sure that if Pantani had simply said, 'ladies and gentleman, I sinned', he would have emerged stronger than before and with more credit. The public would have forgiven him immediately. He is a big star but I knew him when hardly anyone else did. He has changed: we used to chat in the peloton; he was always motivated. Now, he makes these inflated statements which smack of unhappiness; he has it in for everybody; he practically picks himself for the national team, going over everyone's head despite having just pulled out of the Tour. Is that right? I hope that, in retrospect, he'll be able to admit, even privately, that he has gone about things in completely the wrong way.

The Olympic road race was a mini-fiasco for all five Italian riders, on a flat course manifestly ill-suited to their strengths. As usual, the most biting criticism was reserved for Pantani.

The day after Marco's return to Italy, 30 September, I was due to marry in Pallanza, the town of my birth, on the shores of Lago Maggiore. I was hoping for the perfect late summer's day: I had hired out an open-air nightclub that had a park and gazeboes in its grounds. My grandparents had once owned a shipbuilding yard, which was the inspiration for my father to have beautiful wooden boats laid on to ferry guests to the Borromean Islands in the middle of the lake. Marco had landed at Milan's Malpensa airport on 29 September, returned to Cesenatico for a few hours' nap and at five in the morning was back behind the wheel. The ceremony was to take place at eleven o'clock and the first guest to arrive at the church was none other than Marco Pantani – complete with straggly beard and cap, but there nonetheless. Clearly the sun had not accepted our invitation for it was pouring with rain. But, soon, the town mayor, a family friend, had called to offer me the use of the park villa because the 400 guests would never all squeeze under the saturated gazeboes. I walked up the church steps and I remember that Marco's was the first kiss I received. He was thrilled and hugged me again before entering the church. He stayed for the whole day with Christina, some friends, his parents and his aunt. He had come in his Ferrari, whose interior and dashboard had been completely flooded. For once, he had no intention of risking an accident by leaving that evening. He left the car at my brother's house and arranged for Ferrari to pick it up. He stayed the night in Baveno then headed back to Cesenatico with Christina the following day. His presence was the greatest gift he could have given me on that day which meant so much.

9

A New Team for
the Pirate

My problems at Mercatone Uno didn't diminish with the passage of time. In the autumn of 2000, Luigi Valentini told me that the season had gone better than expected – with Stefano Garzelli's Giro d'Italia victory and Marco's double stage win at the Tour de France – but that, with my role in the team confined almost entirely to taking care of Marco, he should pay my salary, not Mercatone Uno. I replied that I also performed duties for the team: I acted as the manager, the press officer, the logistics manager. Valentini retorted that they didn't need a press officer, that he could offer to reimburse my expenses, but that Marco would have to pay me. To tell the truth, money was the least of my concerns at that time – far behind Marco being able to count on the fact that I was representing his interests and smoothing relations between him and the team, and making sure that factions didn't form. I decided not to tell Marco about Valentini's demand and just to relay the bare bones of the meeting.

But Marco and the team continued to grow apart. Whenever I spoke to Cenni that winter he would resort to his familiar refrain about me 'needing to bring in money'. Shortly before Christmas, I called Roberta Gasperoni, media relations officer of the Mercatone Uno corporation, to ask her where to send my photo and curriculum vitae for publication in the team brochure. She replied that I was no longer the team manager then wished me a cursory 'Happy Christmas' before putting down the receiver. I immediately called Valentini, wanting answers: our recent conversations suggested that my position was under review purely for economic reasons, not for the role I had. I told him about my conversation with Gasperoni, upon which he admitted having forgotten to tell me that Romano Cenni no longer wanted anything to do with me. I took this to mean that I was sacked. I didn't say anything to Marco, who was in Saturnia, simply because I didn't want to ruin the end of his year.

At the beginning of January I decided to meet him to discuss the situation. My husband, Paolo, came with me. It was 6 January: 'Marco, I don't want to cause you any problems, because usually it's a manager's role to solve them. If Mercatone Uno doesn't want me, I'll never stop being your friend. In the meantime, start looking for a manager who is more to Mercatone Uno's taste. Talk to Cenni about it.'

Marco was vexed that I was now even beginning to question myself: 'Listen, you have no problems as far I am concerned: I'm happy with you, I'd tell you if I wasn't. If Cenni has decided to reject one of my co-workers, let him choose his own and I'll choose my own. But I want to understand why he's done this first. Because I can smell something fishy about this – it's as if Gimondi and Martinelli have got you kicked out. When I get back from Saturnia, I'll go to talk to Cenni.'

After meeting Cenni, Pantani tentatively explained that the boss was frustrated with me because I hadn't brought him a sufficient return on his investment. He also made it quite clear that Gimondi and Martinelli didn't want a woman in the team. Especially Gimondi. The team management was to remain their business: I could stay on as Pantani's manager, but not team manager.

At the beginning of 2001 I was involved with organising the presentation of the team, largely because, after finding a new co-sponsor, SBS, I could hardly be excluded. But over the months that followed my role was quickly reduced to that of spectator. I had taken the brush-off very badly, but there was nothing I could do. Marco continued to tell me that I needed to stay close to him, to support him. I did my best to show my face at as many races as possible but I was now picking up the bill for my own expenses and I didn't want to intrude too much on Marco's personal space. After a while, it was him who asked me to lend a hand behind the scenes because, incredibly, the team had an inadequate supply of leisure clothes and shoes.

In between races, I struck a clothing deal on behalf of the team with a company called Unlimited, whose owner was a close friend. Now we needed to find a footwear supplier, as relations with current sponsor Asics had badly deteriorated. This kind of problem drove Pantani mad, loathe as he was to compromise on his or the team's image. I promptly set about looking for a supplier. 'By doing this, you'll be helping me,' Marco said. 'Don't think that you're directly helping the team. You're doing this for me.' One day that spring, in an impromptu meeting in his hotel bedroom at a race in Spain, he told me: 'I know it's hard for you, but you have my full support. Please help me out. There are already loads of problems with my team-mates. When I sit down at the dinner table I want to do it with my head held high.' He felt like the family father and breadwinner who didn't want his children to go short of anything. Here was further proof of his greatness: all of the riders went to him with their grievances and he made them all his personal campaign. This was precisely why the feeling of gradually having lost credibility with his team-mates was perhaps his greatest source of suffering in the final few years of his career. Once upon a time, he wielded great influence within the team, but for some time now his requests and suggestions had been falling on deaf ears or were rebutted with one excuse after another. Marco didn't want to operate a dicta-torship – he simply wanted to help bring the team together with his charisma. He wanted to revive the spirit of sacrifice and unity around the captain. But that family atmosphere within the team which Luciano Pezzi had created back in 1996 was destined never to be rediscovered after Pezzi's death.

Leblanc blocks the path to the Tour

The first part of the 2001 campaign was far from ideal for Marco. In late April, he lined up at the Giro del Trentino with his heart set on a victory which would provide a much-needed boost to his morale ahead of the

Giro d'Italia, even if a triumphant return to the Tour de France was his dearest wish. But during the Giro del Trentino, Marco was floored by some appalling news: Jean-Marie Leblanc, the director of the Tour de France, was inviting neither Mercatone Uno nor Pantani to the Tour. Team-mate Gianpaolo Mondini passed on the message from the Mercatone car in the middle of a stage. Marco was incensed as much by the graceless manner in which it had been relayed to him as by the announcement itself. Mario Cipollini and his team had also been snubbed, and Pantani vented all his contempt for the Tour organisers and their decision to the press. He thought that he had always honoured that race, having won it and 'saved' it when it was staggering towards a bloody and premature end in the drugs-hit 1998 event, and he was disappointed by Tour's lack of respect and recognition.

I don't have to remind anyone how Marco won the Tour in 1998, the year of his Giro–Tour double but equally of the Festina affair and the rider's strike. Leblanc had pleaded with Marco to help him see the race through to Paris and Pantani had obliged. Fabrizio Borra had told me that – in the final two weeks of that race, so fearful had the teams become of further police raids that there wasn't so much as a strip of aspirin in their luggage. The 'cleanest' Tour, if that's what you can call it, was without doubt the one which Marco had won. Hence his profound bitterness now: 'That's life for you: you give, and when you need something in return they slam the door in your face. I need the Tour for my mind and my motivation, to spur me into action, but for these guys its strictly business.' Granted, neither Pantani nor his team was doing particularly well, but this wasn't what lay behind the Tour de France's decision: they didn't want him associated with their race on account of his ongoing battles with the Italian judiciary and the reflected infamy this could bring upon Leblanc and the Tour. If there was one thing which terrified the organisers it was the threat of yet more scandals. This fear, it seemed, far outweighed any debt of gratitude they might – although probably didn't – feel towards Marco.

I tried more than once to get through to Marco that what happened in cycling was no more than a microcosm of everyday life, i.e. that injustice was rampant in both spheres. What this didn't take into account, though, was that at Madonna di Campiglio Marco had effectively been robbed of his bike, which was akin to taking away his sole means of expression; in the same way that you kill a painter if you take away his paintbrush, that day Marco felt himself die. What followed thereafter was even harder for him to bear, because he fell to earth with a thud, suddenly among the ordinary people, into a reality with which he wasn't familiar. Marco was always at races, travelling from country to country, hotel to hotel – anywhere but where normality continued its relentless plod. For Marco, any problem, be it an argument with his girlfriend or parents or a disagreement in his entourage, became an insurmountable problem. Yes, Marco was thirty years old, but he retained a teenager's mentality. I tried to make him understand that what was happening with Leblanc was undoubtedly unfair, but that life was, too, and unfortunately he needed to come to terms with it. By saying this I certainly wasn't vindicating Leblanc, but neither did I agree with Luigi Valentini, who thought that we should accept whatever was thrown at us and stop putting up opposition. For Marco, being barred from the Tour was a real disaster. I'm certain that the news had an adverse affect on the mindset he took into that year's Giro d'Italia.

With the Giro del Trentino over, Marco began to bemoan Mercatone Uno's lack of political influence. He maintained that a cyclist of his stature needed the backing of a multinational company, a much more powerful sponsor and cited the example of Lance Armstrong and the US Postal Service. Cenni also wasn't the sort of 'tycoon' who waded into political issues regarding the team, like, say, Franco Polti of his eponymous Team Polti, or Mapei's Giorgio Squinzi. Finally, Mercatone Uno had no commercial interests and therefore scant influence outside Italy. This, too, left Pantani feeling unprotected on an international level.

The 2001 Giro and the San Remo blitz

As the 2001 Giro d'Italia approached, Marco expressed his desire for me to be present at the race and 'on duty' for the duration of the three weeks. I put it to Martinelli, who said that he had no objections.

Two days before the start, though, Giuseppe admitted that the Mercatone Uno bosses were far from happy about me travelling and staying with the team and that, anyway, there were no vacancies for me in the hotels. I relayed this to Marco and the red mist descended. I tried to calm him down, assuring him that I would find myself hotel rooms on an ad hoc, stage by stage basis. I also made sure that he realised that it wasn't a financial issue because, in any case, I wouldn't be charging my expenses to Mercatone Uno; they simply didn't want me there.

I watched and travelled with the Giro alone. I had got hold of the directory of the hotels where the team was staying and from time to time would call to find out whether there was a free room, which there invariably was. Alone, I would unload my bags, go up to the room, and eat dinner in a quiet corner of the hotel restaurant. I was generally downcast about the state of affairs, but every time I sat down to dinner Marco would turn around in his chair and wink at me from where the team were eating on the other side of the restaurant. Then, as soon as he finished eating, he would get up and come to sit at my table. These gestures confirmed that he was happy I was around and were also enough to make me forget the loneliness and the mental fatigue of following an entire Giro d'Italia. Even looking back now, I still can't fathom the steadfast rejection to which I was subjected by Mercatone Uno at that Giro.

Marco's performance in the race itself was thoroughly undistinguished: he couldn't even keep pace with the leaders, this time assuming his customary first-week position at the rear of the bunch for the entire race. He was doubtless paying the price for a stop-start preparation, but the tension now reigning in the team and their lack of confidence in him also played their part. When the race reached San Remo after sixteen stages and with Marco in seventeenth place overall, almost eighteen minutes down on race leader Gilberto Simoni, Martinelli reached the end of his tether. When I called him that day, he launched into a diatribe the main thrust of which was that Marco had put on weight and that he should pull out now to save some face. He intended to tell Marco exactly same thing. I immediately rushed to the hotel to try to stop him. If he said the same things to Marco that he had said to me, he would destroy him. Martinelli didn't want to argue: he was the *directeur sportif* and he knew how to manage one of his riders. So he stormed off in search of Marco and said what he thought he needed to say. I shut myself away in my room and five minutes later Pregnolato came to see me to tell me that Marco wanted to go home. Marco was in his room, trying in vain to hold back his tears as he repeated what Martinelli had said to him. He was stretched out across the bed, arms and legs spread wide, tears trickling down his cheeks. I suggested that he stay that night and leave the race tomorrow to avoid all the sniping about him 'running away'. I wanted Martinelli to assume responsibility for his decision in front of the press: it was him who didn't want Pantani at the Giro. Fortunately, Marco agreed to pull out only after a rest-day press conference the following day in which he would explain the reasons for his abandonment.

That day, the managing director of Mercatone Uno, Ilaro Ghiselli, was dropping in to visit the team. Ghiselli and Gimondi wanted to convince Marco not to abandon the Giro. I explained to them that it wasn't Marco's decision but Martinelli's. As if by magic, the situation was turned on its head: they told me that Martinelli had assumed that Marco didn't want to race anymore. Ultimately, Marco was to stay in the race, but he felt disheartened.

We would later thank our lucky stars that Marco hadn't carried out his threat to leave that evening. Shortly after it was established that he would be staying on, the hotel reception was suddenly swarming with smartly dressed men who I assumed to be in San Remo for a conference or something of the like. They turned out to be investigators from the Italian drugs police (NAS), who were about to conduct searches of the riders' rooms. Marco wasn't unduly perturbed and nothing was found in his room. We knew, however, that, had he abandoned the Giro, the newspapers would have written that Marco had pulled out due to a tip-off about the police raids. The NAS stayed until two or three o'clock in the morning. I can remember Cipollini being angry because they had broken his children's toys to see if anything was hidden inside...

We finally went to sleep and the next morning Marco's suitcases were already packed for his return to Cesenatico. Suddenly we were given a message, sent by Mario Cipollini, to the effect that there was to be a riders' meeting because they had decided to boycott the rest of the Giro d'Italia. The cyclists had espoused the war on doping and it went without saying that the NAS had to do their job, but there were ways of going about it: the NAS had shown excessive arrogance while conducting the 'blitz' and the riders had been treated like real criminals.

Marco had been among the last to find out about the meeting and was ready to head home in the car with Pregnolato when he was notified. I found him in reception and, assuming that he would be attending, wanted to squeeze in a pep-talk to guard against yet another PR faux pas: 'Marco, please, if you want to be involved...' 'I must go because it's my duty. If the riders hold a meeting, it's only right that I'm there, too. I can't run away. I'm no coward.' I warned him: 'That's to your credit, but remember: listen to what the others have to say, express your opinion, but don't act like the mob leader, don't put yourself in a difficult position for the sake of being their spokesman. Remember what happened when you did it at the 1999 Giro. Don't do it again.' 'Yes, Manu, don't worry, but it's really a disgrace. We can't go like this. It's my duty to fight for my sport.' Gimondi didn't want Marco to play any part in the meeting, and of course it was my fault that he intended to. My intuition told me that something serious was about to happen.

Back in the hotel, I later found out that the riders had drafted and signed a press release communicating their decision to stop the Giro d'Italia. That statement was about to be made public when Candido Cannavò suddenly bowled in and took control. Marco later told me that when he had tried to talk, the Gazzetta director had politely invited him to refrain, 'because he had already caused enough trouble as it was'. Cannavò had then set about changing the riders' minds, saying that he had spoken to the team sponsors, who had inferred that stopping the race would do no-one any favours in the long run, while if the riders pushed through to Milan, they would back them. Cipollini, who had led the dissenters – not least because he had been a victim of the heavy-handed search tactics – now changed his stance and claimed that Cannavò was right: the Giro had to finish in Milan and they must channel their efforts to take cycling in a different direction. A meeting would be held in Rome to establish a code of ethical behaviour. The net result was that Pantani was depicted as the rebel who had stirred up the other riders and made stopping the Giro his own personal crusade, while Cipollini was hailed as the saviour of the race and – why not – the entire sport.

Marco was disgusted at his peers' unwillingness to support his efforts to change the sport. There was no coherence. The other riders thought that, being rich, Pantani had nothing to lose, while they needed to remain in the sport to support their families. From their point of view, it was best not to fight a system which was stronger than they were; pragmatism – and hence conformity – were the best insurance policies. For Marco, in contrast, it was a matter of principle. He couldn't bring himself to accept the hypocrisy which increasingly seemed to dictate in cycling.

He left San Remo and the 2001 Giro that afternoon a forlorn figure, sparking my fears that he would again drown his sorrows in cocaine. He returned home with Roberto Pregnolato and that was the last I would see or hear of him for some time. Meanwhile, Pantani's former rival from their amateur days, Gilberto Simoni, secured his first ever Giro victory five days later in Milan.

The proposed meeting to establish an ethical code was to be held in the second week of June at CONI (Italian Olympic Committee) headquarters in Rome. Marco didn't want to participate but I insisted that he attend such an important meeting. Pantani had been vehemently criticised after the San Remo blitz when he hadn't started the following day's stage. Twenty-four hours later, the *Gazzetta*'s front page headline read: 'Cipollini the saviour of the Giro. Result of the blitz: nothing found in Simoni and Cipollini's bedrooms'. Nothing had been found in Pantani's room, either, but they hadn't taken the trouble to point it out. Someone, however, had seen Roberto Pregnolato throw a plastic bag out of a bedroom window, which at least meant that Marco could be conveniently incriminated by association.

This didn't stop Marco heading for Rome with Martinelli, but he would soon wish that he hadn't bothered. It was a disaster. Not only was he stopped by police and stripped of his licence for speeding on the journey, but the meeting on the ethical code was spectacularly inconclusive. Marco realised that everyone present pretended not to see what it suited them not to see, plastering over the cracks but refusing to address the problem at its root.

A new team?

The summer came and went and our relationship with Mercatone Uno and the team had apparently deteriorated irremediably. With Martinelli, it was daggers drawn, while with Gimondi, there had never been any dialogue, so little had changed. I set up yet another meeting with Marco at home to work out how to go forward. I had reflected long and hard on the situation and had realised that there was no scope for bridge-building at Mercatone Uno. I lacked credibility and power, so I proposed to Marco that we create a new team with an innovative management model. His response was enthusiastic: 'OK, Manu, let's create the Formula One of cycling. I'll get the riders together, I'll take on every imaginable responsibility and you take yours. We'll ask Mercatone Uno if they want to sponsor us. If not, we'll look for someone else.'

I explained to Marco that we would take on new, different staff, which would hopefully add to his motivation. We had visions of a three-year project, perhaps alongside an academy team full of emerging talent. When his career was over, Marco would be able to pass on his energy and expertise to the young riders. Most importantly, though, he would no longer have any reason to be dissatisfied with the team and its management and he would no longer feel that they lacked faith in him. In short, we would recreate an atmosphere around him which was conducive to success on the road.

We would acknowledge Mercatone Uno's input and their support of Pantani over the years and we would offer to relieve them of the responsibility for managing the team. It would be impossible to go on as we were, but it would also be unthinkable for him to ride for another sponsor in view of his sentimental ties to the company and colours. Giorgio Squinzi had practically offered him a blank cheque to sign for Mapei after his 1998 Giro–Tour double but Marco rejected it in favour of remaining with Mercatone Uno. More than once, Cenni had made it clear to Pantani that he resented the amount of money he had cost the company, to which Marco would reply that it was him, Cenni, who had offered him such a hefty fee to stop him moving to Mapei, so his conscience was clear. Marco believed that he had given the team at least as much as he had received financially, if not more.

Beyond these considerations, it seemed to me that the idea of a self-governing team was the right one to force Marco to take responsibility and therefore restore his motivation. At that time, the most important thing – the doctors agreed – was to keep him on his bike, otherwise, he would soon start drifting again.

I decided that he should be the one to talk to Cenni. I was in Rome for work, and tried to call Marco several times to find out how the meeting had gone. I finally tracked him down at around ten o'clock that evening. His voice was very quiet and I didn't draw much comfort from his words. He said that Cenni wanted to carry on, but that he was hesitating and perhaps the owner of the Saeco team, Sergio Zappella, was interested in merging Saeco with Mercatone Uno. A meeting would be held to discuss the possibility. Also, Marco got the impression that Cenni was leaning more towards Gimondi and Martinelli than to him, although, again, as Marco told it, the evidence for this was somewhat vague.

A second meeting took place, attended by Pantani, Cenni, Zappella and Franco Cornacchia, the Mercatone Uno financial director. Marco called me immediately afterwards: 'They want to reform Mercatone Uno and they're willing to putt in about £1.7 million apiece. They need a manager. Cenni doesn't want to be in control of team affairs – he just wants to be the sponsor. Franco said that he could give us a hand to begin with but we need a manager. Are you up for it?' I replied instantly: 'It would be an honour, but are we sure that the budget is in place, sure about everything?' 'Yes, Manu. Look, you go and talk to them about it. Cenni has given me his word – we shook on it. The only problem was that Zappella would prefer to bring in his own people but, anyway, we'll try to sort it to our advantage because I'd rather have people who I trust. You take it on from here. *Ciao*.'

That jaunty farewell signalled the beginning of my nightmare. In my excitement, I leapt back onto the couch and squealed to my husband: 'Paolo! The team is ours. It's marvellous news. We can finally put all of our ideas into practice!' Paolo was more cautious: 'This won't be a walk in the park like you think it will. Are you sure that you want to do it?' 'I'd jump onto a burning pyre for Marco. Don't you worry.'

I went back to Rome and had a first meeting with Cenni. He recapped his conversation with Marco et al and declared that Mercatone Uno was prepared to invest £1.3 million. Marco had said £1.7 million, but Cenni explained that this figure included £350,000 in bonuses in the eventuality of victory at the Tour or Giro. He was prepared to put it all down in writing. When I asked him about Zappella and whether he was still keen he said that he hadn't made further contact with him and that I should call. I was beginning to notice the growing discrepancy between the dreamlike scenario which Marco had described and the reality now unfolding. Nonetheless, I told Cenni that, after several years of working together, there was no real need for him to put pen to paper on anything yet. I trusted him: Romano Cenni's integrity was beyond question.

In the meantime, Fabrizio Borra had come with me to Marco's house to discuss the make-up of the team. The choice of *directeur sportifs* would be fundamental and was our top priority. We needed someone charismatic, but our options were limited. We considered Giancarlo Ferretti, but there was no way that he would leave Fassa Bortolo. All of the most respected names were already tied to established teams. Also, the last few months under the experienced Martinelli had left Marco disillusioned, and he felt the need to bring in someone with a fresh energy which may rub off on him. 'I don't need a coach who teaches me tactics and race strategies because, without wanting to sound presumptuous, I decide the tactics, doing as I have always done. I need someone who can keep a team united.'

We plumped for Riccardo Magrini. An ex-rider, he had been rumoured to be eyeing a comeback to the racing scene for some time, and already had experience as a *directeur sportif*. Everyone in the sport knew him as something of a free spirit, a wag, and therefore, by extension, unreliable, but his motivational capacities and knowledge of the sport weren't in doubt. And if there was something which Marco needed, it was a person who brought cheer and positive energy. Then there would be Giannelli, Martinelli's long time right-hand man and an organisational whiz-kid. We also thought about giving Massimo Podenzana an opportunity in this, in what would be his first year as an ex-rider; it would be a fitting reward for his loyalty and the sacrifices he had made for Marco over the years. We wanted to build a team around men who had a strong bond with Marco, which made Fabrizio Borra the ideal man to take charge of the medical staff and the masseurs.

I arranged a meeting with Zappella to give him our proposal. My husband came with me to the Saeco owner's Tuscan summer residence. Zappella's reservations centred on the staff and particularly the fact that, in cycling circles, Riccardo Magrini wasn't held in high esteem. Zappella emphasised the difficulty of managing Pantani, adding that if he could be certain that Claudio Corti, the Saeco team manager, was up to the task, he would have gone with him, but that Marco seemed to be very confident of his own staff. If it was up to him, Zappella said, we could give it a try, but he was already negotiating with Corti to preserve Saeco in its current form and he would need his German shareholder to approve the concept of the Mercatone Uno–Saeco merger. We went to lunch and Zappella made the telephone call to Germany before my eyes. I don't understand German, but I heard the name Marco Pantani mentioned at least thirty times. Zappella proposed a toast: his German shareholder was excited about the project and now we just needed to be more specific about the riders involved and the management structure. It could be considered, therefore, that he had accepted our proposal, even though some of the finer details still had to be ironed out. I returned home highly satisfied after we had promised to speak again a few days later.

Zappella seemed to have good reasons to want the Mercatone Uno –Saeco merger to come off. At the end of that 2001 season, Zappella would lose Cipollini, who was bound for Vincenzo Santoni's Acqua e Sapone team, and Saeco clearly needed to replace him with another big name, a leader. Zappella had also said that, to placate Corti, he could give him the budget to create a new team sponsored by another of his brands, Gaggia. I was giving Magrini, Giannelli, Podenzana and Marco – who was preparing for the Vuelta a Espana – regular updates on how the negotiations were progressing. In the meantime, I was also trying to tie things up with Mercatone Uno. I had no experience as managing director of a cycling team, so Franco Cornacchia stepped in as a financial consultant, although the ultimate responsibility to negotiate and seal the deal with both Saeco and Mercatone Uno remained mine. Having Franco at my side simply made my job easier and sheltered me from some of the criticism which would no doubt come my way.

We quickly went about registering the new company and drawing up contracts for the riders who had been with Mercatone in 2001. It was now almost September and most team's 2002 rosters were already being finalised. In Italy, most wheeling and dealing in view of the following season takes place during the Giro d'Italia, which meant that we were already playing catch-up. Igor Astarloa and Marco Velo, for example, had already made alternative arrangements despite having reassured Marco that they would wait for him, even if it took a year. Others simply accepted the first offer that came their way.

A few weeks later, Zappella called me to say that there had been a misunderstanding: the German shareholder thought he had said 'Fassa Bortolo', and now, hearing Pantani's name, had rather turned up his nose. I found it hard to fathom: I had heard Marco's name very clearly and repeatedly pronounced during Zappella's phone conversation, and I had no recollection of Fassa Bortolo being mentioned. It looked for all the world like an excuse. In fact, before giving me a final confirmation, Zappella had decided to wait until after the Vuelta: if Marco went badly, he would be forced to reconsider the plan.

As if this wasn't enough, rumours had started to intensify to the effect that Martinelli would move to Saeco to take up a position as *directeur sportif*. Marco began to suspect that Saeco had lost interest and it soon proved that he had suspected right.

To top it all off, the Vuelta was a catastrophe. We still had no written agreement with Mercatone Uno, Saeco finally pulled out of talks, and no agreement was struck with Gaggia, either. Yet, we were now fully

committed to a project for which I bore a large share of the responsibility, and whose initial budget was now more than halved. Marco
wasn't aware of the sudden downturn in our prospects and I didn't
know how to tell him. In the end, I decided to be completely open with
him and tell him exactly what had happened with Zappella. I tried to
reassure him, promising to roll up my sleeves and look for other
sponsors in time for the new season. It goes without saying that, come
October, it's far from straightforward to find companies willing to stump
up over £1 million with their marketing budgets for the following year
long since set in stone. There was also the not unsubstantial problem of
asking companies to invest in a project so heavily dependent on Marco
Pantani. To listen to them, you'd think that everyone had faith in
Pantani, but no-one was willing to put their money where their mouth
was. It's always easier to find sponsorship in companies ruled by a single
person: Romano Cenni, for example, would make his decisions on the
back of his love of cycling and because he believed in Pantani, even if
his board of directors didn't agree. The risk was his and so, logically,
should the decision also have been his. The modus operandi is very
different in a multinational or in a company with a flat management
structure, where the marketing manager stakes his future on the
choices he makes. Who, in that situation, would invest in cycling and
a project linked to Marco Pantani? Had the gamble failed, whoever
instigated it would lose his job.

Unfortunately, it was easy for those outside the sport to overlook the
fact that the fundamental issue wasn't whether Pantani won races or
not. His public profile alone would have mobilised the media's attention
and this would have justified the investment in PR terms. In my opinion,
if a sponsor wants the image of a star athlete associated with its brand,
it should never bank on that athlete's sporting success. Victory is only
the icing on the cake; an investment based solely on this is too volatile.
Pantani epitomised the athlete who could always bounce back, a man
with granite resolve, a leader – and this alone made him endorsement
gold. Also, when things are going well, anyone can be a sponsor of a
top sportsman. It's when things start to go badly that an investor's
true qualities emerge. I think that for a sponsor to remain loyal to a

champion and keep faith with him even in hard times is an excellent reflection on the company's image. Who could criticise that kind of approach? And yet, it was far from easy to bring prospective sponsors around to this way of thinking.

Here is what really happened in those weeks and months. Cenni had shook my hand, telling me that he was confident and that he would soon draw up a contract with Cornacchia. The contract was taking its time to come through and in November we would have no choice but to submit it to the UCI, the sport's governing body. Cornacchia made me an offer which kept me awake every night for three weeks. I was presented with a contract which basically said: the offer is for £1.3 million plus £350,000 if Marco wins the Giro and the Tour. In addition to this, there were countless clauses stipulating all sorts of penalties, in particular for Marco abandoning races. Cenni also wanted Marco to act as guarantor in the eventuality of financial difficulties and to underwrite a performance guarantee as further insurance. Cenni's crux was this: until Madonna di Campiglio, we gave him money and he asked for guarantees from us, but since then Pantani has never been the same so now it's us who want guarantees. Their reasoning was flawless, but I couldn't understand why Cenni wouldn't say all of this to Marco's face. Everyone claimed that they had faith in Pantani, that Marco would always be able to count on them but when it came to making things official, their attitude changed radically. I fought long and hard to get clauses in the contract relaxed but all I really managed to do was to eliminate the personal risk to Marco. It nonetheless remained a punitive contract and explaining it to Marco would be a delicate operation. At the very least, he would lose some of his faith in Cenni who for him had always been a model of coherence and correctness.

Marco had given Mercatone Uno levels of exposure that would have been very difficult to replicate in advertising without investing far more money. I knew therefore, that there was never any reason for me to blush about championing Marco's cause with Cenni, but Mercatone Uno maintained that the opposite was true. I signed that contract because at the time I had no other choice and, finally, I plucked up the courage to explain this and what the contract entailed to Marco.

If, before creating the team, I had known how things would pan out, I certainly would have adopted a different tactic and made different decisions, but then all of this was easy to say with the benefit of hindsight. What I've never been able to accept is Cenni's failure to clearly outline his real intentions to Marco during their first meeting in that August of 2001. It wasn't very correct on his part to present us with that kind of contract in mid-December, knowing that we would have no choice but to sign it and accept the conditions it laid down.

Doing a quick sum of the penalties which had been imposed and Marco's fragile mental state, his inconsistency and the likelihood of him abandoning races, I had nightmares. My faith in him, however, remained intact, so I set about looking for a co-sponsor in the hope of making us less financially dependent on Mercatone Uno. I paid for a team of marketing consultants to go in search of investors out of my own pocket. Despite their impeccable credentials, all they managed to obtain were promises, none of which later translated into a firm commitment and money; there were faxes, signed letters and even pre-contract agreements galore but none of them were ever honoured.

In the meantime, another bombshell had dropped on our heads from the Vuelta. Auro Bulbarelli, an Italian TV commentator, happened to mention in one broadcast that Giannelli, who was to be a lynchpin of the new team, wouldn't be involved with Marco Pantani's team the following season. He wanted to take a sabbatical, a pause for reflection. Giannelli hadn't told me anything. I asked him for an explanation and he, very diplomatically, made it clear that Martinelli was calling him every day to make him feel guilty about having agreed to stay with Marco. Giannelli was a very sensitive person and rather easily influenced. On one hand, he was being harangued by Martinelli, to whom he owed a debt of gratitude for having always looked after him, and on the other hand he was very fond of Marco. He didn't know which way to go and in the end he just opted out completely. Marco took it very badly, partly because of the way we had found out, but also because it left us exposed from an organisational point of view: Magrini was coming from a long absence from the racing scene, while this was Podenzana's first job as a *directeur sportif*.

We didn't let the ongoing problems with the sponsor and the staff deter us. Pantani, Magrini and I decided to go to Paris for the presentation of the 2002 Tour de France. Marco was at his most dapper in a gorgeous suit. He proudly took his place among other past and present greats and got a fine reception. Attending the Tour presentation didn't mean that he was taking it for granted that he would be invited to the 2002 race, but it was a way of making the first move and extending an olive branch. Magrini and I were trying to coax some of the pride and arrogance out of Marco and instil a mite more diplomacy in its place. People in the sport immediately realised that something had changed: Marco was conducting his dealings with the press and the rest of the milieu in a completely different manner. After that presentation, we were very encouraged because, in spite of all the problems we were up against, Marco was enthusiastic and determined, and the changes in his behaviour gave us grounds for confidence.

With Giannelli now struck off our list, I contacted Marino Amadori, who had just managed the Gas Sport Team to victory in the women's Giro d'Italia and who came with a ringing endorsement from Alfredo Martini, the former Italian national coach. He came in as our second *directeur sportif*.

The contract with Mercatone Uno was still a worry. I only hoped that Cenni didn't abandon us. Not only would it be another slap in the face for Pantani, but the livelihoods of other riders, masseurs, mechanics and an entire group of people would be placed in jeopardy. But for the moment, my faith in Cenni held firm.

Up to that point, Cenni would not allow anyone at Mercatone Uno to challenge his belief in Marco or the decisions which concerned him; Romano would almost invariably reject suggestions from Franco Cornacchia and other colleagues if he thought that Marco stood to be penalised. He could make up his own mind and he knew Marco well enough to rely on his instinct. When things started to go badly, however – as had undeniably been the case in 2001 – it seemed as though his advisors and in particular Cornacchia were seeing all of their predictions fulfilled. Consequently, Cenni had to give them freedom of action and back their demands for a more hardline approach.

The team's first steps

The team's first training camp of that winter took place in November in Montecatini Terme in Tuscany. I recall that it went well and Marco left Montecatini fit and happy – so happy in fact that I almost had to pinch myself. I can remember telephoning my mum, my dad, my husband and Marco's parents on the way home to Milan. I was proud because I had never seen him like that, perhaps not even when I first met him and we had started working together.

Over the next few days, Borra, who was in charge of the medical staff, tried to contact Marco to arrange some meetings. Marco wasn't answering his phone, which was usually a sure sign that something was amiss. We finally tracked him down and arranged to meet him in Cesenatico a few days later. On arrival at his house, I immediately got the feeling that something had changed: he wasn't himself, he was absent and nervous. Fabrizio and I asked his parents how they saw the situation. Paolo, Marco's dad, told me that he was doing quite well, although there was still the odd dip in his mood. When I said to Paolo that we were managing the team on our own, he didn't react well. He asked me if we intended to 'go bankrupt', but at the time I didn't grasp the true meaning of what he said. I would understand later, when it was too late.

In December, we were to hold a second get-together in Terracina, on the coast between Rome and Naples. The team had already gathered when Borra called to make me listen to a message. There was a moment of silence, then he read out the text message which had just arrived on his mobile from Marco: 'Dear Fabrizio, I give you permission to tell the doctors about my psychological problems and my cocaine habit. Please help me.' My world collapsed. Throughout 2001, there had been no mention of cocaine with Marco. He seemed to have resolved the problem, the odd occasion when I had my suspicions excepted. At no time, though, did he seriously shown signs of having relapsed, especially after the summer.

With Marco apparently healthy, until now there had been no reason for us to alert Magrini to his past troubles. Now, however, he too needed to know what he was taking on as the *directeur spotif* of the new team, so he was duly informed.

The message was significant because it represented that first time that Marco was openly and very clearly admitting that he had a serious problem with cocaine. Beyond the first confession that he had made to me in November 1999 – when he had exaggerated, saying 'I'm a drug addict. There's no way out' – here, finally, was the basis for a plan of treatment. This time there was an explicit plea for help on his part, which we could welcome; Marco was at least showing some self-awareness, albeit about something very negative. When, together with him, I had made the decision to reform the team I was convinced that, if the problem wasn't entirely resolved, it was vastly reduced in its dimensions. Fabrizio showed more bravery than any of us. He said that he would take care of Marco. He didn't think that it would be a wise move to tell the team doctors because they might well get cold feet. Instinctively, he decided to make Marco's health his personal responsibility, went to fetch Marco from Cesenatico and brought him to Terracina where the team had just come together. When Marco asked for help, he always made you feel full of strength. You thought that you could overcome any obstacle if it meant helping him. It was when he didn't ask for help and shut himself off that he made everyone around him feel powerless.

Having arrived in Terracina with Fabrizio, Marco barricaded himself in his room. He didn't want to see anyone. In the end, Fabrizio was forced to tell the doctors everything, leaving them free to resign if they wanted to, but reaffirming that we needed them. Doctors Vezzani and Manari told us that we could count on them and Vezzani immediately tackled Marco, explaining that from that moment on Marco would have to conform to their demands. At first, Marco seemed frightened and refused to talk to anyone, but it was almost as if he were waiting for precisely that kind of resolute approach. When I arrived in Terracina later that week, I bumped into Marco as he was leaving a session with his masseur, Raniero Gradi. A true Tuscan, Magrini's friend and an exceptional human being, that year Gradi had taken Pregnolato's position as chief masseur. Pregnolato's conduct wasn't to the taste of lots of people, including journalists, and Mercatone Uno had made it clear that they didn't want his contract renewed. Also, we were set on a comprehensive overhaul which meant that he, too, had to be moved out. From that moment on, Raniero became a key figure in our attempt to restore Marco to his former self.

When Marco saw me, he shot me a furtive glance, and later, in the hotel reception, sat with his legs crossed and his elbows on his knees, he said: 'You're disappointed in me, eh Manu? I've let you down. You're always having to run around after me and you thought that everything was OK. I've betrayed you. I've let you down.' He confessed that things weren't going well with Christina either. This was his obsession. 'Christina doesn't understand me,' he complained. 'She's abandoning me: she doesn't want me any more. Without her, I can't live. If I can't make her happy, it means that I've failed again. Yet again. But now, with the help of the doctors, we'll get back on the wagon.'

Manari and Vezzani's prescription was as follows: a permanent training camp and a room-mate cum guardian in Marco's room at all times. We plumped for a young man who was a member of Manari and Vezzani's staff, a physical coach but also and above all a motivational psychologist. Marco didn't accept the arrangement: he didn't want to sleep in a room with someone he didn't know. In fact he hadn't even been sleeping in a room with other riders for some time. He came to me to complain, apoplectic, vociferously making his point then slamming the door as he left. But Manari and Vezzani were immovable. They struck a compromise: for the first few days, Marco would simply speak to the person who had been assigned to him, but they wouldn't share a room. In any case, we soon realised that we wouldn't be able to stay at Terracina, as we had begun to notice peculiar comings and goings around Marco. Manari decided to rent an apartment for Marco at Lerici, several hundred kilometres up the coast on the Tuscany/Liguria border. It looked like a good solution, for its proximity to Podenzana, who lived in nearby La Spezia, and to Magrini, and it was also only a short drive from the doctors' base in Reggio Emilia.

Keeping tabs on Marco was a full-time job in itself, but we also had to deal with another 'problem rider', Valentino Fois. Signing Fois had been another of Marco's crazy ideas. As well as having been banned from cycling for doping offences in the past, Valentino had other problems – I'm not sure how serious – but he had certainly earned a reputation in the sport for his erratic behaviour. When we had decided to give him a chance, the decision had been roundly ridiculed and criticised, but Marco wanted to help him, wanted to give him a life raft which in this case would be the bike. I tried to make Marco understand that before you can help someone, first you need to be strong yourself. Bringing in a rider with his own issues to resolve would be risky both for that athlete and for Marco. The scenario almost repeated itself in January 2003, when Marco urged us to take on the Spanish climber Jose Maria Jimenez, who would wind up dead from a cocaine overdose in a Madrid clinic later that year. Marco wanted to help 'El Chaba' after the Spaniard had been offloaded by Banesto. Davide Boifava, naturally, vetoed the move. But Marco simply wouldn't heed my warnings about Fois, and it's also hard to tell a person they are wrong when they are trying to be charitable.

Just before Christmas, I went to visit the apartment in Lerici with Marco, Borra, Manari, Podenzana, Gradi, Fois and Brignoli. Marco didn't like it: he thought that it had a sad air about it – one of those apartments on the Ligurian Riviera which are only occupied in the summer; it didn't feel lived in and therefore wasn't welcoming. I checked into a nearby hotel and immediately asked whether there were rooms available to accommodate the team for an indefinite period. There were, so the next day, the whole platoon moved in en masse, their sole objective to raise Marco's spirits on his return from training sessions and to help him stave off the blues.

With the Christmas party season in full swing, I got a call from Marco's father: police officers had turned up at the house to deliver official notification that Marco was once again under investigation. There were two counts of indictment: at Montecatini Terme, just over a week before the San Remo blitz at the 2001 Giro, a syringe containing traces of insulin had been found in the room allegedly occupied by Pantani; and at San Remo, Pantani was suspected of complicity with Pregnolato in the sale and use of doping products, after witnesses had seen the masseur throw a bag out of a hotel window.

No-one knew how to break the news to Marco. Pregnolato wasn't the only masseur from the 2001 team under investigation, either, and there were also mechanics involved. Our sentiments mixed disbelief with desperation and, to make matters worse, we still didn't understand the nature of the allegations. Finally, Marco was informed. He reacted better than expected. Perhaps the other irons we had in the fire meant that his mind was on other things and gave him some perspective. He shrugged that the lawyers would take care of it. By now, he seemed to be almost immunised against whatever the magistrates wanted to throw at him, preferring not to take too much notice and to focus on training; he certainly didn't welcome the news, but neither did he let it get him down. That Christmas at Lerici was a generally happy parenthesis: both the Hotel Europa and its owners were very charming, the location was tranquil and secluded from prying eyes and curious *tifosi*, and Marco was bathed in affection. Danilo Manari's little girl had designed T-shirts which perfectly illustrated our 'adventure': Marco and the rest of us were looking out of the portholes of a yellow submarine, with the famous lyrics of the Beatles floating above our heads: 'We all live in a yellow submarine...'

Marco's shyness was something which, despite his fame, he never really conquered. He didn't like spending time in other people's houses because he felt too awkward and embarrassed. Despite this, we managed to persuade him to spend Christmas with Massimo Podenzana's family. Massimo later told me that, after appearing uncomfortable at first, Marco had let his guard drop and he'd been fantastic company, just as he had been when he and Massimo often roomed together at races prior to Madonna di Campiglio. In the week of New Year, we tried to make sure that Marco was never alone. Spending the holidays a long way from home and in a hotel is enough to make anyone miserable, so the group tried to rally around him and inundate him with positive energy. We went to elaborate lengths to foster a sense of unity: every year, it was tradition for the masseurs and mechanics to receive a gift from the team, and that Christmas I had commissioned special watches featuring the Pantani logo. We gave one to everyone as a small gesture which would hopefully help to create the spirit that Marco needed. Moments like these reinforced our sense of pride and belonging to a strong, united group. Only the senior staff were aware of the seriousness of Marco's problem, but no-one, up to that point, had hesitated in trying to help him.

We had just handed out the watches, with everyone gathered around a table, when Marco made a request: he wanted a day of freedom. He had promised the doctors that he would follow their regime, but he wanted a day's 'leave' to go home for New Year's Eve. He had managed to contact Christina, who seemed willing to give him another chance and he couldn't contain his excitement. A friend from the nearby town of Massa, Franco, owned a well-known fashion boutique and had given Marco a gorgeous Pignatelli suit. It was to be a special evening, and he wanted to look special. We, on the other hand, were all very worried and quite honestly set against him going to Cesenatico. But he couldn't be dissuaded, and we couldn't force him to do anything even though we needed to be strict to help him out of the black hole he had fallen into. Until that day, everything had gone smoothly, but now we were petrified. It would have been pointless trying to dictate to him because ultimately Marco would always do what he wanted and we could have undermined all the good work we had done up to that point.

Marino Amadori took him back to Cesenatico. It was one of the most nerve-wracking New Year's Eves I've ever experienced and sadly, we soon found out that our fears were more than justified. I saw in 2002 in Milan with my husband, and the following morning the phone rang:

Ciao, Manu, it's Christina. You've got to go to Marco's house to pick him up, because he's hurting himself there. He came to my place but I've thought about it and I want to live my own life. I don't want to be with him for the rest of my days. I want to make my own choices, take my own path. I know that being with him requires a lot of patience and sacrifices, but I don't want to make sacrifices. I don't want to devote all of my energy to helping him, because I want to think of myself. I'm sorry but I've decided that I don't want him any more. He's at home harming himself. Please go and fetch him.

She cut me off before I had a chance to reply. Yet again, my world came crashing down around me. Straight away, I called Fabrizio Borra to tell him to hurry to Marco's house. I also called Manari, who was on holiday in the mountains with his family. Fabrizio rushed to Marco's villa. They spoke at length and it quickly emerged that the meeting with Christina had left Marco devastated. He had turned up convinced that they could start anew, but she immediately shot him down by telling him that, if he wanted, they could spend the evening together but no more. She had found someone else. Throughout their time together she had never been happy, she said. She had spoken in terms which were harsh, cynical and also vulgar. The lack of subtlety and respect she had shown Marco appalled me, while he couldn't believe that she could be so unkind. Manari, meanwhile, said that he would cut short his holiday and drive straight to Marco's – a journey which took him several hours. Later he told me that Marco hadn't seemed too bad. Marco had promised to listen to him and end his relationship with Christina once and for all.

2002: An uphill struggle

A further training camp had been scheduled to start in Reggio Emilia on 2 January. Part of the team's new strategy was a policy of maximum transparency. On a medical level, Fabrizio Borra had decided to achieve this with a highly innovative organisational 'model' which extended to internal health and dope tests. Precisely because there were still so many suspicions hanging over Marco, Dr Manari suggested that we perform the classic blood tests periodically requested by the UCI not in the private laboratories that most teams used, but in public hospitals. That way, the doubts surrounding Marco might finally be banished.

On 2 January, Fabrizio Borra came with Marco to the hotel in Reggio Emilia. That evening, the team had lunch together and was also joined by the head of the cardiology department of the local hospital. Marco was edgy – he kept disappearing to the bathroom, he was permanently clutching his phone, and he kept telling us that he absolutely must go to bed because he had an early start in the morning. He didn't want to spend the rest of the evening with the team and seemed distressed. I tried to talk to him and he replied that what had happened with Christina was irreparable and that as a result he was thinking of giving up riding: without her, he would never pull through and he had been humiliated by her walking away. He was carrying on more as a favour to us than anything else. He wanted to spend time thinking about whether to retire or not. They were shocking words, especially with all the responsibility we had taken on vis-à-vis the other members of the team. I asked myself whether Marco could possibly be irresponsible enough to desert a project like this.

He was due to report to us at 8.30am the following morning. First, he would undergo the blood tests at the hospital, then board a flight to Spain, where hopefully the January weather would be more conducive to training. The previous afternoon, I was relaxing in my hotel room when I heard a knock on the door. It was Manari, who was furious with Marco. I asked him what had happened. Manari had seen Marco walk out of the hotel and get into a white car with a Ravenna number plate which had clearly been waiting for him. Shortly afterwards, he had seen Marco get out of the car with some sort of container and head towards the hotel entrance. Seeing Manari, he had got back into the car, gone around the block, then come back with his hands in his pockets with no package in sight. The doctor had stopped him and asked what he was doing, to which Marco replied that he had just been for a drive.

Listening to Manari, the seriousness of the situation began to dawn on me: it was no longer a case of occasional relapses and a decisive intervention was needed. I instructed Manari to look for Fabrizio Borra and to go with him to read the riot act to Marco. Manari and Borra told me that their conversation with Marco had quickly become very impassioned. He wouldn't stop bashing the wall with his suitcase, yelling that they had violated his privacy, that he hadn't been doing anything, and that he was ready to take the blood tests the next morning.

We could do nothing but hope for some good fortune and, perhaps, a miracle. The following morning Fabrizio called Marco to tell him that it was time, but there was no reply. Several journalists had also turned up at the hospital, obviously aware that Marco would be taking blood tests even if they didn't yet know about his cocaine problem. The strong media interest was an unwanted side effect of our transparent new approach, although we had stopped short of informing the press that Marco would be going to hospital for tests, judging it unnecessary. We had a medical team who had agreed to help Marco, but we intended this, and not self-glorification, to be their only goal. However, just the previous day, one of Manari's assistants had already granted an interview to a local paper in which he proclaimed himself to be Marco's new coach.

Marco wasn't opening the door. He wasn't ready. We went into the room and found him in a terrible state. As well as cocaine, he had started using crack. At that stage I didn't even know what crack was. I rushed to the hospital to try to defuse the tension which was building. I said that Marco had been ill that night but he would still be coming to take the tests in a short while. Privately, I was terrified that a journalist might go to the hotel and blow our cover. The medial staff were now also realising what a huge responsibility they had taken on by agreeing to help Marco.

I went back to the hotel and called an emergency meeting in my room. Manari thought that we needed to persuade Marco to go public: he should reveal the exact nature of his problem – only that way would we be able to start concentrating on his recovery again. There is no doubt that it would have been the best solution for everyone, if only Marco would agree to it. It would have meant relief from the ever-present threat of a scandal and from the anxiety of having to deal with Marco. But, above all, the damage to Marco's image would have taken on a secondary importance, which would have helped him on a thera-peutic level. But Marco refused point blank, not for the first time: the idea of being at the centre of yet another scandal terrified him. In fact, in his mind, any further loss of face would lead him to suicide.

Later, we came in for a lot of criticism for not having made Marco's problem public earlier. Journalists thought that if we had talked, Marco would have stopped running away and hiding. I agree that it would have been better for everyone, especially for those of us who were trying to help him, and whose anguish would have been considerably alleviated by a public admission. But the real problem is trying to understand how it would have affected Marco's treatment. It would have been easy to answer those who said, 'If Pantani doesn't dope anymore, he won't win anymore!', by pointing out that his problem was a different one. But who gave us the right to do that, trampling up and down on someone's feelings, simply as a means of explaining away Marco's disappointing results? I wanted to protect Marco, not hurt him even more. Protecting Marco meant keeping him away from the eyes of the world and the curiosity of the media, which is what he wanted. Protecting him meant finding a solution with doctors, experts, and people who were capable of dealing with such a delicate situation. We had invested our love, our devotion, our willingness to make sacrifices, and the rest of the world didn't need to know what Marco's problem was.

Manari, though, continued to stress the need to go public. He suggested that we then take Marco to a commune in Sardinia. The whole world would discover Marco Pantani's dark secret, but at the same time it would see him improve and hopefully recover. Vezzani strongly disagreed: He wanted to consult a toxicologist and work with him to establish whether Marco could carry on racing and whether cycling could be a form of therapy or whether it would represent an obstacle. The search for a specialist had begun in Terracina and would prove far from straightforward.

10

The Slow Road Back

My prime concern at this point, on the cusp of the 2002 season, was Marco's health. By now, I knew his personality inside out, and I knew that without his desire and his determination – the very same qualities which had allowed him to lift himself up after every setback thus far in his career – we wouldn't see any improvement. I knew that nothing would make me give in and as long as I was Marco's manager, financial pressures wouldn't permit it: if sponsors discovered the truth, what would happen? If nothing else, they would accuse me personally of being a fraud. I was torn: if I lifted the lid on Marco's problem I would be betraying him, but if I said nothing I would be betraying my intellectual and professional honesty. Moreover, if I had been the only person with something at stake, I could have lived with any consequence, but other people's destinies and livelihoods were tied to mine, Marco's and the team's. The doctors were already accusing Borra and I of having neglected to give them a true impression of how bad Marco's problem actually was, but in all honesty, if we had known how ill Marco was – and if we had had his consent – we wouldn't have tried to hide anything. As I have already mentioned, nothing we had seen in 2001 gave us any inkling of how dramatic the situation was about to become.

I made a decision. I knew that Romano Cenni had always thought of himself as almost a second father to Marco. I also knew that Marco had confided in him, albeit perhaps not unreservedly or explicitly. Cenni would later confirm to me that Marco had not gone beyond talking about his problems with Christina, who he said had gone off the rails, but there was no mention of cocaine. He probably assumed that Cenni already knew or understood. Together with the doctors and the other senior members of staff, I decided to reveal all to Cenni and to ask him whether he was with us or against us. In other words would he help us or would he rather shut the team down once and for all. We could go to him with clear recommendations from the medical world to the effect that Marco should continue to ride. Unfortunately, Marco's lack of motivation dictated that this was easier said than done. I was worried about how Cenni would react, worried that he might castigate me for having known yet keeping him in the dark. But I had a clear conscience. I knew what had happened, how it had happened and I was prepared to do anything to solve Marco's problem. At that moment, my common sense told me that openness was the best policy. I asked Magrini to call Cenni, who immediately told us to report to Mercatone Uno HQ.

We went to see Cenni late in the evening, having spent the day in Lerici taking it in turns to 'supervise' Marco in our attempts to keep him calm. We failed miserably on that occasion and, frankly, neither of us knew how to react. 'Get out of my room! All of you, get out!' Marco screamed. 'I don't want to see you, leave me in peace. I'll sleep on it then we'll decide what to do. I don't get a moment's peace here.' Once we had sat down with Cenni, some two-and-a-half years after Marco consumed his first doses of cocaine, we explained exactly what had and what was happening. Romano was speechless. Instinctively, he asked first whether Marco would ride the Giro d'Italia. We said that the doctors couldn't promise anything: Marco would be continually monitored and Cenni would receive daily updates. We were under no illusions, however, that we could turn Marco's life around overnight with any amount of support or guidance. We would test his urine continually and make sure that he adhered to an appropriate treatment programme. We would make enquiries about treatment clinics in Italy, Spain or the United States, while knowing that without Marco's committed co-operation there was little hope of a positive outcome.

Cenni thanked us for our dedication but, as I had feared, reproached me for having known about Marco's cocaine habit and not telling him earlier. I replied that I hadn't wanted to reveal such an intimate detail of Marco's private life but that as soon as we had realised that he had become a fully fledged addict, we hadn't hesitated. It also bore pointing out that I wasn't the only one aware of Marco's predicament: Martinelli and other members of the team knew, but no-one had ever broached the subject with Cenni, partly because – as I said – we assumed that Marco had informed him in person. I wound up the meeting by telling Cenni that our only concern now should be finding a solution, whatever our differences of opinion. Everyone else could do as they wished. For example, when Dr Magni realised the magnitude of Marco's problem, he opted to leave the team. No-one else followed Magni through the exit door, but very few members of the team and its staff had the bravery and the desire to stay really close to Marco over the next few months.

The conversation with Cenni left me feeling relieved in one sense. At least, as we outlined his problems to Cenni, it hadn't felt as though we were betraying Marco. Of course we hadn't gone to Cenni to show Marco in a negative light or to endanger his position even more. We did it to find out whether we could count on Mercatone Uno's support in what had become our crusade to help Marco. That evening, despite our earlier clashes with Marco, Magrini and I were relatively relaxed, with our thoughts already drifting ahead to the journey to Spain the following day.

Just dressing Marco in the morning proved to be a feat in itself, as was making his room passably tidy and getting him to the airport. To compound matters, Cenni called me at 7.30am and spoke in a tone which was markedly different from the one he had used the previous evening. He said that Marco had betrayed him, taken him for a ride, and that he couldn't continue to deceive fifty million Italians. I tried to explain to him that Marco definitely hadn't *decided* to become a drug addict, and that he certainly hadn't intended to hide his problem from Cenni or dupe him. In fact, every time he relapsed, he tried to lift himself up again, but the cumulative effect of his disappointments was sapping his strength. He was unable to react, and the problem was exacerbated by this feeling that nothing was being built around him. I remained convinced that our new venture had motivated him and given him a renewed sense of responsibility. The impasse with Christina, however, could not be broken, although Marco now considered it a matter of life and death and more important than anything else. As for the root of his woes, what I know for sure – and the doctors confirmed to me – is that cocaine was only Marco's idea of a quick fix and not his fundamental problem. By the same token, I knew that the cocaine got in the way of our efforts to solve Marco's problems, which were made worse by the effects of the drug. Cocaine was driving a wedge between Marco and his real objectives; it was forcing him into a corner, gnawing away at his ability to regain control of himself. One of the drug's worst effects is that abusers don't acknowledge their illness and, in fact, see cocaine as their only salvation. Marco didn't realise that he had become a slave to the drug: 'I'll give up when I want to,' he would say, but the exact opposite was true.

The car journey to the airport that morning was like a scene from a Shakespearean tragedy. I heard him making strange calls on his mobile: 'They're taking me away. I'm at the airport.' He seemed to be organising a meeting with a dealer to get his hands on a final fill of coke before leaving for Spain. That was my impression and, in fact, when we arrived at the airport, he was quite manic and furious with everyone about the poor organisation. He came up with a million excuses to get away but Vezzani had everything under control. Marco seemed to be waiting for someone, so we tried to get him onto the plane as quickly as possible.

From the airport, I headed straight back to Milan, where I had an appointment with Francesco Cecconi, the sports lawyer, to see where we stood with the investigations in progress, particularly the one relating to Montecatini and the 2001 Giro. There was talk of Marco receiving an eight- or nine-month doping ban. This would ruin his season and Mercatone Uno would effectively 'miss a turn' i.e. receive no return on a year's investment. While I was still with the lawyer, I got a call from Marco: 'I'm in Madrid and I can't work out why I, Marco Pantani, don't have a seat in first class' and with that he turned off his phone. I was caught so off my guard that I didn't have time to reply that internal flights don't have a first class compartment. It wasn't usual behaviour for Marco, who until then had always travelled in economy with the other riders. It was probably a rogue onset of megalomania in reaction to our attempts to keep him on the straight and narrow. Raniero Gradi, the masseur, met up with the team in Spain and told me that Marco had turned up in a pitiful state, that he was talking gibberish at the dinner table. The doctor had reassured us that he was in no danger, but it was obvious that the devastating effects of cocaine were starting to take their toll. Raniero called me again to tell me that Marco had asked for and reluctantly been given permission to take one of the team cars to go and look for a pharmacy. He had crashed into a bus before he was even out of the hotel car park. Raniero probably wanted advice, but I had none to give. The riders Marco Della Vedova, Riccardo Forconi and Simone Borgheresi were also in Spain with Marco, though not Valentino Fois or Ermanno Brignoli – Brignoli had spent a lot of time with Marco and was now quite exhausted. A few days later I sent Marino Amadori as backup for Raniero. The situation wasn't improving, so I persuaded Vezzani to get on a plane and go with me to Spain.

I arrived at the hotel shortly after Marco had come back from his training ride. He looked wan and bedraggled but he had still managed to do six hours on the road and had dropped his team-mates in the hills. That was the real Pantani. He left everyone speechless. After all that he had been through over the previous few days, he could still defy the laws of conventional science, and when natural talents and training weren't enough, his superhuman tenacity would keep him ahead of all but the most exalted competition. He didn't say a word and kept his eyes on the floor. I tried to approach him but he was almost pushing me away. He was holding himself captive.

I took him to his room and, as we climbed the escalator, asked him: 'So then, Marco, how's it going?' 'Manu, it's awful,' he said. 'I'm too far gone. Christina doesn't want me anymore, I'm done with everything, including racing. I can't do anything anymore.' 'Don't talk nonsense, Marco,' I said. 'Let's try to react. You have to find the strength deep down inside, you have to hit back like you used to in the old days. What do you want to do with me? Abandon me with all these boys, these other riders?' He looked into my eyes and said: 'No, you're right. I can't do that. I promised you that I would take my responsibilities and I'll try to do it, but we have to find the right way, because I can't go on like this.' We went to his room and I tried to be frank with him. For the first time, he discussed his addiction openly, even if he still didn't want to hear himself defined 'a drug addict'. Again, I tried to be gentle with him and make him feel at ease, taking care not to judge him but at the same time hoping to give him a jolt. Sometimes I got the impression that he was deliberately exaggerating his behaviour to shock us and to test our loyalty and our love. When he realised that this tactic only made us dig our heels in even further, that we weren't judging or running away, then *he* was the one who came towards *us*. At the end of that conversation, I called Vezzani and told him to go to see Marco immediately, because I felt that he might be unusually receptive. Vezzani stayed with Marco for around two hours. He made him read books on the effects of cocaine on an abuser's brain and on his mental and emotional health. He told him that he had found a doctor, drug addiction expert and psychologist who would agree to treat him, first providing him with a clear diagnosis and then a treatment plan. Marco said only that he would think about it, although he conceded that it was probably a wise thing to do.

The following day we headed back to Italy to meet Mario Pissacroia, the doctor who Vezzani had mentioned to Marco. To persuade Marco to come with us, we used the pretext of a fashion-show to mark the opening of the designer Massimo Rebecchi's new showroom. Rebecchi was a friend of Marco's and had supplied the team's smart clothing for the 2002 season. After the show, we arranged to meet to Pissacroia, who came across as an excellent doctor, in a hotel in Reggio Emilia. A university professor and the author of groundbreaking texts on toxicology and psychoanalysis applied to subjects with addictions rooted in depressive disorders, Pissacroia had practices in Rome and Florence and was a hospital consultant in Reggio Emilia. He submitted Marco to a three-hour initial assessment followed by a series of psychological and attitudinal tests. Pissacroia concluded that Marco's profile was that of a person who had been suffering from depression since early childhood and who was generally in a precarious psychological condition. He didn't see his cocaine addiction as a major problem at that point. What worried him was Marco's level of psychological distress, on which he intended to focus his work. At the same time, he gave us guidelines on how to keep Marco's cocaine abuse under control.

Our almost immediate return to Spain signalled the beginning of more trying times, especially for Raniero. He was one of the few people who managed to get through to Marco, managing to command his respect even if that meant raising his voice. Marco's attempts to flee the hotel continued, followed each time by explosive slanging matches. At least he was training, and by gradually reducing the frequency of his relapses both his body and mind seemed to improve.

The team returned to Italy for its official presentation and everyone agreed that Marco looked in fine fettle. He was relaxed, revitalised and apparently highly determined. Even Cenni was pleased. As promised, we gave him regular progress reports on Marco, on his training rides, the distances he was riding and even data on his heart-rate and oxygen consumption. Manari was a stickler for physiological detail and he monitored every one of Marco's training sessions to check that he was improving. We also reported any cocaine relapses to Cenni, having reaffirmed our pledge to be completely honest with him. Sometime around 10 February, Cenni took me to one side and thanked me for the work we had put into the presentation: everyone had given a very favourable verdict and considered it one of the best presentations of the past twenty years. Most importantly, Marco seemed to be back to his old self. For once, Cenni openly recognised our efforts. Coming from a man who until that conversation had always treated me with a certain amount of disdain, those words were the biggest and best compliment I could have received.

The evening after the presentation, Marco claimed to be in contact with Christina again. As usual, this was enough to set all alarm bells ringing. Shortly afterwards, they met up in Venice and spent a wonderful day together. Unfortunately, no sooner had they got back to Cesenatico, than it all turned sour. They argued, so Marco went out with his friends and bowed to the usual temptation. We returned to Spain and towards the end of February the team started racing.

The first hitch with the team arrived shortly afterwards, on our first assignment. I had put Magrini in charge of logistics but I soon realised that, with the best will in the world, he wasn't cut out for organisation. I can remember Marco storming into my room with a bag of popcorn in his hand and announcing that cycling shoes and other items of kit were missing. It was a disaster. I called Biemme, our clothing sponsor, and within two days had managed to get hold of all the equipment we lacked. Magrini, meanwhile, locked himself in his room for days to avoid facing Marco and the rest of the team, who had already begun to doubt his organisational capacities and lose respect for him.

Quitting the Giro

I was also in Spain for the first race of the 2002 season, the outcome of which was largely satisfactory. For the second race, however, I had gone back to Italy, where I received a call from Magrini on the morning of the race. He said that Marco wasn't starting because of a strain in his back. I snapped back that withdrawing was out of the question and that the sponsors wouldn't put up with yet another no-show. I had explained to the *directeur sportifs* what conditions Mercatone had laid down in sponsorship agreement and that we couldn't be too lenient as a result. Also, it was probably just another classic excuse from Marco, who needed to be dealt with more firmly. Magrini spoke to Marco and instead of encouraging him saw fit to tell him simply that 'Manuela [was] pissed off'. Marco grabbed the phone, called me and yelled a volley of insults down the phone. I gave as good as I got: 'Either you get on your bike and start this race or we'll end this here, because I'm tired of being taken for a ride and you're taking yourself for a ride. Forget about strains, niggles, bad legs, bad back, you've got responsibilities, now go and show that you've got balls!' Podenzana told me later that Marco had tears of rage in his eyes as he told me that he would do thirty kilometres then get off. In fact, it was the only stage in which he rode at the front throughout and finished in the leading group. That was the road to go down with him, even though he bore a grudge against me for the next two weeks. In the end, though, he thanked me.

The mix-ups with Magrini continued. Marco was desperate to compete and do well at the Vuelta Valenciana, but the organisers politely informed us that Magrini had forgotten to send in the form requesting an invitation. Marco was rabid. Granted, Magrini had made a hash of things, but Marco was impossible to reason with. For his part, when he found out that Marco had been told about the mistake, Magrini lost his nerve and couldn't react. He was a fan of Marco, he loved him, and knowing that his idol had a problem with cocaine had certainly affected their relationship. Marco berated him for having lacked modesty and boasted that he could organise everything, when in reality that wasn't the case.

Those were difficult times for me, what with Marco's misadventures, the stress of managing the team's admin and finances, the organisational and logistical shortcomings, and Podenzana and Magrini's limitations. In the meantime, Marco began to follow Mario Pissacroia and Dr Manari's treatment fairly consistently. Manari and Borra were trying to get him used to training with a heart-rate monitor and a mask which measured his oxygen consumption. Manari, who was also the Parma football team's physiologist, had compiled a variety of statistics for Marco and showed me that those relating to oxygen consumption were astonishing. There were perhaps only two other cases like him in the world.

With the season still in its infancy, we organised a long training camp at Monte del Re, at the hotel owned by Mercatone Uno, a few kilometres from Cenni's private residence. We were close, but not too close for comfort, to Cesenatico. In that period Marco seemed significantly better. There had been no more relapses and his prospects of riding the Giro d'Italia looked good. He, however, was taking it for granted that he wouldn't be invited to the Tour. After all his ups and downs, the French had a mitigated opinion of the 1998 Tour champion. We did, though, manage to secure an invitation to Liège-Bastogne-Liège and Flèche Wallonne, the double-header of Belgian Classics organised by the Société du Tour de France. Only a few months old and with few results to point to, the team would hardly be in Belgium on merit, but the Tour decided to give us a boost and invite Marco.

In neither race did Marco cover himself or the team in glory: in one he retired and in the other he never moved from the back of the bunch. Realising that some careful diplomacy was probably in order, I went to speak to Jean-Marie Leblanc to explain in person how the team was organised. Leblanc told me that I had a nerve to come to him asking for an invitation to the Tour after the sorry display Marco had just put on in those two races. Drawing on all my pride and bloody-mindedness, I, in turn, tried to convey to Leblanc how important an invitation to the Tour would be for Marco. Naturally I didn't enter into the topic of any personal ill-feeling they might harbour for each other after the controversy surrounding Marco's non-selection in 2001; I just spoke about Marco's bouts of depression and his lack of motivation. I explained the philosophy behind the team, its structure and why we had created it. Leblanc was impressed, but he emphasized that he would make his choices on the basis of what he saw in the races leading up to the Tour and in the Giro d'Italia. Had Marco ridden a good Giro, therefore, the Tour would have been a possibility.

At the Monte Del Re training camp, we completely reviewed and overhauled the team's management set-up: after Magrini's gaffes, Marco wanted to see Marino Amadori take the reins. Instead of lightening the mood, however, the changes only made the atmosphere in the team more strained. My endless search for a second sponsor also kept leading me down blind allies. This was the catalyst for a huge row between Marco and I at Monte del Re in which I threatened to drop everything. We made peace a few weeks later.

It just so happened that in the days leading up to the Giro the first punishments relating to the Montecatini doping enquiry were due to be made public. After all the hard work, it was yet another blow to our morale, as suddenly even Marco's participation in the Giro looked under threat. There were rumours of an eight-month ban. 'Every time I try to get back on my bike and look forward, there's someone who pulls me back. It's as though destiny has it in for me or someone is determined to take away my credibility.'

There was delay after delay until finally the announcement was postponed until after the Giro. Meanwhile, Ermanno Brignoli was suspended for alleged doping offences dating from the 2001 Giro: just a few days short of the 2002 event, Marco's most loyal *domestique* was out of the race. Brignoli had a weak character and was too easily influenced by Marco, but his intentions were always good and he was crazy about Marco. Brignoli himself had seen a whole winter's preparation go up in smoke and his absence from the team destabilised Marco. We set off for the Giro already on the back foot.

The 2002 Giro began, perversely enough, in Holland. From the minute we arrived in the Low Countries it was a turbulent ride, not least because of a long-running saga concerning our mode of transport. A couple of months before we were due to set off, Marco had suddenly piped up that he wanted a team coach at all costs, since all of the other teams had one, while we had a camper van. And Marco Pantani's team couldn't be seen travelling to and from races in a camper van: it was bad for the image and it was uncomfortable on long trips. Marco sent me to ask Mercatone Uno to find and pay for a coach – which to him seemed logical as the bigger vehicle gave the sponsor a bigger surface to plaster with its logos – but I received a blunt 'no'. In their opinion it was a frivolous expense and in PR terms the company preferred to keep a low profile, or at least an unostentatious one. If Marco wanted a coach, he would have to pay for it. We barely had the budget to cover the outgoings we had forecasted at the beginning of the year and even then we had turned somersaults to make the sums add up. But Marco had got the idea into his head and wouldn't be moved, so it was up to me to go looking for a coach.

A short time later, Borra assured me that he could find something second hand from a Formula One team, while Magrini was adamant that he'd take care of it. This was all well and good, but a month before the Giro there was still no coach. In the end it was me who, after doing the rounds of the dealerships in the Milan area, found one second hand, for we simply couldn't afford a new one. It cost us around 200,000 million lira to buy and refurbish. A garage in Varese, in the north-west of Italy, worked around the clock to get it ready for me in time for the Giro. And, apart from the odd cosmetic detail, it really was perfect.

As if this wasn't enough, a few days before the Giro, a 'phenomenon' called Michael Rocky – how else could you define someone with a name like that? – a car salesman from near Cesena, saw fit to tell Marco that he would need bodyguards during the race. According to Michael, everyone had it in for Marco and he should take precautions against the threat of 'attacks'. Michael and three of his pals would therefore make it their duty to watch over him, making sure, for example, that no-one handed him a bottle containing contaminated water. Michael's scare-mongering now made Marco's paranoia all-embracing. We had done all that we could to create a family atmosphere around Marco and now here were his 'friends' – the ones who for some reason disappeared when he was in trouble and only resurfaced when there was a night out in the offing – posing as his guardian angels in front of TV cameras beaming pictures around the world. It was a shameful way to exploit Marco's vulnerability, but they didn't stop there. After a while, they began to draw Marco's attention to the team's organisational flaws. We weren't up to scratch, they said, and Marco needed more support, which they could naturally provide in return for a handsome salary.

So it was that we arrived at the Giro d'Italia with our own high-security escort and the press assuming that I was again behind a cynical ploy to deny both them and the public access to Pantani. Whenever Marco set foot outside the coach or was walked through the hotel reception, he had three shadows next to his own. The more generous brickbats included: 'He should think about winning before he acts like Michael Jackson, and that shambles of a manager should think about managing him better instead of surrounding him with bodyguards.' It goes without saying that I wasn't happy with the state of affairs: a top cyclist should let the public embrace him, almost literally, not keep himself at arm's length. Worse still, we were dealing with arrogance personified. One of Marco's 'crew' even had the audacity to offer his services as the team manager: in his opinion, a woman couldn't manage a team and command a man's respect.

I felt that we were flirting with disaster. In the face of Marco's many demands, all that we could do – I, Fabrizio, Manari and the nucleus of the group – was to try to strike a compromise between firmness and compliance.

That Giro was the second in a row which neither Marco nor his fans would later remember with any fondness. Perhaps even those of us who were familiar with his problems would have expected a little more from him. He had trained hard in the lead-up to the race with excellent if slightly inconsistent results in fitness tests in April and May. Admittedly, the mood that had taken hold of the team shortly before the Giro hadn't helped him. I became so fed up at one point that I ordered Michael and his friends to pack their bags. I was completely exhausted: 'Go home, all of you, because I can't put up with this circus any longer.' I obviously raised Marco's heckles because, predictably, his foot-soldiers marched off to tell him that I'd thrown them out, that I'd mistreated them and so on. Woe betide anyone who upset Marco's friends. He didn't say a single word to me in the last ten days of the Giro. Perhaps for the first time I saw hatred in his eyes when he looked at me. Then, one day, for no apparent reason, Marco suddenly declared that he wanted to change lawyers, that he didn't want Cecconi any more, that he didn't trust him any more. It turned out it wasn't the whimsical change of heart that we had first thought, and that Michael Rocky had given him the idea. Rocky had suggested that he call for his lawyer, who promptly came to meet Marco on one of the rest days of the Giro. Marco told him that he wanted an aggressive lawyer who would stop at nothing to defend him. As Marco's manager, I was duty-bound to attend that meeting, which I had played no role in organising and to which I neither could nor wanted to contribute.

The following day, Marco got off his bike and abandoned the Giro d'Italia. I found him in his hotel room. He told me that he felt empty, that he couldn't go on. He said that he wasn't well – he had been suffering from bronchitis and had had a high temperature for several days – and a whole series of things were demoralising him. That night there was a drugs raid in the hotel and our team doctor, Vezzani, was questioned by the police. A few days later, Vezzani received notification that he was under formal investigation. The raids were almost certainly ordered on the back of the Mercatone Uno rider Roberto Sgambelluri testing positive for the banned substance Aranesp at the start of the Giro. A few hours later – with the usual impeccable timing – we received the latest news from the Trento enquiry: having initially been considered the offended party in the 'crimes' of Madonna di Campiglio, Marco had become the suspected perpetrator and was accused of sporting fraud. When he found out, he could scarcely believe it, remarking ruefully: 'They were just waiting... always on time, our friends.' True to form, he then tried to vent all his anger by turning it on everyone and everything around him. 'We have to start again from scratch here. The team's no good, we need a new sponsor, a multinational. In fact, we need more than one sponsor.'

With great difficulty, I persuaded him to do a press conference. He had no desire to speak to the press, no desire to speak to anyone, he just wanted to go home. In the meantime, he insisted on telling us all that Michael and his friends had assured him that they could obtain an itemised list of telephone conversations from Madonna di Campiglio, and by cross-referencing the details of all of the telephones they would definitely be able to work out who had betrayed him. They would have put anything into his head if it meant that they could fleece him for more money.

Even for someone who by now was used to these sad spectacles involving Marco, the press conference was excruciating: 'I'm leaving the Giro d'Italia, and they won't invite me to the Tour. I'll probably train for the Vuelta, and in the meantime I'll work towards next year. I'll carry on riding as long as I have a top class team, because this one isn't that.'

As usual, we tried to keep him away from Cesenatico. But after months and months of training camps and time away from home, he protested that he wasn't a parcel and we couldn't move him from one hotel to another at will. He wanted to take time out to think, to weigh up whether he could get back together with Christina, and to catch up with friends. The usual reasons, the usual excuses. But obviously no-one could force him to do anything. He went back to Cesenatico and for a few days led the life of a beach bum, apparently with no adverse consequences.

11

Presumed Guilty

That summer I organised for Ermanno Brignoli to stay at Pantani's house in an effort to give Marco some company which wasn't his own demons. 'Il Brigno', as Marco called him, was what you would call a diamond, even though he let Marco influence him rather too much. He was, though, the only one willing to stay with Marco and was genuinely fond of him. Brignoli was with Marco on the day the Italian Cycling Federation's (FCI) disciplinary committee was meeting to decide whether Marco would face a doping sanction. Marco's new lawyer from Rimini, Veniero Accreman, was keen for Marco to attend because in his opinion the Italian Olympic Committee (CONI) and the FCI would have appreciated the gesture and therefore been more inclined to acquit him.

Marco's reaction was typical: in his view, him being there would have no effect on the outcome of the case and would only stoke up more hysteria in the media. He had now done his very own Giro d'Italia of courtrooms and police stations and he was sick of it. He had already been questioned in Rome by the public prosecutor Giacomo Aiello about the syringe found in what was taken to be his hotel room and had been miffed at Aiello's arrogance, which seemed to follow the assumption that Marco was guilty. Marco told me that even the secretary transcribing the interrogation was embarrassed. Marco's temper had finally boiled over: could he reasonably have been foolish enough to leave a syringe in a bin in his hotel room when magistrates from all over Italy were already snapping at his heels? These interviews drove him crazy, which was why, given the option to stay at home, he didn't need time to decide.

In Rome, Accreman began his address by apologising for Pantani's absence and remarking that panic could play cruel tricks on people.

When I heard about this later, I buried my head in my hands. Marco received an eight-month ban.

The Montecatini affair, like many of the others involving Marco, was laced with mystery. In the hotels where the team stayed, it was routine for a list of riders and their room numbers to be displayed in a prominent position in reception. Most teams followed and still follow an identical procedure. The only difference at Merctone Uno was that Pantani's room number was always exchanged with that of another rider on the list. No-one remembered having seen Marco come out of the room where the syringe had been found that 26 May in 2001 in Montecatini Terme. In addition, before Accreman replaced him as Marco's lawyer, Francesco Cecconi had gathered together a series of testimonies indicating that it hadn't been Marco's room. Cecconi also requested a DNA analysis on Marco's behalf because Pantani was certain that the syringe wasn't his. Alas, it would all be in vain as the FCI judges imposed the ban for presumption of guilt, deeming that, if not conclusive, the evidence weighing against Pantani was certainly well-founded.

On 17 June 2002 the FCI's appeals commission lifted Marco's ban in what turned out to be a hollow moral victory for Marco: the International Cycling Union (UCI) reacted to the announcement by appealing to the Court for Arbitration in Sport (CAS) to re-instate the ban, and when they refused, the UCI declared sniffily that they didn't recognise the CAS's authority to impose sanctions anyway. A compromise of sorts was struck in March 2003 when the CAS agreed not to cancel Pantani's ban but instead to reduce it to six months and, hey presto, the UCI decided that the CAS wasn't such a creditless bunch after all. By this time Marco had already served his half-year in the doping doghouse so could return to racing.

Amid all the political posturing, the fundamental issue of whether Marco was guilty or innocent became obscured. I would just like to point out that, later in 2003, at the Giro d'Italia, I met the FCI appeal's commission magistrate who first tried to overturn Marco's ban in June 2002. He merely repeated to me what he had told the press a year earlier: the guilty verdict was inexplicable, since there 'was no certain evidence against Pantani, only assumptions'.

At the time, coming as it did on the back of Marco's horror-show at the 2002 Giro, the announcement of the ban was ruinous for Marco's motivation. I was afraid that Marco could finally implode. Financially, too, we could be facing meltdown, because the team's backers had clearly invested in a team built *around* Marco. Sure enough, some sponsors saw the ban as a license to consider their contracts null and void and to block their payments. This proved what a risky strategy it had been to stake everything on Marco. Belatedly, very belatedly, it was occurring to us that perhaps it would have been a good idea to tuck a few more cards up our sleeve.

This said, we knew that everything we had planned and done that season had been geared primarily towards giving Marco psychological support. Results were our second priority. It's obvious to anyone that a team with several leaders has more potential than one built around a single rider, but, at the time, Marco would have interpreted the signing of another leader to target the Classics as a vote of no confidence. More than once we had tried to get through to him that spreading our risks would also mean lightening his load of responsibility, but he wouldn't entertain the idea; he was happier living under that burden than the onerous hunch that he no longer enjoyed the unconditional faith of Mercatone Uno.

I can remember getting into the car and rushing to Papeete, a famous beach in the upmarket Milano Marittima resort, north of Rimini. I gave Marco the news of the ban, upon which his posture slumped like a beachball deflating, he reached for his motorbike and sped off into the distance. They were a horrendous few seconds.

For several weeks that summer, Marco was simply unmanageable. He said that he was unhappy with the way the team was run and was adamant that we needed a powerful sponsor, a multinational which would give us more muscular support, especially politically. Some friends had given him the idea that he needed a manager with a world-class reputation and world-class financial resources to match. I responded by sending him a letter explaining that I could step down in favour of someone with these qualities if he wished. I reminded him that there was nothing I wouldn't do for his wellbeing and, if I was only to be a cardboard cut-out, an apparition, I'd rather not be in the job; I could and would stay his friend for life in any case. What Marco couldn't do was lay any of the blame for how his doping case had been handled at my door, as he had chosen the new lawyer. Marco justified himself by saying that, even if he had hired the best lawyer in the world, it wouldn't have helped because by now they'd decided to kick him out at all costs.

He eked out one of his customary disappearing acts over several days. I then saw him in Cesenatico for a meeting with Mario Pissacroia, the new psychologist; Tonina and Paolo had told me that their concern was growing and that we needed to accelerate the process. Marco's visits to his sister Manola's house, where he would give full vent to his anger, were becoming more and more frequent. With his nephews, he seemed able to hide his anguish under a kind-hearted veneer, but it didn't take many scratches to reveal the sadness beneath the surface.

Pissacroia persuaded him to go to a private clinic in Rome for a general check-up and detox to purge the ill-effects of a fresh round of cocaine binges. A few days later, I left Milan at five o'clock in the morning, went to fetch Marco in Cesenatico and took him to Rome. It was a struggle, to say the least. When I arrived, he wasn't so much walking as staggering about the house; he was touchy and confrontational, especially with his parents. In Rome we stopped to buy some fruit and some new pyjamas. We arrived at the clinic but he didn't want to set foot inside the door. He wanted me to take him home. Finally Pissacroia arrived and we overcame his resistance. The doctors sent me away, so I got back into the car to drive back to Milan, but a few minutes later Marco called to ask me to go and pick him up immediately because he didn't want to stay. I didn't give in, but four days later I had to go back to fetch him because, after an encouraging assessment, he had asked to go home. That evening he called me two or three times to check that I'd got back to Milan safely, realising that I had driven from Milan to Rome and back via Cesenatico in a single day, a distance of well in excess of 1,200 kilometres. When he worried too much about me, though, I started to get edgy, because I knew that he was doing it to throw me off the scent. The following morning, my suspicions were confirmed when I discovered that he had gone to see his so-called friends, the usual suspects, on a 'shopping trip'. I could easily imagine the rest. He then locked himself away at home for several days, and Brignoli despaired more and more.

The tone was set for the entire summer. I became more and more angry and sent him letters saying that I had to be able to find him before I could manage him. Through Brignoli, Marco made it clear that he wanted to be left in peace, that he needed time to think, and that he didn't want any contact with me for some time.

This gave me the perfect excuse, albeit an unhappy one, to go on holiday to Croatia with my husband. I needed to let off steam. I was absolutely exhausted and for a month I had no more news of Marco. Occasionally, I would call Tonina, who was anxious because Marco had rented an apartment in the centre of Ravenna, around 35 kilometres north of Cesenatico, to be close to Christina. Even his parents weren't seeing him apart from on the odd occasion when he would pop into the snack bar just to say a quick 'Ciao'. I can't say for sure, but while Tonina told me that he had looked surprisingly good whenever she had seen him, I don't think a day went by that summer without Marco taking cocaine. On 26 August, while my husband and I were on our way back from Croatia, I got a message on my answering machine: 'Ciao, it's Marco. I wanted to know where you are, how you are and tell you how I am, so if you want to come and see me in Cesenatico…' I called Tonina, who asked me to visit as soon as I could: Marco had come back from Ravenna, he was in bad shape again and her dismay was growing.

That week Marco was involved in a car crash, one of the many which, like his drug taking, became the punctuation marks of an otherwise shapeless existence. His mind had been anywhere but on the road, under the effects of cocaine and yearning for Christina. Soon, these accidents became another bane of his life which continued to haunt him until he died and added to his conviction that fate and other people were conspiring against him. I can remember one of the many sleepless nights he spent at my house, and him asking: 'Why do they always accuse Pantani? I have never hurt anybody. I've pulled people out of accidents! Why do they always judge me so harshly?'

The morning after Tonina's call, I was already in Cesenatico. I saw Marco as I had never seen him before. All hope, all life seemed to have drained out of him. He admitted: 'I've gone into a tunnel which you wouldn't believe. I'm becoming so exhausted that it's scaring me. I'm scared that I don't have the strength to go back. Pissacroia's useless, too.' He didn't even mention cycling anymore, nor the team, nothing. And his usual obsessions – Christina and his feeling of emptiness – were only exaggerated by the effects of the drug.

Between them, doctors and clinics didn't seem to have offered an effective solution. I decided, then, to turn to an athlete in my agency's client portfolio, Renato Da Pozzo, originally a mountaineer who had now moved into other extreme sports. I knew that Renato had rented a house in Norway where he treated people with stress or drug problems with his very own twist on outward bound therapy. There were three key ingredients in his recipe for physical and psychological wellbeing: total immersion in the unpolluted Norwegian countryside, exercise and meditation. His aim was to restore the link between body and mind, the human being and nature. His name for the project – 'Thanks Mum', with 'Mum' meaning 'Mother Nature' – was almost a statement of a mission to recreate the innate harmony which modern life had taken away from his subjects. I explained all of this to Marco and persuaded him to go to Norway.

After that conversation he called me, then sent me a text message which I'll never delete from my mobile phone. It said: 'Manu, you're my number one friend!'

I made all the necessary arrangements with Renato and decided to go with Marco. We had booked to fly from Milan to Oslo. The following morning we would take a connection from Oslo to Bodö and then from Bodö to Narvik. Narvik is a tiny village in the extreme north of Norway: here, we would hire a car then drive across the fjords to the house which Renato shared with his girlfriend. The day we were due to leave, I drove to Cesenatico with my husband. On the way, Marco called, sounding quite bizarre. When I arrived he was in a terrible state. While his parents were busy packing his suitcase, he opened the front door and greeted me with a fusillade of abuse: 'Last night I heard on the news that there had been an accident and that Christina was involved. You lot didn't tell me! It's your fault. Last night Christina came to see me, she left me a list of everyone who was guilty and your name was on it.' At this point, my husband butted in: 'Marco, if Manuela has done something, tell her and we'll solve this right here.' 'You shut up, you're on the guilty list, too.' He was completely out of his mind. At first, we tried to keep him calm, but this was an extreme sport in itself and soon I was exhausted. I threatened to go back to Milan and cancel the trip, but he kept saying that he wanted to go. I didn't feel like spending time alone with him, but at the same time I didn't want to leave him with his parents who were imploring me to take him away because they didn't know how to deal with him any more.

My husband and I looked at each other: we had the same idea. Paolo would come with us to Norway. He called work and asked for a few days holiday. We drove back to Milan and stopped just long enough to pack his suitcase then all three of us piled back into the car and headed for the airport. Marco slept at every given opportunity: in the car on the way to the airport, on the plane, in the taxi on the way to the hotel. He ate, slept and gulped down pills. In Olso we boarded a plane bound for Bodö and from there took another flight to Narvik. Paolo had to literally hold Marco to keep him on his feet.

We hired a car then set off for Renato's house. The landscape was spellbinding but I was afraid that it wasn't the best tonic for Marco in his current state of mind. When we arrived, he started to get cocky: 'How the hell can anyone live here? Madness. I'd never stay here.' Renato set about tackling the problem head on, explaining the difficulties often encountered by a sportsman who can no longer channel his energies in the right way and how devastating this can be. He talked to Marco about how the system had created him then destroyed him. 'You're someone who can't hit back when you're attacked. They knew where to aim, where to strike, but you need to respond with actions. If you choose cocaine, be aware that cocaine has these effects.' He didn't pull any punches: 'If you want to self-destruct, buy yourself a lorry-load of cocaine, go away somewhere and do what you've got to do. Don't involve everyone in your private enterprise. If you turn to other people to help you then you have to show some balls, you have to react. Make a choice, you can't have your cake and eat it – involve other people and then do whatever you want.' He was very direct, but what he said seemed to have a profound effect on Marco. He took a few days to decide and, in any case, Renato didn't have an immediate vacancy. It therefore became a fact-finding mission. We went back to our hotel and that evening Marco seemed willing, although he was already slipping in veiled criticisms of Renato and his company. The following morning, he knocked on my door at nine o'clock, looking as though he had seen a ghost. 'I couldn't find you. I thought that you'd abandoned me, because I'm not staying here.' He was terrified.

We spent three or four days touring the fjords, each framed in a landscape as desolate and symbolic of Marco's current outlook as the next. We then stayed for a couple of days in Tromsö, the town where tourists flock every winter for a spectacular view of the Northern lights. Rather than go straight back to Italy, Marco wanted to visit Christina's sister in Copenhagen, where we duly spent a couple of days traipsing around the city in almost funereal silence. Marco spent a long time talking to Christina's sister, clearly in the hope of yet another truce. Perhaps because he was under our surveillance 24 hours a day, and despite his generally dark mood, we noticed that he was getting better every day over the ten days we spent in Scandinavia. Slowly, ever so slowly, a certain inner mettle seemed to be returning.

We flew back to Italy and he asked me if we could go with him to Saturnia for a few days. He wanted to relax, discuss our plans for the future and his cycling career. To be truthful, I was more interested in his personal recovery than a sporting comeback, but I said yes. We left for Cesenatico and went to see his parents who were happy to see that he was so much better than in the week before the trip to Norway. We had time for a quick snack then set off for Saturnia. We stayed for around ten days in Marco's beautiful house – a small, pink cottage perched on a hill rising under a blanket of olive trees – living the 'country life' among the humble, uncomplicated local people. We even worked like them. I said to Marco: 'You're a bit spoilt, you don't do anything. You have to learn to appreciate what you have, take care of it and not make your dad do everything.' The next morning I got up, did some housework, then we cut the grass and collected it in bundles. We toiled to the tune of laughter. When we weren't giggling, Marco worked like a demon, as though instead of scrub he was scything away at the people who had hurt him. Then, at four o'clock we showered and went to the spa baths in town, where we stayed until eight o'clock in the evening, thinking. It became our daily routine. At dinner, we talked about everything, from morality to people in the team to sponsors to manners to the depth of sentiments. Marco was blessed with great sensitivity, although often he found it difficult to express. He had many passions, but after the events of Madonna di Campiglio he had changed and lost interest in cultivating his interests, such as fishing and hunting. After ten days, the idyll ended and I would have been returning to another version of domestic bliss in Milan were it not for the ongoing problems with Mercatone Uno which now needed to be addressed.

Some time later that summer, I went back to see Marco in Saturnia, where he had stayed, to discuss our plans with regard to Mercatone Uno and other matters. In the intervening period, I had detected a change in his voice on the telephone. I arrived at his house and found him there with some friends from Cesenatico. He hardly needed to tell me that he had relapsed. I was so angry that I barely set foot inside the porch before getting back in the car and going back to Milan. He spent that autumn oscillating between Copenhagen – in another desperate attempt to rebuild his relationship with Christina – Saturnia and Cesenatico. It certainly wasn't one of his happier periods.

Cipollini's proposal

At around the same time, Mario Cipollini's victory in the World Championships in October 2002 briefly looked like shaping the destiny of Marco's career. In the weeks leading up to the race, Vincenzo Santoni, manager of Cipollini's Acqua e Sapone team, had privately organised to meet Cenni to propose a merger between Mercatone Uno and his sponsor. Simply put, he had told Cenni that he wanted to help

Pantani because he believed in him. Cipollini soon got wind of the possible fusion and declared after winning the Worlds that he wanted to help Pantani and wanted him in his team. In the public's eyes, the ever popular Cipollini therefore looked like the one who had taken the initiative to help Pantani; in private, Cipollini had apparently been nonplussed with Santoni's idea.

When I told Marco about Cipollini's cupboard love, he laughed: 'Yeah, come on, another one of Mario's specials. At the 1999 Giro he called me at midnight to organise a protest against the overlapping blood tests, then I was left hanging out to dry on my own because he and the others wimped out. He called me about stopping the Giro in San Remo after the raids in 2001, when I had already pulled out of the race, but in the end Candido Cannavò won him round and he became the saviour of the Giro. And he was the one who had dragged me into it to put our weight behind the protest! Let's forget about the ethical code and things like that: Cipollini's always turned his back on me.' As if any translation was needed, Marco meant that he didn't attach any weight to what Cipollini said.

At around the same time, Fabrizio Borra had privately asked Marco whether he could massage Cipollini, who had basically head-hunted him. Working with Cipollini, Fabrizio had managed to build that relationship of mutual trust which often forms between a professional cyclist and his masseur. On this basis, Fabrizio told me that Mario seemed sincere and that, together with his team-mates Giovanni Lombardi and Mario Scirea, he really wanted to try to help Marco. I let myself be convinced and I tried to explain to Marco that it could be the right solution. I had also persuaded him to attend the Tour de France presentation that autumn. The 2003 Tour would mark the race's hundred-year anniversary and all of the 21 living Tour champions were to gather for the event. On the day of the presentation, Marco had a long conversation about depression with Greg Lemond, whose son had suffered from the illness. There was no need to say anything to 1958 champion Charly Gaul; the two had met before, their mutual admiration was firmly established, and they could communicate with the kind of knowing wink and handshake which said more than any words. Being placed among such exalted company seemed to give Marco some perspective of his past achievements, and, briefly, he felt re-engaged with the sport which he had once loved more than life itself. He was happy.

In Paris, after the presentation, Santoni wanted to talk to Marco about his proposal, but Marco said that before taking a decision he wanted to discuss the matter with Cipollini. He called Mario on his mobile phone. Cipollini didn't seem as enthusiastic as he had after his World Championship just a few weeks earlier, but he nonetheless agreed to meet Marco the following day in Monte Carlo. A few hours later, I got a call from Mauro Battaglini, Cipollini's manager, who was furious at me for allowing Marco to take the liberty to call Mario and not him. I replied that Pantani could call who he wanted and reminded him of our duties towards our clients. I sensed that things weren't going as they should have been. Cipollini postponed the meeting several times through Battaglini, which only added to Marco's cynicism. Every time Cipollini's camp changed the arrangements, Marco looked at me as if to say 'what did I tell you?'

Later, Battaglini was probably called to order by Santoni, who wanted to revive the flagging negotiations. When Marco had told him clearly in Paris that if he was to come to any agreement, it would be with Cipollini himself, Santoni had snarled that Mario did what *he* said in the team so there was no need for Mario to be involved in the talks. In the event, the long-awaited meeting between Cipollini and Pantani never took place, to the immense disappointment of the press in particular. Marco was too proud to make the first move and he also smelt a rat in Santoni's proposal. He would never have signed for Santoni's team without first finding out what Cipollini believed was in it for him.

We returned from Paris and, in Marco's case, to the loneliness of his bedroom – the torture chamber where insomnia was just one of the available punishments, most of which were self-inflicted. That autumn, his relapses became more and more frequent. His parents decided to call on Bianco, a close family friend and a fixture in Marco's life ever since childhood. Marco, like everyone else, admired Bianco's wisdom, and Bianco, in turn, worshipped Marco. Bianco suggested that the two of them go on holiday together with their respective families. They would pack up the Pantanis' camper van and go to Greece on a hunting trip, Bianco said. Marco accepted and so the five set off.

Meanwhile, I tried to realistically consider our prospects for the following season. Cenni remained convinced that the only way to rouse Marco was to put him alongside a rider like Cipollini. That year, Mario had won Milan–San Remo and the World Championships, he was still highly motivated, plus it would be a huge coup in PR terms to unite Pantani and Cipollini, by some distance the two biggest personalities in Italian cycling. Cenni went as far as to say that if we wanted Mercatone Uno's help, Cipollini must be on board. Marco would prefer me to look for alternatives, which might change Cenni's mind. First, he sent me to speak to Bjarne Riis, manager of the Danish CSC team, in his villa near Lucca. I also spoke to Banesto team manager José Miguel Echavarri, who very politely intimated that he had already had problems with José Maria Jimenez and didn't want another large problem by the name of Marco Pantani. Manolo Saiz, manager of ONCE, said more or less the same thing. We even tried to team up Pantani and Jan Ullrich – in fact there wasn't much we didn't try.

Cenni, though, was steadfast in his view that it was Cipollini or nothing. I gave Marco daily updates and after a while I tried to make him see the light: Cenni had supported him for years, their recent contractual dispute notwithstanding, so perhaps it was time to please him and pursue Cipollini. After several unsuccessful attempts, I got Marco to speak to Mario on the telephone. Cipollini seemed sincere and Marco said to him that if they were to do it, they had to do it together. Cipollini added that *they* should manage the team and not Santoni, otherwise it would be a disaster. Marco finally gave me the green light: 'Go ahead with it. Just as long as everything is clear.'

I soon spoke to Santoni and out of correctness sent him a fax detailing all of the verbal agreements made together and Marco's conditions: his salary (much lower than Marco had expected); the riders who Marco wanted in the team, i.e. Ermanno Brignoli, Daniel Clavero, Roberto Conti and Fabio Fontanelli; the masseur Raniero Gradi and the *directeur sportif* Marino Amadori. Meanwhile, Franco Cornacchia, the Mercatone Uno financial director, had aired his misgivings about the possibility of us working with Vincenzo Santoni. In the sport it was well known that Santoni had gaping holes in his balance sheet and there were suspicions that he was eyeing a Cipollini–Pantani link-up primarily because it would allow him to cover his debts. Indeed, Pantani would have brought a substantial lump sum of around £1.6 million from Mercatone Uno. Others doubted Cipollini and Pantani's motives: Cipollini was coming off a superb year and many commentators doubted that he could rescale the same heights; in Marco's baggage, meanwhile, there was not only Mercatone Uno's money but a string of run-ins with the courts and his cocaine problem, which was by now the subject of persistent rumours in the sport. I was afraid that it would turn out more or less like this: the team would welcome Pantani and the Mercatone millions, but if problems arose the blame would be placed squarely on Marco's shoulders, while Cipollini would maintain his saintly reputation.

Cipollini's strong personality could also cause divisions, for both Cipollini and Pantani would want their say on the composition of the team in major tours and in particular how many *domestiques* they were each assigned. Overall, the proposal offered more negatives than positives. However, I didn't want to thwart Cenni yet again and so very discretely asked Cornacchia to have a quiet word in his ear about Santoni's financial problems. This made sense, too, because it was Cornacchia who had done the background checks on Santoni. Suddenly, though, perhaps because he didn't want to get caught up in the negotiations, Cornacchia claimed that he no longer wanted to be involved with the cycling team. He would help draw up the contract, he said, but he recommended that I go to see Mercatone Uno's lawyers first.

By this stage I was demoralised, but I reminded myself of my objectives, or rather my objective: to look after Marco's interests and no-one else's. I did everything I could to make Santoni confirm the terms of the agreement in writing. Santoni didn't want me sitting in on the talks alongside Cenni, but I wanted clarity on Marco's position before the signature of the sponsorship deal between Santoni and Mercatone Uno. It was Marco, after all, who had 'provided' the sponsor. The evening before the contract was due to be signed, Santoni called me to announce that he might have another sponsor and that he wanted to make a few last-minute amendments to the terms of his agreement with Cenni. I replied that Cenni was a no-nonsense kind of guy and that he didn't like double-dealing, but that Santoni was free to proceed as he wished. I just wanted the contract signed as quickly as possible. Santoni called me the following day to demand ownership of Pantani's image rights: they must belong to him, as Cipollini's did, and not to Marco as I had requested; there was no room for inequalities between the two, said Santoni. My response was that if Battaglini had made Cipollini sign an unrewarding contract, that was his problem. Pantani's image rights had to remain his own. We could then agree to discuss separate terms for every single occasion when Santoni wanted to sell the rider's image to a sponsor. Pantani, though, would have the final say. This was one issue on which I wouldn't compromise.

I got into the car and hurried to see Cenni. I warned him that Santoni had probably signed with another sponsor and that he would more than likely come back and try to entice him into a bidding war. I was only going on what Santoni had told me, rather cryptically, and Cenni was entitled not to believe me. I also reiterated that I would not sell on Pantani's image rights. Cenni agreed that I shouldn't back down. Then I had an idea: if the purchase of Pantani's image rights was a pre-requisite for Santoni forming the team, then I would sell the rights to Mercatone Uno and they would decide how they wanted to manage them. It was the least I could do, I told Cenni, as recognition of their devotion to Pantani over the years. Cenni approved. I stayed there with him to wait for Santoni, who arrived almost two hours late. Cenni was baffled. He had even invited the Italian state broadcaster RAI to film the signature of the contract.

We sat down around a table and Santoni began by apologising for the delay. Cenni, Cornacchia and the respective lawyers nodded in acknowledgement. Santoni certainly wasn't pleased to see me there. The talks ran aground at the first mention of Pantani's image rights. Santoni continued to insist that Pantani and Cipollini should receive identical treatment, while I emphasised the difference between the two. Santoni finally lost his rag and suggested that Pantani was no longer worth anything and I wouldn't make any money out of his image. He maintained that only he could rebuild Pantani's career and that in my hands he wouldn't get back to his best. I couldn't understand him: why did he want Pantani's image rights if he thought that he was finished as a rider? I excused myself for a minute or two because Marco was calling my mobile from Greece. He wanted to know how the meeting was going. He told me not to cave in, said that he trusted me and confirmed that he wasn't prepared to sell his image rights to anyone: he was already bringing £1.6 million worth of sponsorship to the table, so what more did they want? The wrangling came as no surprise to Marco. Cipollini had already warned him that Santoni wasn't the best man to head up the operation. I returned to the meeting and relayed what Marco had said about his image rights. Cenni said that we should move on to the other terms of the contract because, for one thing, an RAI camera crew was waiting outside.

Santoni, though, was categorical: without Pantani's image rights, there would be no deal. His agreement with his mystery 'other' sponsor – whether signed or not at this stage – put him in a position of strength. Santoni then had the gall to say that it was a question of sentiment and not money: he and Cenni were pursuing a common goal to save cycling, he said. Not even Cenni could believe what he was hearing now. He stood up from the table and told Santoni to stop being so bloody sanctimonious.

I drew breath and thought that I'd finally got what I had wanted. I was wrong. Having calmed down, Cenni returned wanting to resume the talks and with a view to putting pen to paper the next day. Everyone could go home to gather their thoughts in the meantime. It was then that Cornacchia suggested Mercatone Uno buying Marco's image rights and managing them in the same way that Juventus had started to do with their star striker, Alessandro Del Piero. In other words, Pantani would retain ownership of the rights but Mercatone Uno would have the first option on selling them to third parties. It would have been a perfect solution for Pantani, too, but Santoni didn't want to know. He agreed with Cenni: all decisions should be postponed until the following day.

After the meeting, Cenni and I found ourselves alone, and he immediately turned on me: I was obsessed with Pantani's image rights,

I had never brought any money into the team and neither would I bring any this time. He hit me with a barrage of insults. I asked him to wait just another fifteen minutes, then he would see who was right. At that exact moment Cenni's mobile started to ring. It was the journalist, Pier Bergonzi, from the *Gazzetta dello Sport*, calling to ask for an update on the negotiations. Cenni wasted no time in laying the blame for the ongoing stalemate on Santoni and I, but then assured Bergonzi that he would soon make sure that a deal was done. After an uncomfortable silence, Bergonzi informed him that Santoni had just reached an agreement with another company, the travel agent Domina Vacanze. Cenni turned white. The humiliation would be hard to live down: he had been made a fool of in his own back yard.

We went to dinner at Monte del Re and Cenni was too proud to thank me straight away. The next morning, Valentini called me to express his thanks for having saved not only Pantani but also Mercatone Uno's reputation. The press took an opposing view: they said that I had shattered the *tifosi*'s dream of seeing Pantani and Cipollini in the same team... I was too preoccupied with Marco's wellbeing to pay any attention. And with Mario Cipollini's – I could have pointed out – because riding in the same team would have been catastrophic for both of them.

A few days later Cenni proclaimed that, having reflected on the way that Santoni had caught him out, he had decided that he didn't want to leave the sport on a such low note. He told the press that he wanted at least another year. Cornacchia responded by suggesting Davide Boifava as team manager. Meanwhile, I still hoped that we could raise more money than Mercatone Uno were willing to put up alone by linking up with Jan Ullrich or the CSC manager Bjarne Riis – even though it wasn't in Mercatone Uno's interests to sponsor a foreign team or to hand over its budget to a team that it wouldn't directly control. Marco wasn't jumping for joy at the prospect of being reunited with Boifava, with whom he had fallen out before leaving Carrera, but he finally agreed, at my prompting, realising that it was the 'least bad' of the alternatives on offer. Boifava assured me that he was genuinely fond of Marco and had great faith in the project. He seemed sincere, so I

shelved all contingency plans and decided that we should go with
Mercatone Uno as our main sponsor. I discussed it with Marco, who
from Greece said that he trusted me. Boifava already had a small second
division team sponsored by the Scanavino wine merchants, who, he
said, could come in as the second sponsor of the new Mercatone Uno
team. The team wasn't automatically invited to the Giro d'Italia, the
Tour and other prestigious races, but Davide promised that, with his
connections and Pantani in the team, there would be nothing to worry
about. Cycling, he would often say, needed Pantani and this need
would open doors.

Mercatone Uno wanted to confine me to a role as Marco's manager
now that Boifava would be taking charge of the team. A veteran of thirty
years in the sport, Boifava had built a reputation as one of the shrewdest
managers in the business and had friends in high places at the UCI. He
even promised to pull some strings to have Marco's ban reduced.

Marco returned to Italy after the Christmas and New Year holidays.
In early January, he booked an appointment with a doctor friend for a
nose operation. In the fall in the 1995 Milan–Turin, among other
injuries, his nasal septum had been displaced and this had affected his
breathing ever since. Snorting cocaine may well have aggravated the
problem. On the same visit to the doctor, Marco also had his ears surgically pinned back. Remembering how Lance Armstrong had ribbed him
during the 2000 Tour de France, he joked: 'Now I'll descend faster and
the American won't be able to call me 'Elefantino' [Dumbo] any more!'

Next, he flew to the Balearic Islands for the first training camp of the
winter. He seemed a changed man: he had returned from Greece with a
poise which he seemed to have irretrievably lost, he was good-natured and
accessible. He had agreed to share a room with another rider – Fabiano
Fontanelli or Roberto Conti depending on the day – after years of
demanding a single room. He was transformed. Boifava was overjoyed, as
were the other riders. Their excitement and determination suddenly
soared. But shortly before the second camp in the Canary Islands, Marco
paid a flying visit to Cesenatico and probably had a relapse. I say 'probably'
because in the first few months of that year I had taken more of a back
seat because, as I already mentioned, Mercatone Uno had asked me to

make way for Davide and my presence at training camps and races could have hindered the development of Marco's understanding with Davide.

But it wasn't long before the cracks began to appear. As mentioned earlier, Davide had promised Marco that he would speak to UCI president Hein Verbruggen in an attempt to reduce the length of his ban. As a first step, we met up with a high-ranking official in the Italian Cycling Federation (FCI), Claudio Santi, with a view to patching up Marco's differences with the authorities and working with them to rehabilitate his image. The diplomacy led nowhere: when Marco finally was eligible to ride, he was denied an invitation to the Tour of Murcia in Spain, for which he had prepared assiduously, and the Tirreno–Adriatico and Milan–San Remo in Italy. Both the Tirreno–Adriatico and Milan–San Remo were organised by RCS, also the owners of the Giro d'Italia, which raised the almost unthinkable possibility of Marco being shut out of the Giro. It was becoming obvious that Boifava couldn't keep his access-all-areas promises and Marco, realising this, began to lose patience.

One of the most delicate aspects of our new deal with Mercatone Uno was the issue of Marco's salary. Mercatone Uno had offered a figure significantly lower than what Marco had received in previous years. It might have been a reasonable estimation of Marco's worth on the road, but it grossly underestimated the value of his image. I arranged a meeting with Cenni and Marco came with me. Cenni shook his hand and said to trust him: for now, he would have to settle for what he was being given, but if things went well Cenni promised that he would be generous. Marco felt reassured and went away satisfied with what at this stage was a gentleman's agreement.

After that meeting, Marco spent several weeks with team-mate Daniel Clavero, first in his house in Madrid then at his seaside villa in the south of Spain. Things were going smoothly, with the exception of Marco's relationship with Boifava: after the broken promises, Ermanno Brignoli had been thrown out of the team to Marco's disgust, he still hadn't received the lightweight wheels he asked for at the start of the year, and Boifava's confident noises about reducing his ban had come to nothing.

Marco made his belated 2003 début at the Coppi e Bartali stage race in March and immediately raised hopes with a fine performance. He then returned with Clavero to Spain, where the only thing that he binged on was training. He relapsed very rarely if at all that spring. In the week before the Giro del Trentino, a key Giro d'Italia warm-up race, Boifava granted him a visit to Cesenatico which Marco had requested on the pretext of needing to see Christina, who had disappeared for months but was suddenly back in town. Marco told me that Christina had got in touch again because she needed some advice on a mortgage. It seemed an unlikely tale to me, but Marco had decided that he would return from Spain via Cesenatico to meet her. It's highly probable that the evening ended in yet another row and that Marco tried to console himself on a night out with his friends. The upshot was that the following day the team had to think up an excuse for Pantani not starting the Giro del Trentino. Marco again retreated to Spain, away from temptation and media scrutiny. The relapse had jeopardised a large part of his training, but the team doctors were still cautiously optimistic. It was Boifava and the team's morale which were worst affected.

We set off for the Giro d'Italia. Marco was highly motivated and the mood in the team buoyant. But things immediately took a turn for the worse. That year, I had been asked not to follow the race with the team, but the evening after the first mountain stage, I received a call from Marco. I was shocked, because when he left for the Giro he usually blocked out everything; he wanted to concentrate solely on the race and never took his mobile phone with him. He was screaming down the phone like a madman. Ever since February he had been asking Boifava, also the owner of the team's bike supplier, Carrera, for a special bike with lightweight wheels, which he wanted to kit out with a revolutionary seven-speed gear system from Shimano. Not only had this never arrived, but the bike Marco found himself riding on the morning of the first mountain stage was similar to those he had used as an amateur a decade earlier. Even worse, the seven-speed gear system turned out to be incompatible with the bike's frame. He was already furious when he pulled up alongside Stefano Garzelli – now riding for Vini Caldirola – at the start and saw that his team was riding on Carrera bikes – manufactured by Boifava – with state-of-the-art wheels and the Shimano gear system. I include these details simply in the interests of historical accuracy and our objective understanding of what happened at that, Marco's last Giro d'Italia.

Marco saw Garzelli ride away from him and I'm sure that he thought: 'They're creating the new Pantani. Garzelli shaves his head like me, his team's jersey is yellow like Mercatone Uno's and Boifava supplies his team's bikes and mine, only his are new and mine old-hat. Plus, everyone knows that Boifava is advising Garzelli behind the scenes.' He confided in me: 'Now everyone knows that I have a coke problem. There's no point in them saying that they believe in me; if they want to create the new Pantani, why don't they just say that and stop making me look like an idiot? Because I make mistakes, but I'm giving it everything I've got: I've been away from home at training camps for months. I'm doing everything I can, giving the team exposure. I'm battling my demons, and it's not all my fault if I've got lost in this tunnel.' Even Cipollini was astonished when he saw Marco's bike and – with the stage ill-suited to his sprinting talents – loaned Marco his pair of lightweight wheels for the day.

Marco was given more reasons to be bitter in that Giro. Every evening he would call me with a new complaint, asking me to pass it on to Cenni. I went to see Romano to explain that Marco felt snubbed and that, when he had taken the matter of the bike up with Boifava, he had been told that before making demands he should learn to behave like a true professional. Boifava hardly needed to elaborate but he seemed to have been waiting for this opportunity: he left Marco in no doubt that he was referring to Marco's cocaine addiction. Cenni agreed that Marco was entitled to feel aggrieved, but said that he couldn't argue with Boifava about Marco's lack of professionalism, at the Giro del Trentino at least. Admittedly, I replied, there was no denying Marco's past mistakes, but, equally, now that he was making every effort to win the Giro d'Italia, it hardly made sense to neglect him citing his drug habit as the reason. I also explained what I now believe was Marco's real problem for years, namely the stigma of being labelled a drug addict. This could undermine not only his already fragile motivation but also his credibility within the team. Cenni took note: he was a cycling fan, he loved Marco and he had grasped the significance of the references to Garzelli. On the other hand, it was his responsibility to mediate and he couldn't defend Marco at all costs, including that of turning the rest of the team against him.

Despite the distractions, Pantani rode well and, had it not been for a tangle, ironically with Garzelli, on the descent off the Sampeyre climb on stage 18 in the Piedmontese Alps, Marco would probably have finished in the top ten overall two days later in Milan. Instead he had to settle for fourteenth, at almost thirty minutes down on winner Gilberto Simoni, and the unparalleled affections of the fans. In one valley on the penultimate stage near Lago Maggiore, an elaborate flower-bed spelling Pantani's name greeted the peloton in every village. Early in that stage, Giovanni Lombardi suggested to Marco that he ask the race leader, Simoni, if he could let him break away from the pack, but Marco refused to rely on any such charity. He launched attack after attack, each one sending a tidal wave of noise gushing through the valley. I was beside myself with excitement and hardly dared look at the television screen. I wanted to see him cross the line alone with his arms aloft. It felt as though I was the one pushing on the pedals. Simoni ended up closing down Marco's final attack to win the stage. If the applause was muted as the Saeco rider uncorked his champagne on the podium, it was cacophonous as Marco crossed the line 44 seconds after Simoni. It was the same wherever Marco raced throughout his career, and no current rider enjoys adulation quite like it.

On one of the last days of the Giro, I was called to a meeting with Romano Cenni, who now seemed prepared to do anything for Marco, even help him to find a way into the Tour de France. The Tour organisers had considered Mercatone Uno unworthy of a wild card to start the race for the third straight year, which left them looking for a short-term merger with a team already qualified by rights.

Also towards the end of the Giro, Marco said to me one morning: 'Kids look into my eyes wanting to see a role model... But what am I?... I represent a world wrapped up in pure hypocrisy, which I wasn't strong enough to rebel against. Until I can reclaim my dignity and unite all of my fellow riders to restore some honour to cycling, I don't feel like I deserve this much love and admiration.' The depth of his feelings was sometimes remarkable. Often, he would call me in the evening after a mountain stage that hadn't gone as well as he'd wanted to reassure me that before the end of the Giro he would pull out something special. He could be so touching at times and I, in turn, told him not to worry: 'Marco, sweetheart, even if you haven't won anything this has been one of your best Giros. From the fans' point of view, you have no obligation to win. They love your riding, your honesty, your commitment and your grit. You excite them, move them, and they love you for that.'

Since his death, I've often thought about the times when Marco's words would offer glimpses of what I believe to be the secret of his tragedy: the life he had sacrificed to realise the dream of becoming cycling's undisputed 'king of the mountains'. He was born to be number one and he had succeeded thanks to enormous sacrifices, an exceptional capacity to go beyond the pain barrier and amazing sporting talent. All of a sudden, one day he felt as though he were thrown off a pedestal as high as a skyscraper by the world to which he had devoted his life. Cycling had abandoned him, dumped him in a corner, treated him like any old criminal. Stereotyped him as the dope-cheat par excellence.

I still ask myself *why* Marco and why, after Madonna di Campiglio, did some people assume that he had been a fraud all along. He had been winning almost since the day he started racing as a boy, he had saved the Tour de France and won it in its 'cleanest' year. He had revived a flagging sport, mesmerising millions in front of their TV screens all over the world. He could and should have fought back but he didn't have the strength to. As if this wasn't enough, he had spiralled into drug addiction, perhaps after a friend or friends had told him: 'take some of this, it'll do you good'. Cocaine wasn't just a bad habit for Marco. It had eventually become an incurable illness in its own right which had forced him into a corner and enslaved him to his own nightmares and insecurities. Marco used cocaine as a punishment for having let everyone down, for having lost his girlfriend, for having exposed his family to the criticism of the press, and out of his fear of having lost honour as a sportsman and as a man. He had gone into his shell and was frightened to come out and face judgement. He felt ashamed of having accepted the rules which his sport had bent and moulded according to who it wanted to save and who it didn't. These thoughts and the questions they raised tortured him. And he wanted answers. He had been tossed away like a rotten apple, apparently the only one. Meanwhile cycling went on its merry way, seemingly following the script of the Sicilian dramatist Luigi Pirandello's famous comedy about role-playing, *The Rules of the Game*.

It's hard to image how much Marco could have suffered in the last few years of his life. The thought of not being able to alleviate his pain drove me crazy. I couldn't come up with answers to his questions. Words were no longer enough. Nor was love. And strictness certainly wasn't. Marco wanted to shout out his desperation but the fear of no-one believing him had taken away his voice. He had a mountain to climb to reclaim his dignity and for once he was destined to come up short.

After the final stage to Milan, he was invited to appear on RAI's post-race analysis programme, *Processo alla Tappa*. He arrived on set clearly agitated and anxious to be interviewed straight away so that he could head back to Cesenatico. Christina had come to see him twice during the Giro, leaving him under the mistaken impression that she wanted them to get back together. Marco had even toyed with the idea of buying a house in Spain and going to live there with her. That evening he couldn't wait to go back to see her. He left Milan in a car with Marino Amadori, who later told me that Marco called Christina several times on the way to Cesenatico, but without success. When she finally did pick up she told him that they wouldn't be seeing each other that night because she would be at the nightclub in Siena where she was once again working as a podium dancer. Marco was distraught. They met up the following evening. That was apparently when she told Marco that she didn't want to be with a drug addict, then she promptly left.

Marco suffered a relapse from which he never really recovered. It was as though he couldn't accept yet another failure, this time a senti-mental one. Moreover, he was convinced that other people had driven them apart and that, had he not been robbed of his dignity, the relation-ship with Christina would have worked. He was also afraid for her.

Every now and again he would call her to see if she needed money, to find out where she was working, and whether she needed a car or some help to pay the rent on her flat. He was always very thoughtful towards her – sometimes unbelievably so – which added to Marco's parents' frustration.

12

The Lonely Pirate

Through the thick and ominous clouds hanging over Marco and the team's future in 2003, there was one cloud with a silver lining. At the beginning of the year I had visited Marco and the team at the ritual winter training camp in the Canary Islands. I had constantly felt nauseous, which I took to be a symptom of some kind of mild food poisoning, perhaps from some rotten seafood. I went home and, after a few days, my husband and I were overjoyed to discover that our first child was on its way. I phoned Marco: 'Marco, guess what, are you sitting down?' And him: 'You're pregnant!' He was ecstatic, surprisingly so as I knew that he could often be jealous and quite possessive with friends. I also think that he was afraid that this new responsibility would limit the time and attention I could devote to him. When Marco returned from the training camp and we held a first team meeting in Brescia, we went together for a post-operation check-up on his nose and eyes and I showed him the first ultrasound scan of my son. In his excitement, Marco started preparing for his role as adoptive uncle: 'I'll be Uncle Fester', he would say, coining the nickname which he later insisted we use in the last days he ever spent in my house.

Although I was pregnant, I continued my work as usual. I went to see Marco at the training camps, I fought tooth and nail to have Brignoli reinstated when Boifava and Mercatone Uno didn't want him, and I was present in Lecce for the start of Giro and for a few of the later stages, naturally taking the necessary precautions.

It was during the summer that Marco again disappeared off my radar. After the Giro d'Italia he waited for Mercatone Uno to give him an answer on whether he could compete in the Tour, as we had already discussed with Cenni at the Giro. Marco was sure that the only solution would be for him to temporarily join a team which was already invited to France. There were two avenues worth pursuing in his eyes: the first was Jan Ullrich's Bianchi team, whose financial difficulties left it needing investment of exactly the type which Pantani's presence might attract; the second and more plausible option was a fusion of Mercatone Uno with Stefano Garzelli's Vini Caldirola which would end when the Tour did. Marco said that he would speak to Stefano in the hope of coming to an arrangement.

He was prepared to do anything to go to the Tour. It wasn't flattering, relying on other people's favours and Marco would naturally have preferred to go to the Tour through the 'main entrance'. It wasn't a superiority complex that he was trying to maintain, only his dignity: Marco always drew an analogy with someone who bought a degree certificate and hung it on the living room wall. 'I want to go to the Tour on merit. I think that I *do* deserve to go after doing a creditable Giro and – although I didn't win – showing that I was improving in the last few stages. I could be in top form for the Tour.' Deep down, he felt as though he had earned the right to go to France. At the same time, other factors demotivated him completely: for example, the fact that Cenni would be forced to pay out of his own pocket for him to join another team, the fact that Mercatone Uno didn't realistically rate his chances at the Tour, and the realisation that another team would only take him on because they needed Cenni's money. It was neither Cenni's nor anyone else's fault. Everyone did what they could and there didn't appear to be any better solutions, but Marco was, as ever, uncomfortable with the idea of compromising.

He felt that the prevailing mood in the Mercatone Uno team was now one of resignation to, and not enthusiasm about his presence. He found this immensely frustrating. Also, Christina had given him the brush-off yet again on his return from the Giro and his relationship with Boifava had deteriorated badly on account of Davide's treatment of not only him but also me. Since the start of 2003, I had kept the low profile that Cenni and Cornacchi had advised, and left the management of the team to Boifava, the expert. I had decided to follow their advice, but what annoyed me most, not so much for me as for Marco as my client, was the sense that I was being used as the ball in one large-scale game of ping-pong. I would go to Boifava with a question and he would tell me to see Cornacchia; I would go to Cornacchia and he would tell me that Boifava was the boss. Wherever Marco was concerned, it was always the same. They seemed determined to pass the buck, and I couldn't tolerate it. It was also frustrating to raise an issue with them on Marco's behalf and always come away empty-handed. Marco needed Mercatone Uno to demonstrate their faith, but, while I wouldn't tire of seeking it out, I couldn't raise my voice too much because everyone knew about Marco's personal problems. It was sad to see how his cocaine problem could be used to blackmail him, not so much by Cenni as the rest of the entourage.

People in and around the team continued to phone Marco that summer, but not many had the courage to visit him at home. Davide Boifava made one attempt, if I'm not mistaken, to explain that if he wanted to Marco could go to the Tour, but there were still issues to resolve. Cornacchia, on the other hand, was frightened of being left to struggle with a hornets' nest if Marco failed. The net result of all of this – together with other conspiring factors – was that Marco lapsed into what with hindsight was a terminal state of depression. He started to avoid everyone, even that human safety belt which Roberto Conti, Fabiano Fontanelli, Daniel Clavero and Marino Amadori had buckled around him.

Sometimes Marco was plain unlucky, sometimes just foolhardy. After the Giro, I had helped Boifava to organise a holiday in Sardinia for the riders and their wives. I told Marco that, if he wanted, he could invite Christina. She declined, humiliating him yet again. Keeping him away from Cesenatico was extremely difficult. Every day either Fontanelli, Conti or Amadori would knock on the door of his villa, and sometimes they would be lucky enough to catch a glimpse of Marco. That was assuming he wasn't staked out behind a locked bedroom door, which was more normal. When he did finally reappear, he was invariably in a desperate state. He was alone, terribly alone. Where were his friends, the real ones, the unconditional ones? There was almost no way to quell his desire to be alone. But then real friends usually hold firm and don't wait to be called. We didn't know which way to turn. Now in the final stages of my pregnancy, I went to Cesenatico. Marco was in a disastrous state and seeing him, I suggested to Roberto and Fabiano that they talk to professor Giovanni Greco, an expert in the field of drug addiction working at the Ravenna general hospital, not too far from Cesenatico. Marco agreed to meet him, with his usual reluctance, and to be treated by him. Greco only confirmed the prognosis given to us by Mario Pissacroia, with whom we had stopped working in July 2002 because it seemed to us that his advice was always the same and didn't produce results. Moreover, at the end of the 2002 Giro d'Italia Pissacroia had implied that I should give up with Marco. Pissacroia couldn't envisage him ever beating his addiction.

I was in Spain for one of the pre-season training camps, when one of the team's doctors, Danilo Manari, called me to tell me about an article which had just been published in the *Gazzetta di Parma* newspaper. The report was entitled 'False psychiatrist exposed' and for legal reasons referred to the false doctor only by his initials, M.P. Reading on, I was left speechless. The devil was in the details and the details seemed to point to Mario Pissacroia. Apparently, the suspect had been working as a psychiatrist for years, with countless publications, doctorates and university posts to his name but not even the most basic qualification – a degree. Marco was understandably disgusted and his faith in doctors took another knock. Perhaps this explained why he tried to goad and provoke Greco more than once. Fortunately this professor, at least, was far too confident in his ability to be intimidated by Marco's attacks.

It wasn't only the weather that was sometimes stifling that summer. I spent hours on the telephone to Tonina, who would fill me in with detailed reports on Marco's behaviour. He would talk and talk and his delirious ramblings were no longer confined to his usual obsessions, like Madonna di Campiglio. Sometimes they took leave of reality altogether. Yes, he would still mention Madonna di Campiglio and Christina, but his language was becoming more and more cryptic. Fed up with Boifava's attitude, he didn't want to talk or hear about the team. To his mind, Boifava had taken him to the Giro and failed to treat him like a leader either in the race or psychologically. I don't want to judge – I simply want to illustrate what Marco was feeling.

I spoke to his Dad: we had to find Marco a confidant, a psychological bodyguard. The matter was made even more urgent by the fact that I was due to give birth at any time. The best idea, we agreed, was to hook him up with someone who knew the going-out scene in Cesenatico but whose only agenda was to keep Marco away from drugs. We asked Michel, a local lad who sometimes went fishing or hunting with Marco. He said that he was willing, which made me feel somewhat reassured. In the meantime, Greco had recommended a doctor in Parma, who Marco duly went to see for an assessment, which lasted several hours. His view was that the best solution would be a specialised clinic where Marco would undergo intensive therapy supplemented by group therapy. Can you imagine? The clinic was in London, which immediately threw up the language problem. We even considered hiring an interpreter. By that stage there wasn't much that we hadn't considered. Naturally Marco refused. The doctor said that we needed to be patient, because without Marco's consent we couldn't do anything. I went back to Milan and continued to get progress reports from Tonina and Michel several times a day.

Marco stayed in Cesenatico for a few weeks then announced that he wanted to go to Saturnia. He no longer wanted to see Fabiano, Roberto or anyone else on what had become his visitor's rota. He wanted to be with people outside of our 'support group', like for example a certain 'Tramezzino' (literally 'Sandwich'), a jeweller from Rimini, a close friend and an ardent cycling fan who had visited him at the Canary Islands training camp the previous winter. Marco asked Tramezzino to come with him in the car to Saturnia. Tramezzino leapt at the opportunity – anything to spend time with Marco. They set off, and within two hours of them arriving I received a call from a Tramezzino. His voice was taught with panic and despair. As soon as they had arrived, Marco had locked himself in his room and told his friend that he wanted to be left alone and free to do what he wanted. Tramezzino didn't know what to do and didn't want to shoulder the responsibility for whatever capers Marco might get up to. I called Tonina and Paolo, who drove to Saturnia that night.

When they arrived, Marco was in his room and Tramezzino was immobilised. Paolo practically had to carry Marco and bundle him into the car. They called me, at a complete loss, and said that we couldn't go another day without organising some form of regular, intensive treatment. That instant I called Giovanni Greco and asked him to find a clinic because we couldn't carry on as we were. Greco arranged for Marco to be admitted to the Parco dei Tigli clinic near Venice the next day. Paolo and Tonina now faced the usual problem of persuading Marco. They called me time after time on the way back from Saturnia, pleading for help. My husband categorically forbade me to get in the car and drive to Cesenatico, so I tried to advise them over the phone. When they arrived back in Cesenatico, Paolo called me and almost screamed, out of relief, that Marco had agreed. I also cried for joy, knowing that we had found the best solution in the current circumstances.

That same evening I got a call from Roberto Conti, who had been contacted by a journalist whose name he didn't want to reveal and who had somehow found out about Marco going to the clinic. I worked out that the journalist was Angelo Costa, the cycling correspondent from the *Resto del Carlino* paper which covers Marco's native Emilia-Romagna region. I was literally inundated with calls from journalists wanting confirmation of the news. At that moment I didn't really know what to say, because without Marco's authorisation I could issue neither a confirmation nor a denial. I called every other member of the team and staff and begged them not to reveal anything. I then managed to contact Marco and suggest that, with a bombshell about to land in our lap, the best course of action would be to write an open letter signed by him.

The following morning journalists were already camped outside the clinic. I later found out that as soon as Marco walked through the front door another patient recognised him and asked him for his autograph. Paolo had called me seconds after dropping Marco off to warn me that it didn't seem like the most suitable place. Unfortunately he proved to be right as someone inside the clinic immediately notified the journalists that Pantani was indeed in the building. Taking my advice, Marco duly explained in an open letter that he was in the clinic to receive treatment for an unspecified problem and asked that he and the other patients in the clinic be shown respect and left in peace.

A couple of days later, he phoned me, outraged at the fact that a number of journalists, including those working for the TG5 television news, had said on air that he was being treated for drug addiction. 'Who did it? I want that bastard's skin!' he hissed. Marco never talked about cocaine and Giovanni Greco had a hard time helping him to admit the real nature of his problem to himself and other people. Until then, in fact, Marco didn't admit that he was ill, partly out of shame and partly out of pride. He talked only about depression, which to his mind had been caused by what happened at Madonna di Campiglio and of which the cocaine habit was only a by-product.

He sent me text messages from the clinic telling me that he was contemplating his future. I said that, if he wanted, I could start trying to build a new team again, because I had met people who had asked me to draw up a business plan for a team and who wanted to invest a significant sum of money. His response was ambiguous: 'I've thought a lot about my future as an athlete and I need to work out whether there's anything worth fighting for. I want to work out what Mercatone Uno and Cenni are doing. Most of all, I want to think about the past and only after that will I decide what to do.'

He was bitterly disappointed at how the promise of that year had evaporated. He was full of resentment and was afraid both that he had been used and that his illness had been used as a weapon against him. To top it all off, now Cornacchia didn't want to pay and, in fact, wanted to renegotiate the salary that had been agreed at the start of the year because Marco was clearly not going to ride a full racing season. Cenni also contributed to making matters worse by supporting Boifava. Marco now decided that he didn't want to see anyone except me. Although it was August, I was in the middle of moving house and was days away from giving birth, I took the car and went to visit him in the clinic without telling anyone. We spent a wonderful few hours together and I was brutally frank. 'Marco, your priority now has to be your life, not cycling. You can leave Italy – you liked it at Clavero's place, so you can buy a house in Spain. You decorate it, furnish it, put your heart and soul into it and make it your own, not like the anonymous house you live in now, which says nothing about your personality. You'll make new friends, you'll get on in life…' The problem was bringing him into contact with new people. If only he had found a woman, a real woman who loved him unconditionally. Maybe only that could have saved him.

The plan was to create a new life for him, a new environment, to surround him with real friends. Clavero was one of these, and he had one huge factor in his favour: he lived a long way from Cesenatico.

'We need to give your life new bearings,' I said. 'You need to develop new interests, then we'll see: if cycling is your life we'll persevere with it, we'll build on what's left of your career; we'll learn from your successes and your mistakes; we'll decide whether you still want to ride for Mercatone, go to another team or create a new team from scratch…'

There were many options open to us, but they all relied on Marco wanting to change. Finally I said: 'There's no point in you lying, to yourself, to me, to everyone else, betraying people all the time. Where do you think cocaine is going to get you? You've become a drug addict and I don't say that with contempt, I say it with bitter regret. You behave in a way which is unrecognisable from how you used to be; you tell lies, especially to yourself. You can't stop hiding behind this thing.'

I tried to be as direct as possible, making him understand that life is hard for everyone. When he insisted on going back home with me to Milan that very day, I warned him: 'You have to stay until the therapy's finished. Even if you don't believe in it, I don't care: it's a process which you have to go through. You have to learn to finish things instead of always stopping halfway. Since we started trying to get you better, you haven't finished one course of treatment. It's tantamount to pulling out before you even start sprinting for the line.' That evening, he didn't leave with me, but he did call with this message: 'Manu, it's Marco. I wanted to thank you for today because you really showed some guts. I needed to hear those things: no-one had ever said them to me before. I'm happy now that we're going to work on my recovery together, because I can't go on like this. I need air, I need to breathe, I need a life. You're right – I'll give it everything I've got.' I was happy, but I had heard the same speech before and I knew that it wouldn't be as simple as Marco made it sound. Sure enough, the next day, the bizarre, disjointed messages started arriving again. I could sense that something was wrong. He sounded dazed: 'Manu, something strange has happened and you simply must come to fetch me.'

I immediately called Paolo, my husband, because I didn't feel like going on my own. Marco was emaciated, not so much clothed as draped in a white T-shirt and his hands gripping the protective bars over one of the windows like the convicted criminal some still made him out to be. No sooner had I greeted him than he said: 'Call Nevio now. I want to go on holiday to Cuba.' 'What?!' Nevio seemed like the original shady character, or at least that was both mine and Marco's parents' opinion. Marco had insisted on bringing him to that year's Giro to drive the team coach, and this left both me and Mercatone Uno open to criticism from all sides. Marco had admitted that Nevio had been in prison for some fairly unedifying conduct, but I only found this out after the Giro.

I had already turned on my heels to leave when Marco ran after me saying that he wouldn't go away with Nevio, but he at least needed to tell me what had happened. A group of patients in the clinic had knocked on his door telling him that, if he had some money on him, they could get hold of some cocaine. He then started to pull the wool over both mine and my husband's eyes, telling us one lie after the next. The bottom line was that he didn't want to stay in that clinic. He had clearly taken cocaine, although he denied it. I didn't want to know how he had got his hands on the drug – that was just a detail. That said, I was outraged by how easy it was to sneak drugs into a clinic where addicts went to detoxify. I made this point in no uncertain terms to the doctor: I would have expected to find out from them that he had been 'using', certainly not from Marco. What was clear now was that we needed to get Marco out of there. We called Giovanni Greco, the only doctor Marco trusted, and he told me to bring him back to Milan, where we would decide which course of action to take next.

We arranged with the clinic for Marco to be smuggled out that evening and for a statement to be released saying that Marco had finished his treatment. I took Marco to Milan without telling anyone, which prompted accusations that I had gone to fetch Marco on my own initiative and had taken him away from the clinic. My house still wasn't fully decorated and my husband had to borrow a camp bed for Marco to sleep on. Marco accepted gracefully, but made me swear that I wouldn't tell anyone; I later teased him about how I could photograph him asleep on the fold-up bed and sell the picture to the papers...

The days went by peacefully: Marco slept deep into the morning, after which we ate breakfast on the terrace overlooking the Trenno park, and during the day Paolo tried to engage Marco in conversation, encourage him to read or go for walks. Simply put, we tried to make him feel at home. We managed to get in touch with an old friend of Marco's, Carletto, who came from Milan but used to go on holiday to Cesenatico and who Marco wanted to see again. At around that time, Vasco Rossi, the 'doyen' of Italian pop music, was due to play a concert at the San Siro stadium and I managed to get hold of two tickets for Marco and Carletto. They had a great time on a rare, carefree evening for Marco.

Marco stayed with me for around ten days. Then I gave him a lift back to Cesenatico and we called Dr Greco to arrange a meeting. Greco repeated that Marco should be kept under permanent supervision, but that I, being pregnant, wasn't the person to do it. Anything linked to childbirth also brought back bad memories for Marco: as I have already pointed out, he was blackmailed by a woman claiming to be the mother of his child shortly after Madonna di Campiglio. Some time before that Christina had already had an abortion. We decided that Paolo should spend a few days with him in Cesenatico. I think, though, that he had already started using cocaine again: he was unusually thoughtful, and I recognised some of his telltale behavioural patterns. I phoned Michel immediately, and with that call his ordeal began. They went to Saturnia, where Marco's behaviour started to escalate out of control. Tonina went to Saturnia several times to try to bring him back to his senses, but she was powerless. He refused everyone's help. He had become more and more unmanageable, to the point where Michel, in an act of desperation, loaded him into his car and took him to his house in Predappio in the hills behind Cesenatico. There, they went hunting, Marco started to go weight training and he put on twenty kilos. The telephone calls flew back and forth between Michel and I at a rate of around twenty a day, often until two or three o'clock in the morning.

13

The Long Goodbye

In the latter part of that summer, Marco's health and spirits seemed to improve, at least according to what Michel and Dr Greco told me. Apparently, there were no relapses. But sadness continued follow him like a shadow and cycling remained a taboo. Hoping that his aversion to his bike was temporary, I busied myself with yet another attempt to create a team with a new sponsor, inquiring about buying the rights ownership of the ONCE and Banesto teams – both of which would be automatically qualified for the 2004 Tour. It was all in vain. As soon as Banesto team boss José Miguel Echavarri heard Pantani's name, he sensed that my proposal was all about creating a vehicle for the umpteenth Pantani comeback and broke off the negotiations.

The same thing happened with ONCE chief Manolo Saiz, who even tried to bypass me completely to get his own paws on a prospective sponsor with whom I was already in talks. I had decided that I would say nothing to Marco about the project until I was sure of his intentions. I was never speaking to him directly at that time and all news of him came from Michel.

One day Michel passed Marco a phone call from an old schoolmate. Marco made a joke about how much weight he had gained: 'Now I'm an ex-cyclist – I've put on twenty kilos.' They both laughed. This friend of Marco's was a journalist from the *Voce di Cesena*, which the next day published a report under the headline – 'Pantani retires' – quoting the choicest soundbites from what had been an informal telephone conversation. Pandemonium broke loose and it seemed as though every journalist in Italy was calling my phone. It was in situations like these that I realised what an important figure Marco was. 'But how on earth can

Pantani decide to retire and announce it through a local newspaper?' was a popular question. What had been intended at the time as a throwaway line had somehow morphed into a scoop about Pantani's retirement. Marco asked me to publish an official denial, to make clear that it had been no more than a joke to a friend. If Pantani had wanted to quit cycling, he certainly wouldn't have gone about it like that. As Marco said: 'I always said that I would leave just as I arrived: on tiptoes.'

He decided that he would come to see me in Milan and, within hours, everyone knew his next destination. I called Marco to ask him how come Auro Bulbarelli, RAI's cycling commentator, knew where he was going, who he was seeing. He replied that it was impossible. In reality, Michel had mentioned to a friend, the owner of a well-known restaurant near Cesenatico, that when Marco returned from training that day he would give him a lift to his manager's house in Milan. Within hours, practically every cycling journalist in Europe had been briefed. Over the years, Marco and I spent hours wracking our brains in an attempt to figure out how these leaks came about, and our conclusions invariably pointed to Marco's entourage or his circle of friends in Cesenatico. It didn't matter that the journalists knew that Marco was coming to Milan, but the fact that the press seemed to be able to track his every move caused him terrible anxiety.

He arrived at the house and immediately congratulated me on giving birth to Filippo on 1 October. The first message that I sent after the delivery had been to Marco. It was seven o'clock in the morning, but he called me back straight away, clearly thrilled: 'Manu, did you not see that I sent you a message earlier?' I checked and found his text: 'Last night I said a prayer. I love you all, a big kiss to all three of you.' It was the first message I had received that day and it moved me to tears. I was discharged and a few days later he and Michel came to see me at my parents' house on Lago Maggiore. He brought two presents for Filippo – a beautiful silver music box and a wonderful silver necklace with a star-shaped diamond pendant. He put it around Filippo's neck and said: 'Dear Filippo, this is Uncle Fester's present, a necklace with a star – the symbol of fragility.' Only then did I notice that Marco had an identical one, which he pointed towards then winked at me.

I tried to talk to him about work, about the possibility of a comeback, about my ideas for a new team. Marco needed to be motivated, inspired: 'I need to be able to ride the Giro and Tour. We've suffered too much. If it can work, then that's fine, if not then let's not delude ourselves any longer because I'll be happy to stay at home. In fact, it'd be a weight off my shoulders, because that's what cycling has become for me – a weight.'

Marco was particularly relaxed that day. Later that evening, at the San Siro, Internazionale were due to face their great city rivals Milan, and being an AC Milan fan, Marco had asked whether I could rustle up some tickets. A very dear colleague, Stefano Traldi, duly managed to find him two tickets for the VIP enclosure. Marco and Michel were due to meet Stefano outside the stadium to pick up the tickets but Stefano had a hard time recognising Marco, he had put on so much weight. A few days later Marco told me that before the game he had also bumped into Walter Gallone, cycling correspondent for the *Messagero* newspaper, who had also looked at him blankly at first. 'What do you mean you don't recognise me?' Marco scolded Gallone. They made small talk for a minute or so and Walter could barely conceal his delight, having not seen Marco since his last race at the Giro. No-one could have imagined then that he would be the last journalist Marco would ever talk to before his tragic death, least of all Walter. At the end of the game, Marco felt that he should call Stefano to thank him for the tickets. This type of gesture was quite unusual for him, but when everything was going well he behaved like anyone else and could be incredibly thoughtful and sometimes even grateful.

The trips to Cuba

A few days after Filippo's birth, Marco and Michel flew to Cuba for a hunting trip. It all went well but no sooner had they returned to Italy than Marco's antics began to prove too much for Michel, who found that he could no longer keep Marco in the house. I want to be very careful here: I've spent whole days with Tonina discussing the doubts we had about Michel. She was afraid that Marco was paying for his silence. I, however, am sure that Michel was only motivated by his desire to help Marco that autumn and winter. Many people have said that Michel was short of money and that this was his only reason for spending time with Marco. It's true to say that certain incidents in that period could have given this impression, although Marco wasn't stupid and sooner or later he would have begun to ask questions and certainly not allowed himself to be duped. The first signs of friction nonetheless started to appear. When Marco spent one night at his friend Nevio's house, Michel was so furious that he was adamant that he didn't want to let Marco back into his house the next day. Marco drove aimlessly around Cesenatico for a while then finally called me to ask if he could come to stay. I could hardly say no, but Michel was angry with me for agreeing.

Marco arrived in the middle of one Saturday night and kept me up to itemise his problems with Michel and his doubts about him. He was rather vague, but I listened, while knowing that much of what I was hearing was the usual litany of excuses to deflect the blame away from himself. When Marco was on the defensive he would turn his contempt on other people as a matter of routine. I said to him that Michel may well have behaved badly towards him on this occasion, but that he should be grateful for everything else Michel had done and that he didn't have to spend time with him if he didn't want to. Marco changed the subject and told me that he had fallen in love with a Cuban girl on his holiday and that he wanted to go back there. I tried desperately to dissuade him.

One option was to ask Giovanni Lombardi to invite Marco to train with him in Spain. Lombardi lived in Madrid but was working with me on my plan for a new team, which often brought him to Milan that autumn. Lombardi came to meet Marco on a Sunday and they spent the entire day talking about cycling. Marco seemed to want to start riding again and he let us persuade him to go to Spain with Giovanni. I called Daniel Clavero, asking him to keep Marco in Spain, to distract him with training and to take him with them to Argentina for a training camp. That way, if the team came to be, Marco could take his time to decide whether to carry on riding or not. At the very least, he would be spending some time in a healthy environment.

He left for Madrid but only stayed for a few days. When he got an idea into his head, he was immovable: from Spain, he flew to Cuba and I later found out that Nevio would join him there. I can't be certain, but I would guess that it had all been concocted in advance. On the day he left for Cuba, Marco asked me to keep him updated on how things stood with the team. Unfortunately, his mobile always rang out when I tried to call him, ensuring that I completely lost track of him for a few days. I was naturally beside myself with worry and didn't know who to call. It was Marco who finally re-established contact by calling his father: 'Send someone to get me because it's getting messy here.'

I tried to find out more from Roberto Pregnolato, who I knew had been contacted by Marco from Cuba and had found him an apartment through a friend who worked for the sport and tourism department of the Cuban government. Roberto told me that Marco wasn't well and that he needed medicine which he couldn't find over there. I asked Michel if he was prepared to fly to Cuba. He said yes, but he wanted Marco's parents to pay him handsome compensation for making the trip. When Marco heard this, he was livid, but also disgusted: the issue was always money... How could he know who were his real friends when everyone seemed to be looking after their own interest? It was one of the puzzles which Marco never worked out how to solve.

I found out from Michel that when he arrived Marco really was in a pitiful state – ashen-faced, contemplating an apartment strewn with furniture which he had either knocked over or destroyed. What really happened in Cuba remains a mystery, although from what I've been able to gather from various sources, it seems that Nevio and Marco clashed, perhaps because Nevio's suppliers had given him badly cut cocaine. Doctor Greco confirmed that on his return from Cuba Marco was showing illusionary symptoms. His behaviour was bizarre, and may have been brought on by the consumption of impure cocaine. It was during this final trip to Cuba that Marco filled the pages of his passport with the muddled but poignant lament which I would later read out at his funeral. As Marco's depression had deepened over the years, he had become an obsessive if erratic note-writer. What he wrote in Cuba probably told us more about his psychological chaos, which by this stage made Marco incapable of constructing coherent sentences, than anything else, but still a few familiar themes emerged:

I have been humiliated for nothing and for four years I've been in every courtroom… Cycling has paid a high price and lots of riders have given up their hopes of justice. I'm hurting myself by writing down the truth on my passport so that the world will realise that all of my peers have been humiliated in their own bedrooms, with cameras hidden to try to ruin families. How can you not be hurt by that? … I know that I have made mistakes with drugs, but only after my life as a sportsman, and above all my private life, had been violated. I hope that my story serves as an example to other sports; rules are necessary but they need to be the same for everyone. There's no other profession in which you have to give your blood and take tests at night, in your own home.

Go and see what a cyclist really is and how many men endure the most torrid sadness… This document is the truth and I hope that a real man or woman reads it and defends those of us campaigning for equal rules for all sportsmen. I'm not a fraud; I feel wounded, and everyone who used to believe in me must speak out.

Michel brought him home from Cuba and the rapid degeneration of their relationship continued. Marco was out of hand and Michel's determination to stop him bringing cocaine into his house led to endless rows. I also fell out with Michel over his habit of calling me literally dozens of times a day and causing me great anxiety in the process. He even called Tonina to tell her that there was a dealer who was hassling Marco and who it was up to her to hunt down. There were too many things that didn't add up with him – too much confusion, too many contradictions.

The final Christmas

Marco spent the Christmas of 2003 – which was to be his last – at home with his parents. The festive spirit was in short supply, but Marco had made it clear to Tonina that relations with Michel were at an all-time low and that he didn't want to stay another day with him in Predappio. Michel, meanwhile, tried to convince Tonina that Marco should stay with him. One day, at the house in Predappio, a confrontation between the two had escalated to the point where Michel had Marco up against a wall and with his hands around Marco's neck as he tried to force him to throw away a bag of cocaine. Marco had been shocked and frightened by Michel's aggression. The situation had now become untenable, so much so that, along with Giovanni Greco, we began to reconsider the option of treatment in London. But the problem remained the same: without Marco's consent all of our efforts were and would continue to be in vain.

It was Marco's birthday on 13 January and a group of friends had arranged a dinner in Predappio to celebrate. It was a disaster. Marco was manic: first he clashed with old school friends Carletto and Simone, then spent the entire evening arguing, humiliating himself and being humiliated. When it was all too much, he called me: 'Manu, I can't stand this any more. Now my parents are here, too, I can't breathe, they won't let me live. I need to live again. I can't stay here. Can you come and get me. Take me back to your place, please. Now. Please do something.' Mentally, he was exhausted, crushed, and so were his parents. For Michel, that night was the final straw: he no longer wanted anything to do with Marco. I was in my office and called my husband, who rushed to Predappio to 'rescue' him. I hoped that spending time with a new-born child and in a family environment could give him back some perspective. I still hoped that I could persuade him to check into a clinic to detox. That was now my only objective, and frankly I couldn't see any alternative.

On reflection, with such a young baby, if I had known that Marco was in such a terrible state that night I wouldn't have let him into my house. But over the days that followed Marco turned out to adore Filippo, showing just how sweet he could be. The responsibility on me, though, remained huge, because Marco was now shockingly ill. I wondered how anyone could get into that state. When I had been living and working in close contact with him, there may have been the odd relapse, but now I had the impression that he had been taking cocaine non-stop for months. He had already lost fifteen of the twenty kilos he had put on through weight training.

When he appeared before me at the front door on the night of his birthday, pain and anguish were etched all over what was now a skeletal face. As usual, he dispensed with the formalities and got straight to the excuses, angling for a mixture of sympathy and under-standing. I certainly didn't want my house to be a soft option, a place where Marco could indulge himself and be indulged. Neither did I want him to play on the fact that, after five years of battling and suffering with him, my resolve may have been waning. I immediately asked Dr Greco for advice on how to deal with Marco – what medicine he needed to take and what approach I should adopt with him. In those first few weeks of 2004, Tonina often complained that Greco didn't devote enough time or attention to Marco. But not even Greco had a magic formula: as I have stressed on numerous occasions, without Marco's explicit co-operation any recovery attempt was doomed to fail.

The camp bed in the new lounge where Marco had 'slummed it' the previous summer had been replaced by a comfortable sofabed. Marco slept solidly there for around a week, only getting up to eat and take medication. On the rare occasions when he was awake, he took care to make a nuisance of himself: 'Does your husband have to be here? He's annoying me. Paolo, what are you doing on the computer?' 'I'm paying bills.' 'But wouldn't it be quicker to go to the post office to pay them? Go on, you're annoying me.' It got worse: 'I'm not convinced about your husband. There's something about him. Even when he came to pick me up in Predappio... I think firemen are spying on us. There are spies in here.'

Marco was very jealous: he loved Paolo, but he was also afraid that he might monopolise my attention. On one occasion, my mother tried to tell Marco how fond I was of him, but Marco just shrugged. I already had Paolo, he said, and there was Filippo, too. Unfortunately, not only was he jealous, the cocaine also made him paranoid and gave him hallucinations. Giovanni Greco's suspicions after seeing Marco on his return from Cuba were supported by a growing body of evidence, not least his lengthening stream of delirious consciousness.

I kept urging Marco to change his mind about the clinic, but he still refused categorically. I suggested going back to Renato Da Pozzo, who had moved back to Italy since our unsuccessful trip to see him in Norway in 2002 and was now working as a 'life coach'. I was sure that Renato could work with Marco, perhaps taking him abroad on some form of 'voyage of self-rediscovery'. Being an athlete himself, Renato knew exactly where to intervene, not only from a physical point of view but above all psychologically. Renato used to tell me that if an athlete's adrenaline isn't channelled in the right way, it can cause ruinous damage.

He came to meet me at home. I knew that Marco wasn't in an ideal frame of mind, but we had no more time to lose. There was nothing civilised about the start of the meeting, but gradually Renato's directness started to embed messages in Marco's brain. Renato's basic thesis was that sport and competition should be seen not as an end in themselves, but as a means to achieve the sense of wholeness which comes not from victories and performances but from self-awareness and wisdom. He gave Marco his interpretation of his fall from grace, blaming the sports system that creates stars only to then destroy them when it serves other interests. Even so, he said, what had happened to Marco didn't justify or excuse his crisis and his cocaine addiction.

Renato therefore suggested a process which would allow Marco to reconnect with his soul. The first stage would be a full detox under the supervision of a doctor whom he trusted; then, day by day, they would work towards restoring his inner harmony. Renato made it quite clear that second thoughts and slips weren't allowed and would lead to the programme being called off. Da Pozzo thought that Marco should prove his commitment by going public and keeping his fans up-to-date with his progress via an online diary. It was the only way for him to re-establish his lost credibility and shout out to the world what he really thought sport should be. It was also the only way to activate his plan to rebuild and decontaminate cycling, the sport to which he had dedicated his life. Marco wanted to shake off the tag of 'dope cheat' and say everything that he hadn't been able to say up to that point.

Marco seemed enthusiastic and I called Tonina straight away to tell her. She suggested that I arrange for Marco to leave with Renato as

soon as possible because she knew that it wouldn't take much for him
to change his mind. I gave Renato a lift back to his house and when I
came back, Marco's motivation was not only intact but seemed to be
growing: he confidently reaffirmed that he would follow the programme.
The only drawback was that Renato couldn't leave for another week, and
this gave Marco ample time to get cold feet, which is precisely what
happened a couple of days later. I reminded him that I was becoming
tired of his fickleness and that he wasn't helping himself, but he just
waved me away. He felt different a few days ago, he snapped, and now
he didn't believe in Renato's project any more. Renato was aghast and
demanded to be paid for the assessment even if we weren't going
ahead with his plan.

It goes without saying that professional people need to be paid, but
when Pantani was involved everyone seemed to eye up the jackpot.
Renato quoted exorbitant fees, justifying them by claiming that he
offered a unique service. I didn't even feel like trying too hard to
persuade Marco: if he suspected that the person who was supposed to
be helping him was trying to make money out of him, the therapy
would become counter-productive and he would lose his faith in me,
too. Renato's project was very attractive, but he made an arrogant
salesman and Marco had realised that.

A few days later I sent a text message to Tonina which read: 'Your
son is a wonderful person. If he was always like he is today, it would be
a dream come true.' After a settling-in period at my house, which in
truth had been highly unsettling for all concerned, Marco had started to
improve. And when he wasn't down, he really was a joy to be with.
I called one of my close friends, Fiorella, a head of department at the
nearby Pallanza hospital, asking her if she could do a blood test on
Marco. The results came through a few hours later and were perfect.
Marco breathed a sigh of relief, but I soon came to regard those tests
as a mixed blessing. Granted, physically, there was nothing wrong with
Marco, but this allowed him to cling to the belief that his real problem
wasn't cocaine but making sense of what had happened at Madonna
di Campiglio. The tests had also reinforced Marco's conviction, obviously
false, that his body was indestructible. Only five weeks earlier, on

6 December, the former Banesto rider, Marco's friend and fellow climbing ace José Maria 'El Chaba' Jimenez had died of a huge heart attack induced by a cocaine overdose. Initially, Marco was petrified, but within minutes he was denying any similarity between him and the Spaniard: his heart, he sniffed, wasn't like Jimenez's. He was fearless.

For the time being, his confidence in himself appeared justified by his unusually cheerful mood. We spent some memorable days together talking and setting the world to rights, helping my husband Paolo in the kitchen and strolling in the Trenno park with Filippo. Marco was the perfect, sweet-natured uncle. One day I was in my bedroom when I looked down the stairs to see Marco and Filippo on the sofabed in the lounge; Marco had his head on a cushion and was holding Filippo's tiny hands and gesturing towards the television as if to say 'watch this'. I took a photograph which I'll treasure for the rest of my life. That picture is worth a thousand words about Marco's tenderness, but its symbolism is also heartbreaking: it shows two opposite lives, one belonging to a child's at the beginning of his journey and the other to a 34-year-old man nearing the end.

Marco's good humour was enjoying a long stay of execution. I was keen to seize the moment and, on the advice of Gianfranco Josti, who was still my guru on cycling matters, contacted the former rider Alcide Cerato. Marco had met Alcide on one of his visits to Saturnia and they had talked at some length. Despite having ridden predominantly in the 1960s, Alcide still knew cycling inside out and, like Marco, was a keen hunter. I thought that Marco could benefit from spending time with him and duly tried to set up a meeting. Unfortunately, Alcide was spending a few days in Brazil on business so the meeting had to be postponed until he came back. I wasn't too worried: I had the distinct impression that Marco was regaining some perspective and some balance by staying with me and I deluded myself that there would be plenty of time for Alcide to join Marco's 'support system'.

The days had become reassuringly uneventful. We went to visit my parents on Lago Maggiore and Marco still seemed content, oddly content, but it wasn't long before the danger signals began to creep back. Like the day when he said whimsically: 'You know, I could see myself going away to live like a hermit. I'll buy a house in the mountains and live like Charly Gaul.' Gaul was in many ways Marco's precursor, a sublimely gifted climber who had won the 1958 Tour de France and captured hearts with his exploits in the mountains. Plagued by emotional problems in retirement – or, say some, simply left broken-hearted after the break-up of his marriage – Gaul had spent over twenty years living as a hermit in a caravan in the Belgian Ardennes. I knew that Marco identified with Gaul, but I also knew that his reclusive 'calling' had less to do with emulating one of his heroes than his desire to be left alone to take all the cocaine he wanted.

One day, my dad took Marco on a walk with a view to suggesting that they spend some time together in my parents' house in the mountains. When they came back and Marco started asking questions about the house, my dad took great delight in ribbing him: 'But do you know how to cook? And wash and clean and do everything else?' Marco looked back at him, stunned but still smiling and asked: 'Dino, why are you asking me these things? You don't really think that if I go I'll bring you along to piss me off, do you? If I go, I'm going alone. I don't want you under my feet!' And my dad: 'Perhaps you don't know me: you're a Capricorn and so am I, but I'm more stubborn than you. If we go, we go together. Otherwise, you're going nowhere.' 'Ah, we'll see, we'll see. Maybe I'll find another house…' Marco laughed.

We went back to Milan that evening and Marco seemed positively euphoric. I knew exactly why: he had already secretly planned a trip to Cesenatico. He told me that he had to go home at all costs to pick up some things, because Paolo had invited him to go ski-ing in the mountains. I pointed out that he didn't need to go all the way to Cesenatico to get his clothes – we could buy some new ones at a shop in Milan. I was terrified of Marco going back to Cesenatico. We tried to stop him but in the end had to accept a compromise of him taking my husband's car as long as he guaranteed that he would leave in the morning and be back by the evening.

The reconstruction of the magistrate investigating Marco's death indicated what incredible speeds he must have driven at in order to complete that 700-kilometre round trip. We know now that he stopped off at a bank in Cesenatico to withdraw no less than 12,000 euros, bought cocaine from a dealer, then rushed home to say a quick 'ciao' to Tonina and pack his suitcase before returning to Milan that evening. At home he also found the time to shower and shave; usually that in itself was a good sign because when Marco was 'using' he wore shabby clothes, didn't wash and didn't shave. That evening Paolo and I heard strange noises coming from his room. Paolo went to check on him and saw nothing incriminating but plenty to arouse suspicion. The following day we realised that Marco had been up all night and he admitted that he had betrayed us. We got him to hand over the cocaine, which we threw away. He assured us that he had handed it all over, but that obviously wasn't the case. We would follow him everywhere, look in his suitcase and in his pockets, but Marco always managed to hide a few grams somewhere.

Over the next few days he became gradually more aggressive, partly because we gave him no peace and constantly badgered him to give us his drugs. On one evening that week I invited my close friend Federica Panicucci and her husband Fergetta to dinner in the hope that it might provide a distraction for Marco. I had asked him to be on his best behaviour but in fact he was at his provocative worst all evening; it was impossible for Federica not to notice that something was horribly amiss.

I hoped that Marco would react better to guests who were his friends more than mine, so a few days later the invitation went out to Carletto – the friend from the Milan derby – and his sister, who had shared a short-lived summer romance with Marco one year when she was on holiday in Cesenatico. Carletto's sister is a lovely girl, a nursery teacher. That evening she spent a long time watching how I handled Filippo and spoke only briefly with Marco, but even she noticed that something was wrong. After Marco's death, Carletto made a confession to me about that evening. At around the same time, I had been trying to persuade Marco to buy an apartment which was for sale not far from my house. Marco agreed that he needed to be near to me, because I was 'a moral reference point'. The architect of the apartment had also designed and sold me my house, so I asked him to show Marco around. That evening

Marco told Carletto that he wanted to buy the apartment for the sole reason that he needed somewhere to go to take cocaine in peace whenever he wanted. Carletto retorted that instead of staying in my house and ruining my life, Marco would be better off in a hotel. After Marco died, Carletto bitterly regretted having given him that piece of advice. I tried to console him by reassuring him that he had only been speaking as a friend, and if things had ended up the way they did it certainly wasn't his fault.

Man on the run

Unfortunately, apart from the odd bright moment, Marco was becoming more and more difficult to live with. He continually tried to provoke me and insulted my husband, who, he said, always followed him to the bathroom and wouldn't leave him alone. We were running out of patience and ideas. Through Dr Greco, I made an appointment for Marco to be assessed at the Le Betulle clinic in Appiano Gentile, a suburb to the north-west of Milan. It was a Friday. I sat in on the assessment, conducted by Dr Furio Ravera, which lasted around an hour. Ravera described to Marco how cocaine forces an abuser into a corner or hole and how he had expanded on this theme in his book *A Void in the Soul*. Marco turned white and said that he had been there, or at least close. Ravera replied that it could be a very dangerous condition without the guidance of someone who knew the way back.

Marco suddenly seemed terrified and started to put up his defences, of which cockiness was one. No doctor had been able to cure him yet, he smirked. I tried to make excuses for his cynicism by telling Ravera about our problems at the clinic in Rome and at the Parco dei Tigli near Venice. Ravera said that he could vouch for the professionalism and competence of his clinic and outlined the nature of the therapy he offered. From stone cold, Marco's response turned lukewarm and he grudgingly agreed to take the weekend to mull it over. He would decide on Monday. On his way out of the clinic, he slammed the door and burst into tears like a little boy. I squeezed his hands tight: 'Marco, just this time, do what I tell you. You'll see, we're doing the right thing. I'm not telling you to stay here for a year. You have to detoxify your body and the therapy will last a fortnight or twenty days, then we'll start from scratch, we'll go back to Saturnia, we'll do whatever you want. But you need to clean your blood. You need this help.'

He looked at me and gave his word, although added through his tears that Ravera had no right to tell him that he had a void in his soul. I tried to explain that he had misunderstood and that Ravera meant something quite different, but I also realised that it was better not to insist too much and to let Marco vent whatever he was feeling. For the duration of the journey back to Milan he just gazed forlornly out of the car window. Filippo was crying and Paolo drove with one eye on the road and one disconsolate eye on me in his rear view mirror. Marco started muttering to himself: 'I'm not going behind bars like a junkie. I want my freedom. If you snort cocaine they label you a druggie, but I'm not a druggie. It's society that's drugged. They've ruined me. I hated drugs and look at the state I'm in...' Tears welled in his eyes – great, glistening tears which spoke of sadness and desperation. When we were home, while Paolo took Filippo for a stroll in the park, Marco started to talk to the television set and wouldn't stop provoking me. He wasn't going back to the clinic, he said. That evening I called his parents. They had to come to Milan. We had to make a decision.

The house was a mine of tension. Marco wanted to be left alone. Paolo and I tried to reason with him but the wall had gone up. He pushed us away. Sometimes he could be soft and submissive, but now he was aggressive and arrogant. Our continued pleas only had the effect of making him want to leave: he wanted to check into a hotel and be left in peace. I screamed at him: 'You're going nowhere. You're not disturbing anyone here, you're just destroying yourself, your wonderful self, the person we love like a member of our own family.' He responded by writing a letter which I kept, and will keep for the rest of my life...

I'm getting out of here – there's too much hospitality. I don't want to cause you problems, I just want my space where I can go to make my mistakes. I want a space to make my mistakes, I want to be treated like

an adult who is capable of deciding to make mistakes or not in his life.
I don't want people coming to get me and rescuing me all the time like
a child. I'll call my parents, I'll call the doctors – I know where they are.
I'm going to the hotel over the road.

I didn't want him to go. At the same time, though, I didn't want him
taking cocaine in my house and I insisted that he check into a clinic to
get treatment. Eventually, I persuaded him to stay one more night. The
following day his parents arrived from Cesenatico. The responsibility of
keeping him in my house in his current state was now too much, and I
was frightened that the following Monday he would refuse to go to the
clinic in Appiano Gentile. Instead, he would hole himself up in some
hotel where I wouldn't be able to find him. I called my mother-in-law to
ask her to come and take Filippo away for a few hours, which set
Marco's alarm bells ringing and made him even more edgy. Almost as
soon as they arrived, he began to argue furiously with his parents. They
no longer knew where to turn, either. I sensed that it was time for
desperate measures and called the clinic in Appiano Gentile to ask if
Marco could be checked in that evening. They replied that if Marco
wasn't willing then it probably wouldn't be wise because they didn't
want him causing a scene in reception.

Tempers were not so much being frayed as lost completely. I could
only take so many of Marco's now incessant insults before I also
erupted: 'Here in my house, you show some respect! We took Filippo
away not because we're scared of you but because we want to talk to
your parents and make sense of what's going on. You can stay here, but
only if you obey certain rules.' Marco didn't wait to hear what these
conditions were before refusing the offer. 'If you go,' Marco's father
warned, 'you're coming home with us.' The argument then resumed
with even more venom than before. Tonina was so distressed that she
fainted and I had to call an ambulance. Fearful of being recognised by
the paramedics, Marco fled. He took nothing with him and said nothing
of where he was going.

My husband went to the hospital with Paolo and Tonina while I
stayed at home and began to clean frenziedly, at the mercy of what I'd

later realise was a panic attack. I was afraid that there might be cocaine still hidden somewhere in the house. I could even smell it.

Paolo and Tonina returned from the hospital some hours later and immediately went back out into Milan to look for Marco. I started to call every hotel in the neighbourhood but there was no sign of him. Paolo went to work the following day while I headed for my parents-in-law's house on Lago Maggiore, where Filippo had slept that night. I couldn't bear to stay at home. I was afraid of everything. I was really shaken up. At around two o'clock that afternoon the telephone rang. Anonymous caller. I didn't pick up. Shortly afterwards I listened to my voicemail: '*Ciao*, Manu, it's Marco. As you can see, dogs always come back to their owners. I'm in a hotel. Please can you bring me my medicine? Do me one last favour. *Ciao*, Marco.' But which hotel?! I played the message back several times and tried to trace the call, without success.

I scoured every hotel even vaguely in the vicinity of my house. The following Friday, 6 February, Dr Greco called: Marco had tried to contact him but all he had really wanted was to talk to me. I explained that I was very angry about his behaviour and I asked Greco what I should do. He gave me a phone number for Marco and said that I should come down hard on him: he mustn't be allowed to think that nothing had happened.

The Hotel Touring

I called Marco and spoke in the frostiest tone of voice I could muster. In truth, I found it hard to speak at all, such were my anger and anxiety. Marco apologised for what had happened; he said that seeing my mother-in-law take Filippo away had made him nervous and when his parents arrived he had panicked even more. He asked how his mother was and said he was worried that something serious had happened to her. He said that he loved Paolo and Tonina very much but that the situation had become too much for them to handle. He needed to get away and leave them in peace. He then reaffirmed that his problem wasn't cocaine but the tag of 'druggie' which he was now carrying around with him. He wanted his freedom back, especially his freedom

of choice. 'This week has been tough, but I'm still hanging in there.'
I asked him whether he had attempted suicide and trembled as I waited
for the reply. He hadn't tried anything, just thought a lot and suffered a
lot. I tried to explain to him that, by carrying on like this, he wasn't
behaving like an adult. Finally he asked me to come to his hotel.
I warned him that I would only come if he promised to do whatever I
said. He hesitated, but he needed clothes and medicine. Before leaving,
I packed a small bag containing a tube of shaving foam, a few T-shirts,
some socks, some underpants, and most importantly, a letter:

Dear Marco, I've thought a lot about what happened and I'm still in shock.
I believe in you, but I believe in the Marco who likes himself, not the
Marco who wants to destroy himself. I'm here for you, I've proved that,
but I don't want to lead you by the hand to your grave. You'll never
convince me that cocaine is your destiny, and I'll never accept that you
want to find a place where you are helped to use it or even to contain
your addiction and carry on as you are. You can't continue this way, I don't
believe it, it's not possible. You need to get it out of your system, Marco,
believe me. If you want to start taking this seriously, give me a call.

I went to the hotel and left the bag in reception. Marco was staying
at the Jolly Hotel Touring. When he told me the name of the hotel, I was
lost for words. I couldn't quite believe that, having left my house in the
middle of the night, he had been thinking clearly enough to take a taxi
and ask explicitly to be taken to a hotel on the other side of town. The
choice of hotel was curious but not without Marco's own quirky logic:
when, on 5 June 1999, Marco was told that his haematocrit was over
the legal limit, he was staying in none other than the Hotel Touring in
Madonna di Campiglio; then, on 23 December 2003, on one of several
occasions when he fled Michel's house in Predappio, he had taken
refuge at the Hotel Touring in Miramare, near Rimini, where I later sent
Dr Greco to take him back to Predappio. And now, here he was again
in that damned Hotel Touring...

He called me as soon as he had picked up the bag from reception:
'No, I want to see *you*. We need to get on with the protocol.' 'Protocol'

was the euphemism Marco used to refer to his recovery programme, in the same way that, for him, cocaine was just 'the substance'. 'I've decided to go to Saturnia,' he continued. 'What are my parents going to do?' Paolo and Tonina had in fact already sought advice from the Comunità di San Patrignano – a large residential community for recovering drug addicts near Rimini – and been told to forget that they had a son called Marco Pantani and realise instead that their son was a drug addict and needed to be treated as such; they should move him out of their lives and try to forget that he existed. They decided that a holiday in Greece might give both of them and Marco mutual respite. It's impossible to imagine how much these two parents were hurt by accusations after Marco's death that they had abandoned their son. Too often, people make judgements and pass moral sentences without knowing the facts. If only journalists knew how much damage – irredeemable damage – their words can inflict, they'd think twice before posing as judges and jurors.

Paolo and Tonina have very different characters, but when two people suffer they suffer in the same way. Paolo doesn't show much emotion and could be considered introverted. Tonina on the other hand is an emotional volcano, like Marco. In the last four years of his life these parents gave their heart and soul in their efforts to save their son. Tonina had gone beyond that, beyond the realms of parental responsibility, to the point of tracking down Marco's dealers, threatening them and putting hers and her family's life at risk as a result. If Marco found out, he would tell her not to get angry with them: they were only doing their job and he was the one who went looking for them. But this wouldn't stop Tonina jumping into the car at night and going to look for the dealers to intimidate them and warn them to keep away from Marco. She is a courageous, sensitive woman whose life has been destroyed.

I tried to explain to Marco how his parents were feeling. He saw them as vultures always poised to swoop and take him home – and in the end that's how Tonina and Paolo began to see themselves. But they had no alternative. They told me that they had decided to go away to Greece and I let Marco know; they realised that Marco needed and wanted to be left alone. Marco was delighted: 'Oh, fantastic. That's

great news, Manu. At least they'll have a bit of peace and so will I.
Come and see me and we'll start getting ready for the protocol. I'll go
home, I'll get the car and I'll go to Saturnia. On second thoughts, is
there anyone who can bring my car to Milan? Call Tramezzino.'
Tramezzino refused. After the debacle in Saturnia, he no longer
wanted to be involved. I said to Marco: 'If you want to be treated like
a man you need to be able to go home on your own. You can't always
ask for help left, right and centre.' 'You're right,' Marco said. 'I'll take
a train home. I'll pick up the car then I'll go to Saturnia. First, I want to
see you, though.'

It was barely eight o'clock on the morning of Monday 9 February
when my telephone rang: 'Ciao, Manu, it's Marco. Are you up yet?' Not
only was I up, I was already in my office, I told Marco. 'Ok, so what time
are you coming?' he asked. I wanted to test him, or at least to give him
the chance to be independent just for once, and my assistant, Laura
agreed. I couldn't jump every time he whistled, she said. If he really
wanted me to help him and not just to organise his train journey, he
should hurry up about it. She was right. I told him: 'Marco, can you not
come to the office, because I've got meetings this morning?' 'No,
Manu, come on, you come to the hotel. I prefer it that way. I'll be
ashamed if I come to the office.' I replied that I could be with him for
around two o'clock. 'Manu,' he said, 'I'm not sure that I can wait until
two o'clock. How do I take a train?' 'Marco, you don't even know how
to take a train?' I was deliberately trying to provoke him: if someone
had to tell him how to take a train, he clearly wasn't as independent as
he thought. 'Well, if you really don't want to go to the station you can
always hire a car.' 'But where will I get the money?' 'What do you
mean? You left my house with a stack of money. You can't have spent
it all!' 'Well, you know how it is, a tip here, a tip there. I've spent it all.
I'll pay by credit card.'

The last words that Marco Pantani ever said to me were: 'Manu, listen,
I don't know if I'll wait for you, because I can't bear to stay here any
longer. I'm going down to reception now, I'll pay with my credit card and
I'll book a car. If I don't have enough money I'll call you. We'll speak
anyway, because I'm going to Saturnia and I'd like you, Paolo and Filippo

to come down to visit. We'll go to the spa baths together and we'll start building for the future.' It was the last time that I heard his voice.

After that phone call, I tried to imagine what Marco's plans could be. He seemed to me to be determined to go to Saturnia. I hoped that he would go via his house in Cesenatico to pick up his things and above all his phone so that I could contact him. The following day Tonina told me that Manola, Marco's sister, had been to Marco's villa and detected no signs that he had been there. The days went by. Tonina, Paolo and I spoke several times a day and we started to call everyone who may have seen Marco or could be putting him up. Even his worst friends… he had literally disappeared.

I had no news of Marco until my brother's phone call: 'Lela… Marco's dead!' At that moment, I thought that the world had stood still. I still say to myself now: 'No, it can't be true… Marco's playing a practical joke on me and sooner or later he'll call…' But I know that, sadly, that's not the case. Marco has left us all writhing in that 'torrid sadness', to use the expression he coined to describe his mindset after that fatal 5 June, in that mountain village whose name will always resonate like death bells in my ears: MADONNA DI CAMPIGLIO!